SHORTCHANGED

MARIKO LIN CHANG

SHORTCHANGED

*Why Women Have Less Wealth and
What Can Be Done About It*

OXFORD
UNIVERSITY PRESS
2010

OXFORD

UNIVERSITY PRESS

Oxford University Press, Inc., publishes works that further
Oxford University's objective of excellence
in research, scholarship, and education.

Oxford   New York
Auckland   Cape Town   Dar es Salaam   Hong Kong   Karachi
Kuala Lumpur   Madrid   Melbourne   Mexico City   Nairobi
New Delhi   Shanghai   Taipei   Toronto

With offices in
Argentina   Austria   Brazil   Chile   Czech Republic   France   Greece
Guatemala   Hungary   Italy   Japan   Poland   Portugal   Singapore
South Korea   Switzerland   Thailand   Turkey   Ukraine   Vietnam

Published by Oxford University Press, Inc.
198 Madison Avenue, New York, NY 10016

www.oup.com

Oxford is a registered trademark of Oxford University Press

Library of Congress Cataloging-in-Publication Data
Chang, Mariko Lin.
Shortchanged : why women have less wealth
and what can be done about it / Mariko Lin Chang.
p.   cm.
Includes bibliographical references and index.
ISBN 978-0-19-536769-0
1. Women—Economic conditions.
2. Wealth—Sex differences.
3. Wages—Women.   4. Women—Social conditions.
I. Title.
HQ1381.C52 2010
339.2'2082—dc22   2010000837

1 3 5 7 9 8 6 4 2

Printed in the United States of America
on acid-free paper

FOR MARIAH, CLAIRE, AND SARAH

Contents

Acknowledgments

THE INITIAL IDEA for this book came to me one afternoon during my commute home from Cambridge, Massachusetts. At that time, I was fairly new to Massachusetts and was still actively getting to know the local radio stations. In search of which stations to add to the preset selections in my car, I came across an AM radio station dedicated to financial issues. On this particular afternoon, two day traders were talking about the market (which at that time was still experiencing "irrational exuberance") and I was struck by two things. First, I realized that I knew close to nothing about the stock market and investing. Second, I was struck by the gendered language the day traders used to talk about the market. Being a sociologist, I couldn't help but think that access to financial information and knowledge was surely related to both social class and gender. These initial thoughts eventually led me to the topic of women's wealth. For the initial inspiration that led to this book, I thank these two day traders, wherever they may be.

Just like it takes a village to raise a child, it takes a community to bring a book to fruition. I have benefited from the support and feedback from many people whose contributions both made this book possible and greatly improved the end result. Numerous colleagues gave helpful advice, feedback, and encouragement at various stages of the book and the publication process. I am particularly grateful to Andy Andrews, Denise Bielby, Prudence Carter, Jessica Gordon Nembhard, David Grusky, Lowell Hargens, Ann Hironaka, Jason Kaufman, Stan Lieberson, Meizhu Lui, Sue Monahan, Kathy Newman, Barbara Reskin, Tom Shapiro, Mark Suchman, and Bill Wilson. I also wish to thank Audrey Alforque-Thomas, Stephanie Howling, and Renee Richardson for their assistance in conducting some of the interviews. Terese Leung and Stephanie Howling also provided invaluable research assistance at various stages of the project. Mary Quigley's administrative support and Cheri Minton's technical expertise contributed to the research and writing of the book. My editor, James Cook, always challenged me to revise and refine my arguments and I appreciate his hard work and guidance through the publication process. I thank the many others working behind the scenes at Oxford University Press for their contributions as well. Anonymous reviewers raised important counterarguments and provided constructive criticisms that made the book much stronger. Susan Allan made the words flow more smoothly and removed unnecessary jargon. I am also grateful for the generous financial support from the Russell Sage Foundation and from Harvard University.

I offer my heartfelt thanks to my family. My husband, Paul, provided unwavering encouragement. He never failed to garner enthusiasm for the book, even when I was less than enthusiastic myself. My daughters, Mariah, Claire, and Sarah, may not even realize that this book is a gift to them (and the other girls in their generation for whom I hope this topic will be obsolete). At times, my daughters probably wondered why I spent so much time and energy working on this book, but they were still willing to give me the hugs that sustained me. They kept me grounded and helped me remember what is most important in life. My mother, Marjorie, sister, Michiko, and sister-in-law, Helen, also provided valuable emotional support, even if they did not know it.

I owe the deepest respect and gratitude to the men and women who agreed to be interviewed. Their experiences and voices are an invaluable part of the book and I can't imagine the book without them.

SHORTCHANGED

ONE

The Women's Wealth Gap

What Is It and Why Do We Care?

It is fitting that with the very first bill that I sign—the Lilly Ledbetter Fair Pay Restoration Act—that it is upholding one of this nation's founding principles: that we are all created equal.... while this bill bears her name, Lilly knows this story isn't just about her. It's the story of women across this country still earning just 78 cents for every dollar men earn—women of color even less—which means that today, in the year 2009, countless women are still losing thousands of dollars in salary, income, and retirement savings over the course of a lifetime....

So signing this bill today is to send a clear message: That making our economy work means making sure it works for everybody. That there are no second class citizens in our workplaces, and that it's not just unfair and illegal—it's bad for business—to pay somebody less because of their gender, or their age, or their race, or their ethnicity, religion, or disability.

—President Barack Obama

O**N JANUARY** 29, 2009, President Obama signed the Lilly Ledbetter Fair Pay Act into law. The legislation derives its name from a supervisor at a tire factory in Alabama who, after almost 20 years of employment, received an anonymous note containing the salaries of three other male supervisors. At that time, the sole woman among sixteen supervisors, Ledbetter was the lowest paid person in her position, earning $3,727 per month. Salaries for the fifteen men in her plant who held the same position ranged from $4,286 to $5,236 per month, despite some having less seniority and experience.[1] Ledbetter's salary inequity resulted from smaller raises (allegedly due to discriminatory evaluations), which formed the basis for subsequent raises that resulted in a substantial pay gap over time. After learning of the pay inequities, she filed a wage discrimination lawsuit, and a jury decided in her favor.

The Court of Appeals for the Eleventh Circuit reversed the verdict, ruling that her claim was filed past the deadline of 180 days from when the discriminatory pay decision occurred and that each subsequent pay check did not "reset" the 180-day deadline. The Supreme Court upheld this decision in a 5–4 ruling.[2] The Lilly Ledbetter Fair Pay Act nullifies this ruling,[3] and although Ledbetter will not receive any money as a result of the legislation, the act is intended to help other women fight wage discrimination based on sex.[4]

The Lilly Ledbetter Fair Pay Act illustrates the problem of pay discrimination and the need to eliminate the wage gap between men and women. The gender wage ratio—that is, the ratio of women's to men's median annual earnings—is now at 77.8%, an all-time high, and women under age 25 working full-time now earn 95% of what their male peers earn, almost closing the gap, at least in the early stages of their working careers.[5] More than 25% of women in two-earner families make more than their husbands, and in major cities such as New York, Boston, Chicago, Dallas, and Minneapolis, women ages 21–30 are now out-earning the men their age.[6] In addition to having made impressive gains with respect to income, women are also now more likely than men to complete college.[7] It would seem that financial gender equality may and should be in reach.[8]

While all these economic gains are impressive, they mask a major and often overlooked fault line of women's financial security—the women's wealth gap. Women may make 78% of what men make, but they own only 36% as much wealth. In discussing the financial standing of women in America, a focus on income is misleading because wealth is a much more meaningful measure of economic well-being. In fact, in this book I argue that a women's wealth gap would persist even if the gender income gap were eliminated. There are two basic reasons for this persistence: (1) men have greater access to the *wealth escalator*, which translates income into wealth at a faster rate, and (2) women are more likely to shoulder the financial burden of single parenthood and therefore have less disposable income with which to generate wealth even if they have the same incomes as men. While income is no doubt important to women's economic security, I argue here that we need to shift our attention to gender differences in wealth to understand fully how women might attain financial equality.

What Is Wealth?

Wealth and income are sometimes related, but they are not the same. *Income* refers to the amount of money received by an individual or household during a specific period of time, such as a month or a year. Most people's income is made up primarily of earnings from a job. Other common forms of income are interest on savings or checking accounts, gifts from family or friends, Social Security, government assistance, pension benefits, rent received from property owned, and child support. In other words, it doesn't matter what the source is: any money that enters a person's wallet (or purse) is considered income.

A person's *wealth*, or *net worth*, refers to the total value of her financial and nonfinancial assets minus her debts (table 1.1).[9] *Financial assets* include money held in checking or savings accounts, bonds, the market value of stocks or mutual funds, and money that can be withdrawn from retirement accounts and from some life insurance policies. *Nonfinancial assets* include real estate, the market value of any businesses that can be sold, and other valuable assets such as jewelry or artwork. Debts, in contrast, subtract from wealth and come in a variety of forms, such as mortgages, credit card debt, and student loans. Although most people do not typically think of wealth as being negative, when the value of a person's debts is greater than the total value of her assets, "negative wealth" is the result.

TABLE 1.1.   Types of assets and debts used to calculate wealth

Assets
Financial assets
- All types of transaction accounts (money market accounts, checking accounts, savings accounts, call accounts)
- Certificates of deposit (CDs)
- Directly held pooled investment funds, excluding money market funds (stock mutual funds, tax-free bond mutual funds, government-bond mutual funds, other bond mutual funds, combination and other mutual funds)
- Savings bonds
- Directly held stocks
- Directly held bonds (excluding bond funds or savings bonds)
- Cash value of whole life insurance

(*continued*)

TABLE 1.1. (continued)

- Other managed assets (annuities, trusts)
- Quasi-liquid retirement accounts[a] (individual retirement accounts/Keoghs, account-type pensions [401(k), 403(b), etc.], future pensions, currently received account-type pensions)

Nonfinancial assets:
- Primary residence
- Residential property other than primary residence
- Net equity in nonresidential real estate
- Businesses
- Other miscellaneous financial or nonfinancial assets

Debts
- Debt secured by primary residence (mortgages, home equity loans, home equity lines of credit)
- Debt secured by other residential property
- Other lines of credit
- Credit card balances
- Installment loans (education loans, vehicle loans, other installment loans)
- Other debt (loans against pensions or life insurance, margin loans, loans from individuals, etc.)

[a]Includes the portion that can be borrowed against and is therefore available for use.

Wealth is a superior indicator of financial status because it embodies the total economic resources available to its holder and has several distinct benefits that income does not. For example, wealth gives people a financial cushion to help them make ends meet if their incomes are cut because of illness, divorce, job loss, or emergencies. Savings accounts are probably the best known type of financial buffer, but other assets can sometimes serve this role. Stock can be sold, a home can be used as collateral for a loan, and it is sometimes possible to borrow against a retirement account.

A second important benefit of wealth is that it can be handed down from generation to generation, making it one of the most powerful and entrenched aspects of privilege and inequality. So while an employee cannot transfer the job that provides his salary to his daughter when he dies, the owner of a family business (a form of wealth) can leave that asset to his child when he dies. The ability to transfer wealth is a primary reason that wealthy families remain wealthy from generation to generation.

Third, wealth can generate income that may make its holder less dependent on having to work for a living. For some, wealth may provide the ability to do something that they enjoy but that doesn't pay well. And people with extensive wealth may be able to avoid working entirely.

Fourth, wealth provides opportunities for shaping social and political agendas. Contributions to political candidates, to issue-oriented organizations, and to foundations are some of the ways that wealth shapes the nation's priorities and economic, political, and social trajectories.[10] Through philanthropy, the wealthy may facilitate social change or support the status quo in ways that others cannot. The women's wealth gap is relevant here because men and women have different preferences for giving. Women are more likely to donate to social service organizations that help others in need and to environmental groups,[11] whereas men are more likely to give money to private foundations.[12] The women's wealth gap therefore has implications beyond individual well-being, influencing the broader social, political, and economic priorities and activities of society.

What Wealth Reveals That Income Does Not

Having a high income does not necessarily mean that a person has a great deal of wealth. High-income celebrities such as Burt Reynolds, Kim Basinger, and MC Hammer have declared bankruptcy. Celebrities are not the only high-income people who face bankruptcy. A study of bankruptcy in five states reveals that the percentage of bankruptcy filers with incomes of $100,000 or more ranged from a low of 2.6% in Tennessee to a high of 7.1% in California.[13] While the reasons for bankruptcy vary, such cases illustrate that high incomes and wealth do not necessarily go hand in hand.

The opposite is also true. Many wealthy individuals lack high incomes. As an example, consider the situation of some retired people: they may own outright a house that is worth a great deal of money and thus have no mortgage to pay. They may also have substantial assets in stocks or other securities that are worth a lot of money but that don't provide much income. On paper, these individuals may even be worth millions of dollars, but their *incomes* are actually below average.

Wealth is much less equally distributed than income. In 2004, the top 1% of the U.S. population earned 17% of the total income but owned 34% of the total wealth (see figures 1.1 and 1.2).[14] In contrast, the bottom 40% of the population earned 10% of the total income but owned only 0.2% of the total wealth. In that same year, the wealthiest

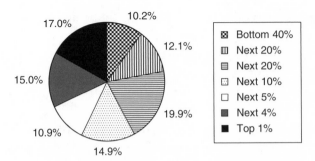

FIGURE 1.1. Percentage of Total Income Received by Percentile Group, 2004. *Source*: Wolff, Edward N. 2007. "Recent Trends in Household Wealth in the United States: Rising Debt and the Middle-Class Squeeze." Levy Economics Institute Working Paper No. 502. www.levy.org/pubs/wp_502.pdf.

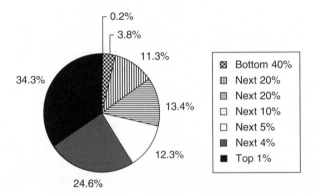

FIGURE 1.2. Percentage of Total Wealth Owned by Percentile Group, 2004. *Source*: Wolff, Edward N. 2007. "Recent Trends in Household Wealth in the United States: Rising Debt and the Middle-Class Squeeze." Levy Economics Institute Working Paper No. 502. www.levy.org/pubs/wp_502.pdf.

20% of households held 85% of the total wealth. The magnitude of income inequality pales in comparison to that of wealth inequality.

Compared to other industrialized countries, the United States exhibits particularly extreme wealth inequality.[15] The tremendous disparity in wealth is the greatest economic fault line in American society and one that is becoming even deeper: between 1983 and 2004, the top 1% experienced a 78% increase in their average wealth whereas the bottom 40% of the wealth distribution saw their wealth decline by 59%.[16] Another way to examine wealth inequality is to compare the wealthiest Americans to the typical American (as represented by the median). In 1962, the wealthiest 1% of Americans held 125 times the median wealth, and by 2004, the wealthiest 1% of Americans held 190 times as much wealth as the typical American.[17]

If we examine how wealth is distributed across society, we can observe inequities that are hidden by the distribution of income. For example, never-married women working full-time earn 95% as much as never-married men working full-time, but women in that group own only 16% as much wealth: never-married men working full-time have a median wealth of $20,000 whereas their female counterparts have a median wealth of $3,150. This comparison is even more striking given the fact that the wealth gap is much larger for never-married women than for other groups of women, even those who experience a much larger earnings gap. In today's tough economy, when layoffs are frequent and unemployment is at record levels, never-married women have a much smaller safety net than other workers. They have very limited resources should they lose their job or face unexpected medical bills or other emergencies.

Clearly, wealth is a much better indicator of economic status and economic well-being than income. It provides a better picture of who is economically vulnerable, who is financially secure, and variations in between.

Why Study Gender Differences in Wealth?

Some may wonder if gender differences in wealth are important. After all, don't most men and women marry, rendering any gender wealth differences relatively unimportant? Actually, about half of all households are headed by single (never-married, widowed, or divorced) persons,[18] which makes the wealth gap between men and women a reality for a large percentage of people. Also, prominent social circumstances prevent women from closing the wealth gap through marriage. First, protection that is offered by marriage will disappear for large groups of women, since about half of all marriages end in divorce.[19] Second, men and women are marrying at later ages,[20] leaving women with more years in which they are self-supporting. In fact, women now spend more of their adult years single than married.[21] In addition, the women's wealth gap is central to understanding the racial wealth gap— particularly for black households—because black women are less likely to marry and to remain married.[22] In short, many men and women spend large portions of their lives unmarried, so the women's wealth gap is quite significant for many. And given the current trends of rising rates of divorce, increasing numbers of children born to unwed parents, and rising ages at first marriage, I argue that the wealth gap is of growing significance. Furthermore, because black women are less likely to marry and are more likely to be single mothers than white women, the racial wealth gap cannot close unless the gender wealth gap closes.

Despite the important role that wealth plays for understanding inequality along racial and class lines,[23] there is no comprehensive study of gender inequality in the amounts and forms of wealth that exist in the United States.[24] One possible explanation for this lacuna is that gender is an individual characteristic; data on wealth, on the other hand, are usually collected at the level of the household or family.[25] And when data are collected by household, the economic or class standing of the members of the household is determined by the head of the household, usually assumed to be the male.[26]

Because existing data on wealth were collected for households and not individuals within the household, studying gender differences in wealth for married and cohabiting persons is particularly challenging. Some may argue that there is no gender inequality in wealth in marriage because husbands and wives are equal owners of marital wealth. Yet a large body of research reveals that household wealth is rarely owned or controlled by all household members equally. Men often make the major financial decisions and control how money is spent or invested. While married couples may pool resources, social scientists have demonstrated that there are unwritten rules regarding the management and control of these joint resources, as well as the freedom to spend them.[27]

Marriage and Wealth

Sociologists studying power dynamics within families have shown that if one partner is economically dependent on the other, the more dependent partner will have less power in the marriage.[28] Since women often earn less than men, they are more likely to be the economically dependent spouse. Women's economic dependency has been identified as a primary mechanism contributing to gender inequality more broadly.[29] For example, economic dependency makes it more difficult for women to leave dysfunctional marriages and abusive relationships.

Even in less extreme situations, a woman's economic dependency often renders her needs or desires secondary since she is not the one bringing in the money. It also sets the stage for further economic dependency. For example, if a couple with a new baby would like one parent to stay home, even the most egalitarian couples will likely decide that, all else being equal, the one who earns less and has lower potential future earnings should exit the labor force.[30] Women's economic dependency thus reinforces the traditional division of labor, in which men work in the labor market for money and women take care of the family. Although women's work at home is important and valuable, it is not financially rewarded. If a woman re-enters the labor market at a later time, her years at home rarely add to her reservoir of job-related skills, and no one in the United States earns pension or Social Security benefits for unpaid caregiving (although people in some other countries do).[31]

Examining many high-profile divorces, such as the very public 1997 divorce of Lorna and Gary Wendt, shatters the assumption that married men and women have equal ownership of household wealth. A highly placed executive with millions of dollars in property, stock options, and more, Mr. Wendt offered his soon-to-be ex-wife a settlement of about $8 million, but she sought $50 million, which equaled half of their estimated $100 million in assets at the time. Although Mrs. Wendt was awarded $20 million in the divorce settlement (more than her husband's original offer), it was a much smaller fraction of the marital assets than the half she had asked for.[32] In commenting on the settlement, economist Myra Strober (then-president of the International Association of Feminist Economics) stated: "When estates grow beyond a certain size, judges move away from equal distribution and over to the old doctrine of 'he who earns it owns it.'"[33]

While divorce settlements vary tremendously, women usually suffer more economic hardship following the end of a marriage.[34] Since approximately half of all marriages end in divorce, any gender inequities with respect to the ownership of household wealth become an unwelcome reality for many women.

Furthermore, although the majority of people do marry at some point in their lives, the average person spends a large proportion of her adult life as a single person. Gender differences in wealth are important for understanding the quality of life for most people. The typical woman may believe that she is sheltered from economic hardship because she is married and shares the family wealth equally, but this is true only for a small proportion of her adult years.

Even if married women do not get divorced, they are likely to outlive their husbands. Contrary to stereotypes about wealthy widows, widowhood is not a financial windfall for most women. The death of a husband is often accompanied by large out-of- pocket medical expenses incurred prior to death, which have often drained savings and sometimes even pushed the household into debt.[35] In fact, the economic consequences of widowhood for women are similar to the economic consequences of divorce.[36] Almost one in five widows lives in poverty, and elderly widows are three times as likely to live in poverty as elderly married couples.[37] The average age of widowhood for women is 60, and in the United States women's average life expectancy is 80 years,[38] leaving about a 25-year gap during which gender wealth differences are likely to have a powerful effect for married women whose partners are absent through death rather than divorce.

Gender Differences in Retirement Wealth

The one area in which gender inequalities in wealth have been studied is retirement wealth. Next to home ownership, retirement assets comprise the largest component of wealth for the middle class,[39] providing a good starting point for investigating the women's wealth gap.

Across all age groups, women have less retirement wealth than men. In 1998, among employed persons ages 18–62, for example, the average amount accumulated in pension plans was $57,239 for men and $25,020 for women.[40] To put it a different way, women had only 40% as much wealth in their pension plans as did men.

A gender gap exists in other forms of retirement assets as well. On average, women have 47% as much as men in their Individual Retirement Accounts (IRAs), with men's average balance equal to $56,429 and women's equal to $26,307.[41] Bear in mind that these figures are for people with jobs. Women are likely to move in and out of the labor force—to give birth and to care for children, to attend to sick elderly parents or other family members—and hence generally have fewer paychecks over their lifetime. This periodic absence from paid labor results in markedly less money in employment-related retirement accounts. The gender gap would be even larger if nonemployed persons were included in these figures.

Gender differences in labor market participation are an important cause of the retirement wealth gap. When examining a cohort of men and women who were 27–35 years old in 1989, economists Bajtelsmit and Jiankoplos found that "the gender pension gap was almost nonexistent…but nine years later women's accumulated pension balances were only 45% of their male counterparts. The most obvious explanation for this change is women's interruptions in labor force participation—and hence pension participation—during the childbearing years."[42] The advantages of compound interest mean that men's early advantage in collecting money in retirement accounts can add up to a great deal of money and a stark difference between their assets and those for women when work life ends.

Perhaps the greatest irony of women's lower retirement wealth is that on average most women actually need *more* resources than men because they have longer average life expectancies. All else being equal, women will need to support themselves an average of 6 years longer than men.[43]

Women Are Not Only Less Rich, but Wealth Poor

Forbes list of the richest Americans in 2009 reveals that eight of the top ten wealthiest Americans are men (table 1.2). Remarkably, of the top 100 wealthiest Americans listed, there were *only eight women*: Christy Walton and family (#4), Alice Walton (#6), Abigail Johnson (#17), Jacqueline Mars (#19), Anne Cox Chambers (#26), Blair Parry-Okedon (#52), and Pauline MacMillan Keinath and Marion MacMillan Pictet (tied for #56).

TABLE 1.2. *Forbes* list of the 10 richest Americans, 2009

Rank	Name	Wealth (millions of dollars)	Source
1	William Gates III	50,000	Microsoft
2	Warren Buffett	40,000	Berkshire Hathaway
3	Lawrence Ellison	27,000	Oracle
4	Christy Walton and family	21,500	Walmart
5	Jim C. Walton	19,600	Walmart
6	Alice Walton	19,300	Walmart
7	S. Robson Walton	19,000	Walmart
8	Michael Bloomberg	17,500	Bloomberg
9 (tie)	Charles Koch	16,000	manufacturing, energy
9 (tie)	David Koch	16,000	manufacturing, energy

Source: *Forbes*, www.forbes.com

The *Forbes* list does more than simply identify the richest Americans; it also offers a social representation of the way that Americans perceive the ownership of wealth. Interestingly, if a wealthy individual is married, only one name appears on the list—usually the husband's—because he is perceived to be the one to whom the wealth belongs. For instance, it was not until Sam Walton's death that his wife's name appeared on the *Forbes* list at all.[44] Christy Walton's name did not appear on the list either until the death of her husband, John Walton (son of Sam and Helen Walton).

Not only are women less likely to be rich; they are *more* likely to live in poverty and to live in poverty for longer periods of time.[45] Women of all ages are more likely to face poverty than their male counterparts (table 1.3), but single mothers face the greatest risk of poverty. The U.S. Census Bureau reports that, in 2006, more than one-third of all women with children under the age of 18 in the household were living in poverty (table 1.4). In contrast, the poverty rate for men with children under the age of 18 was 17.9%, or less than half of the rate for women.[46] The tendency for women to have higher rates of poverty than men was dubbed the "feminization of poverty" in the late seventies,[47] and through the years that term has remained an accurate description of which Americans are more likely to be poor.

TABLE 1.3. Percentages of males and females below poverty level in 2007

Age	Men	Women
Under 18 years	17.9%	18.1%
18–24 years	14.0%	20.6%
25–34 years	9.6%	15.0%
35–44 years	7.8%	11.0%
45–54 years	7.8%	9.1%
55–59 years	7.7%	8.3%
60–64 years	7.8%	10.9%
65–74 years	6.5%	10.8%
75 years and over	6.7%	13.2%
Total	11.1%	13.8%

Note: The Census Bureau measures poverty using money income thresholds that vary according to family size and composition. For further information, see www.census.gov/hhes/www/poverty/definitions.html.
Source: U.S. Census Bureau. 2008. Current Population Survey, Annual Social and Economic Supplement. www.pubdb3.census.gov/macro/032008/pov/new01_100_01.htm

TABLE 1.4. Percentage of families with children under 18 living below poverty level in 2006 by race and gender of head of household

Family type	All races	White	Black	Asian	Hispanic
Male householder, no wife present	17.9%	13.6%	25.8%	19.2%	22.8%
Female householder, no husband present	36.5%	30.2%	43.3%	23.8%	42.5%
Married couple families	6.4%	3.7%	8.7%	7.3%	15.6%

Note: For race, white = non-Hispanic white; black = black only or in combination with any other race (self-identified); Asian = Asian only or in combination with any other race (self-identified); Hispanic = Hispanic of any race (self-identified).
Source: U.S. Census Bureau. 2008. Current Population Survey, table 4. http://www.census.gov/hhes/www/poverty/histpov/hstpov2.html

While 14% of women live in poverty, almost one-third of nonmarried women are *wealth poor*, meaning either that they have no assets at all or that the value of their debts surpasses the value of their assets.[48] The high proportion of women who are wealth poor provides strong evidence that lack of wealth is a major barrier to women's financial stability.

Despite knowing that women are more likely to be wealth poor and that they rarely appear on lists of the richest Americans, we have understood very little about gender differences in wealth for the population at large—until now. In this book, I have gathered empirical evidence to craft a more finely grained picture of the women's wealth gap.

Data

To provide a thorough portrait of the women's wealth gap and its consequences, I use two complementary sources of data. The majority of statistical data that I present on wealth come from the nationally representative 2004 Survey of Consumer Finances (SCF), collected by the National Opinion Research Council on behalf of the Federal Reserve Board.[49] This survey is considered to be one of the best sources of data on wealth inequality, providing an accurate statistical portrait of the distribution of wealth in the United States.[50] One of the distinguishing features of the SCF is that, in addition to having a geographically based random sample, it oversamples high-income households (which are the ones most likely to have a great deal of wealth). Very wealthy people are less likely to show up in random samples because they constitute such a small percentage of the population at large. Because the majority of wealth is owned by such a small percentage of the population, the oversampling of high-income households provides the most accurate view of the extent of wealth inequality and the magnitude of the women's wealth gap. I also draw upon data from the SCF from earlier years in order to provide an overview of how the women's wealth gap has changed over time.

In addition to using the Survey of Consumer Finances data, I also conducted in-depth interviews with fifty men and women. While these interviews cannot be considered representative of the entire population, the purpose of the interviews is to provide insights not available in the statistical data. The twenty-two men and twenty-eight women who were interviewed came from a variety of occupations, class backgrounds, races, and ages. However, all would most likely be found along the continuum from lower-middle to upper-middle class. Their voices are woven throughout the book, and I am extremely grateful for their willingness to share their thoughts and experiences. (I give more details about the Survey of Consumer Finances, the interview sample, and methodology in the appendix.)

Unless otherwise noted, the data I present are for people younger than age 65 (for married and cohabiting households, the age of the older spouse or partner was used). I have two reasons for setting an age limit in this study. First, people generally spend down their wealth when they retire, and some very wealthy people start to give money away on the advice of estate planners as they age. I wanted to focus primarily on those who are participating fully in the economy of earning, saving, and generating wealth, not those who are in a divestment stage.[51] Second, one of my goals in the book is to examine the link between income and wealth, which generally shifts when people retire. Therefore, to simplify, I focus on people who are under age 65. Nevertheless, many of the substantive conclusions I report here will hold for those over age 65 as well, and data for those age 65 and older is available on the book's Web site www.mariko-chang.com/shortchanged.

In determining how to study the women's wealth gap for married households empirically, I considered two different options. The first was to divide the wealth in half, following the conventional understanding that household wealth is owned equally by husbands and wives. The second was to attribute ownership of wealth to husbands and wives based on who is reported in the data as owning each asset (and dividing ownership of jointly owned resources in half). I found neither of these options satisfactory because formal ownership of wealth does not always translate into control over wealth, which is more directly linked with women's financial status within marriage. In addition, most married couples *do* share resources, rendering a division of wealth between couples problematic.[52] In the end, I decided that rather than arbitrarily dividing wealth between married couples in an effort to obtain a quantitative indicator of differences in the wealth of husbands and wives, I would investigate gender differences between spouses in the *control over* wealth using my qualitative interview data.

While it is extremely important for women to have parity with men at the top of the wealth distribution, few people—men or women—have even close to the amount of wealth necessary to be included on lists of the richest Americans. My work in this book is, therefore, focused on the majority of households which fall roughly in the middle, between rich and poor. This focus on the situation of the more typical household will help draw attention to the current situations faced by so many women as they attempt to increase their economic prosperity.

Overview

My intention in this book is to shift the dialogue about women's economic future toward one that includes the importance of building wealth. Chapter 2 provides the reader with important facts about the women's wealth gap. The median wealth owned by nonmarried women is only 36% of the median wealth owned by nonmarried men, but the wealth gap varies in significant ways for women of different ages, races, and marital status characteristics. For example, despite the advances of the feminist movement and the tremendous gains young women have made with respect to educational attainment and in the workplace, the wealth ratio (percentage of wealth owned by women in comparison to men) indicates that younger women are more disadvantaged than their older peers. Furthermore, gender differences in wealth vary by race and ethnicity. More than half of all single Hispanic women living in the United States are wealth poor (they have zero wealth or the value of their debts surpasses the value of any assets). In contrast, 26% of single white women and 36% of single black women are wealth poor.

In chapter 3, I discuss the concept of the *wealth escalator* as the mechanism for understanding why men have an advantage when it comes to translating income into wealth. Chapter 3 also discusses the debt anchor that compounds women's wealth-building disadvantage. Here, I argue that, while earnings are important, the ability to tap into the wealth escalator helps one build wealth much more quickly than by earnings alone. Women's lower incomes place them at a disadvantage in wealth building, but women are less likely to tap into the wealth escalator because of the types of jobs and industries they work in and because of their patterns of labor force participation.

Chapter 4 investigates the effect that parenthood has on wealth for men and for women. Whether married or single, women who become mothers are placed in a "no-win" situation. For every year a woman is a full-time caregiver, she must work five extra years to make up for the lost income and pension benefits.[53] Even if she goes back to work full-time, she will face a motherhood wage penalty. I also discuss a "motherhood wealth tax," which is greatest for nonmarried mothers because they are likely to have custody of children and to have less disposable income to save or invest. As a consequence, the gender wealth gap would continue to exist even if men and women had equal incomes simply because women are more likely to have custody of children.

Chapter 5 examines the extent to which the women's wealth gap is exacerbated or mitigated by the ways that men and women save and invest their money. When it comes to saving and investing, women and men do have different portfolios. Women are less likely to own assets that are considered more financially risky but that also have the highest average rates of return over time: stocks, investment real estate, and business assets. Women are often caught in a financial Catch-22: their lower disposable incomes put them at a disadvantage for building savings, and their lack of a financial safety net means that their smaller nest eggs are subject to depletion in crisis situations. Because of these two factors, they cannot afford the risk and the long time horizon necessary to secure higher rates of return on investments.

Chapter 6 turns to the topic of wealth for married couples. Although it is often assumed that husbands and wives have equal ownership of marital wealth, the interview data suggest a complicated story. While a minority of couples share equal control over marital assets, most couples adopt other strategies. Some couples engage in voluntary specialization, delegating financial tasks in ways that appear to be gender neutral, but in fact leave men with more control over marital wealth. Other couples engage in voluntary separation, dividing money into three categories: *his*, *hers*, and *ours*. Ironically, each method of organizing marital finances can be reconciled with beliefs of fairness and equality between husbands and wives. The outcome, however, is that women are still less likely to have equal access to the financial resources of marriage.

Chapter 7 explains why equal pay and family-friendly policies cannot close the gender wealth gap. Instead, I argue that we need new policies that address the two primary causes of the gender wealth gap: the motherhood wealth tax and women's lack of access to the wealth escalator. These new policy directions include providing paid family leave, integrating caregiving into the wealth escalator, and engaging men in caretaking. I also argue for the advantages inherent in providing additional mechanisms for supporting wealth-building opportunities for single parents, improving women's access to low-interest loans, increasing opportunities for women's entrepreneurship, expanding the definition of assets as codified in divorce laws, and decoupling affordable health care from full-time employment.

This book is *not* a financial "how-to" book for women and does not provide instructions for investing money or increasing one's financial knowledge. It explains how existing social structures—such as Social Security, tax codes, and the motherhood wealth penalties—help men ride the wealth escalator while women who work just as hard are left climbing the stairs or even taking the down escalator. Women's lack of wealth is not simply a matter of individual failures to save or manage money effectively; women are at a disadvantage in acquiring wealth because of the way society has valued certain activities over others and helped some turn their earnings into wealth with much less effort. The purpose of this book is to provide a comprehensive portrait of where women and men stand with respect to wealth, to examine the explanations for and consequences of women's lack of wealth, and to offer possible solutions for improving the financial situation of women, which in turn will benefit not only them but men and families as well.

TWO

Who Has What?

*My aunt . . . died by a fall from her horse when she was riding out to take the air
in Bombay. The news of my legacy reached me one night about the same time that
the act was passed that gave votes to women. A solicitor's letter fell into the post-box
and when I opened it I found that she had left me five hundred pounds a year for ever.
Of the two—the vote and the money—the money, I own, seemed
infinitely the more important.*

—*Virginia Woolf*, A Room of One's Own

VIRGINIA WOOLF'S STATUS as feminist icon might lead some to believe that she would view the victory of women's suffrage as the most empowering event in her life. But no matter how much she valued the right to vote, the freedom that she obtained through financial independence made an even greater impression upon her. Woolf recognized that women's freedom and equality are inexorably tied to their financial self-sufficiency and self-determination. In the 70-plus years since *A Room of One's Own* was published, women have made important strides in their opportunities to earn, as well as in their right to spend and manage their own money. But this chapter will demonstrate that, in spite of these gains, the wealth gap is the fault line of women's financial well-being.

The Women's Wealth Gap

I cannot tell you how much wealth your next-door neighbor has, but I can tell you how much wealth the typical American has. To do so, there are two common measures at our disposal: the mean and the median.[1] Figure 2.1 presents the mean and the median wealth for married and cohabiting households,[2] unmarried men ("single-male households"), and unmarried women ("single-female households").[3] The mean is strongly affected by the small proportion of extremely wealthy people, who pull the average higher. Therefore, to obtain a more accurate picture—one not influenced unduly by the wealth of the few—I deliberately *do not* refer to the *average* person or household; instead, the term *typical* household will be used throughout this book to denote the median wealth of individuals or households.

As is evident in figure 2.1, significant differences in wealth exist among couples (married and cohabiting), single men, and single women. (For simplification, I will use the term *married* to refer to both married and cohabiting couples.)[4] Married households are the wealthiest, with a median wealth of $113,000. The financial advantages of marriage may stem from two sources: the differential selection of individuals into marriage (i.e., the possibility that people with more resources are more likely to marry) and the impact that marriage has on the ability to accumulate wealth.[5] To begin with, married couples may have more wealth because many people wait until they are financially self-sufficient to marry. Married couples also enjoy various economic benefits that make it much easier to build wealth, such as economies of scale—there is only one rent to pay, one electric bill,

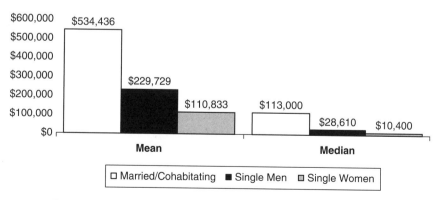

FIGURE 2.1. Mean and Median Wealth, 2004. *Source*: Author's calculations from the 2004 Survey of Consumer Finances for persons ages 18–64.

and so on. In addition, health insurance is often proportionally less expensive for a married couple than for two single individuals. (The wealth-enhancing effects of marriage are one of the reasons that same-sex couples fight for the right to marry.)

For some, marriage may actually instigate a substantial transfer of wealth across generations. One of the interviewees, Sondra, a new-lywed expecting her first baby, provides an account of just such a circumstance:

> When Ben and I got engaged, my parents gave us $15,000 and said we could either spend it on the wedding or use it as a down payment for a house or whatnot.... So we had a small ceremony and reception with only family and close friends and Bill's grandparents also gave us some money as a wedding present...and we had a bit of money saved up...so after we got married, we were able to buy a house right away.

Whereas married households have the most wealth, single women have the least, with a median wealth of $10,400. In comparison, single men have a median wealth of $28,610, a wealth gap of $18,210. To put it a bit differently, single women own only 36 cents for every dollar of wealth owned by single men (this disparity is called the gender wealth ratio).

Another tool used by researchers of wealth inequality is to divide the population into equal fifths, or quintiles, ranked according to the amount of wealth owned, from lowest to highest.[6] If gender did not affect wealth, we would expect to see men and women distributed equally across each quintile. However, as figure 2.2 reveals, women are much more likely than men to be in the bottom fifth of households, with zero or negative wealth (quintile 1), and least likely to be found in the wealthiest fifth (quintile 5).

Figure 2.2 also demonstrates that the majority of people (the bottom 60%, or quintiles 1–3) have less than $109,000 in wealth. While popular culture and the media may imply that there are millionaires around every corner, in reality only 7% of households under age 65 have a net worth of a million dollars or more (figure 2.3). The majority of millionaire households are composed of married couples, but single men are four times more likely to be millionaires than single women.

To take a more detailed look at the women's wealth gap for unmarried persons, it is useful to divide them according to whether they have never been married, are divorced,[7] or are widowed, because there is much variation among these groups with respect to average age, the potential wealth-enhancing benefits of marriage, and the economic costs of divorce (see figure 2.4). The typical never-married woman has

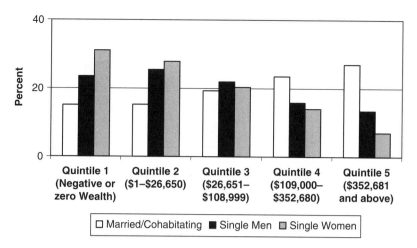

FIGURE 2.2. Distribution of Wealth by Quintiles, 2004. *Source*: Author's calculations from the 2004 Survey of Consumer Finances for persons ages 18–64.

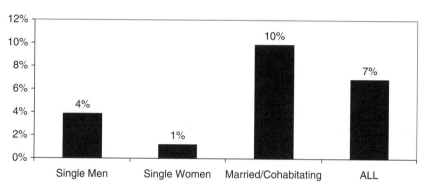

FIGURE 2.3. Percent of Households who are Millionaires, by Household Type, 2004. *Source*: Author's calculations from the 2004 Survey of Consumer Finances for persons ages 18–64.

a wealth gap of $14,000 compared to her male equivalent; the wealth gap for divorced women is about $25,000, and widowed women face a wealth gap of $45,000.

An alternative way of illustrating gender differences in wealth is to describe it as a dollars-to-cents ratio. In addition to examining the wealth gap (the dollar difference in wealth), looking at the wealth ratio helps round out the picture of wealth inequality. For example, a $10,000 wealth gap has a different substantive meaning if women's median wealth is $5,000 and men's is $15,000 than it has if women's median wealth is $340,000 and men's median wealth is

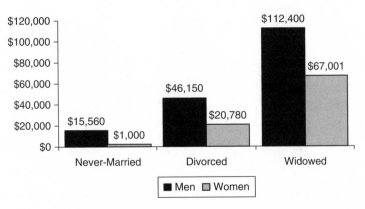

FIGURE 2.4. Median Wealth for Never-Married, Divorced, and Widowed Men and Women, 2004. *Source*: Author's calculations from the 2004 Survey of Consumer Finances for persons ages 18–64.

$350,000. In both of these examples, the wealth gap is $10,000, but the ramifications of that gap in terms of lifestyle and other wealth benefits are likely to be much more consequential for the former group.

The wealth ratio for single men and women is shown in figure 2.5. The typical never-married woman (as represented by the median) owns only 6 cents of wealth for every dollar of wealth owned by the typical never-married man. Divorced women fare better, with 45 cents in wealth for every dollar of wealth owned by divorced men, and widowed women fare best, with 60 cents of wealth for every dollar of wealth owned by the typical widower. Although by no means close to equal, the more favorable position of widowed women is most likely due to the fact that assets that were once shared by a married couple are now owned by the surviving spouse (rather than divided, as in the case of divorce).[8] Nevertheless, while the gender wealth ratio is highest for those who are single because of the death of a spouse, widows also experience the largest wealth gap, with the typical widower owning more than $45,000 more wealth than the typical widow.

Why do never-married women fare so poorly with respect to the wealth ratio? Table 2.1 provides some descriptive information for never-married men and women that allows us to examine factors that are likely to influence the acquisition of wealth. Never-married men have several advantages over never-married women when it comes to accumulating wealth, most notably their higher incomes, their

FIGURE 2.5. Dollars to Cents Ratio of Median Wealth for Never-Married, Divorced, and Widowed Men and Women, 2004. *Source*: Author's calculations from the 2004 Survey of Consumer Finances for persons ages 18–64.

TABLE 2.1. Characteristics of never-married men and women

	Women	Men
Median wealth	$1,000	$15,560
Median income	$22,591	$28,753
Average age	35	34
Percent with a college degree	39%	39%
Percent with a professional or managerial occupation	34%	28%
Percent currently working full-time	64%	70%
Percent self-employed	7%	11%
Percent white	53%	69%
Percent single parent[a]	36%	2%
Percent who own a home	31%	37%
Percent with a retirement account or pension	41%	43%
Percent who have received an inheritance	14%	16%

[a]Single parent is defined as someone having children under age 18 living in the household. This variable does not capture men or women who were single parents in the past, whose children are 18 or older. If the sample is restricted to never-married people under age 40, 41% of women are single parents and 2% of men are single parents.

Source: Author's calculations from the 2004 Survey of Consumer Finances for persons ages 18–64.

greater likelihood of working full-time, and higher rates of home ownership and pension or retirement account ownership. Never-married women have the wealth advantage of their slightly older median age (wealth generally increases with age), but never-married women are also much more likely to be single parents, which reduces their disposable income and hence their ability to build wealth, all else being equal (the effects of single parenthood will be discussed further in chapter 4).

Generational Differences

The growth of the feminist movement in the 1960s and beyond helped bring about social and economic progress for women. Whereas only 35% of women ages 16 and over were in the labor force in 1960,[9] that percentage had increased to 59% by 2005,[10] and many of these workers were mothers of young children. Likewise, women have made tremendous strides in high-earning occupations, and women are now earning college degrees in numbers that surpass men's.[11] Moreover, the earnings gap has improved: in 1960, women earned 61 cents for every dollar earned by men; by 2007, women's share had grown to 78 cents.[12] Younger women are most likely to benefit from the rising economic opportunities for women, and hence we might expect that the wealth gap would be smallest for younger women.

Although wealth increases with age for all household types (figure 2.6), single women experience much flatter increases in wealth by age cohort—that is, women at different life stages (as represented by age group) receive smaller gains than men at each stage. The typical single woman in her 20s begins her adulthood with zero wealth. In contrast, the typical single man in his 20s has $1,100 of wealth. The absolute dollar difference in median wealth is larger for older cohorts, with the typical man 60 years old or older with $79,000 more wealth than his female counterpart.

Despite the tremendous economic improvements facing younger women with respect to earnings, job opportunities, and educational achievement, the gender wealth ratio (the proportion of wealth owned

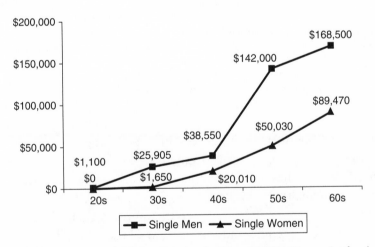

FIGURE 2.6. Median Wealth by Gender and Age, 2004. *Source*: Author's calculations from the 2004 Survey of Consumer Finances.

FIGURE 2.7. Dollars to Cents Ratio of Median Wealth by Gender and Age, 2004. *Source*: Author's calculations from the 2004 Survey of Consumer Finances.

by women in comparison to men) is the most dramatic for women in their 20s and 30s (see figure 2.7). Women in their 20s have a median wealth of zero, and women in their 30s have only 6 cents for every dollar of wealth owned by single men in their 30s. Although the absolute dollar difference in wealth is largest for the older cohorts, in terms of the *percentage* difference, or wealth ratio, younger women are most disadvantaged when compared with men their own age (figure 2.6).

To help us further investigate why younger women are faring so poorly with respect to the wealth ratio, table 2.2 provides descriptive

TABLE 2.2.   Characteristics of single men and women under age 40

	Women	Men
Median wealth	$100	$1,500
Median income	$21,564	$28,753
Average age	30	29
Percent with a college degree	33%	35%
Percent with a professional or managerial occupation	35%	29%
Percent currently working full-time	72%	75%
Percent self-employed	5%	10%
Percent white	57%	65%
Percent never married	68%	77%
Percent single parent[a]	54%	9%
Percent who own a home	27%	35%
Percent with a retirement account or pension	36%	40%
Percent who have received an inheritance	11%	15%

[a]Single parent is defined as someone having children under age 18 living in the household.
Source: Author's calculations from the 2004 Survey of Consumer Finances.

information for single men and women in their 20s and 30s, focusing on factors that are likely to influence wealth. Differences between single men and women under age 40 are similar to those displayed in table 2.1 for never-married men and women: again, we see that men have higher median incomes and are more likely to own homes and pension or retirement accounts. Young women are much more likely to be single parents. Therefore, the wealth gap between young men and women is most likely a result of a combination of factors, including differences in income levels, home ownership rates, pension or retirement account ownership, and the burdens of single parenthood. These factors will be explored further in subsequent chapters.

Wealth Poor: On a Tightrope with No Safety Net

One of wealth's most important benefits is the safety net it provides when income is cut or disappears, as might happen in the case of illness or job loss. It also provides a cushion for large or unexpected expenses such as buying a new car or paying to repair a broken refrigerator. No one wants to plan for the worst, but in today's economic times, in which inequality is increasing and in which layoffs, foreclosures, bankruptcy, and unemployment are becoming more frequent than ever before, it is more important than ever that people have some savings to fall back on.

Christine knows the importance of having a financial cushion:

> Just 3 months after I bought my house, I was laid off. It was totally unexpected and I would have thought it was a joke except my coworkers weren't smiling.... Two weeks before, I replaced the hot water heater and the kitchen floor because it was in really bad shape, so I had some really big bills coming.... I had taken out a home equity line of credit to do some other improvements to the bathroom, but when I was laid off, I put all improvements on the back burner. It was close to 5 months until I got a new job and I was able to do some part-time work during that time. After the third month, I had to dip into the home equity line of credit a bit to pay the mortgage. It really killed me to have to do that, but without it I would have probably had to run up all my credit cards or something and hope for the best.

About one out of three single women, one out of four single men, and one out of seven married or cohabiting households are *wealth poor*, meaning that they have a zero or even negative net worth (figure 2.8). Either these households have no assets at all or the value of their

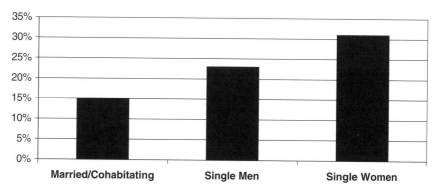

FIGURE 2.8. Percentage of Households that are "Wealth Poor" (have Zero or Negative Wealth), 2004. *Source*: Author's calculations from the 2004 Survey of Consumer Finances for persons ages 18–64.

debts is greater than the value of their assets. The financial profiles of households in this group vary. Some people with zero wealth have no savings and no debt and are likely to be living from paycheck to paycheck. Others who are wealth poor have a small amount of savings, but owe more on their credit cards than they have in their savings accounts. There are also some who appear on the surface to be doing well financially—they are home owners and have what looks from the outside like a solid middle-class lifestyle—but they carry a large amount of debt. Persons who are wealth poor may have faced a period of unemployment, incurred a huge medical expense, or borrowed heavily against their home equity and are now falling behind as their expenses rise and the value of their house and real estate in general declines. Although these hypothetical people may look different from the outside, each is dangerously close to sinking into financial quicksand.

Another way of understanding people's level of financial stability is to see how many months they would be able to sustain themselves if they were suddenly deprived of an income. Financial advisors generally recommend having 6–12 months of income in savings just in case "the unimaginable" should happen. This goal is out of reach for most. On average, single men have 3.7 months of income in savings, whereas single women have 2.1 months of income in savings (figure 2.9).[13] While many individuals would fall short of the recommended 6–12 months of savings, men on average have almost 2 months' more additional income saved to help them weather a spell of unemployment, illness, or other emergency.

It is noteworthy that, with respect to average months of income saved, single men actually have an advantage over married or cohabiting

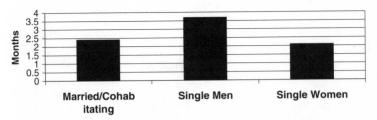

FIGURE 2.9. Average Number of Months of Income in Savings, 2004. *Source*: Author's calculations of the 2004 Survey of Consumer Finances for persons ages 18–64.

households.[14] This finding is extremely important because, in addition to providing men with the ability to endure through tough times, this larger safety net may enable them to take the financial risks that can potentially create greater wealth in the long run.[15]

Eric, a single man in his late 30s, explains how he was able to build his now-successful business:

> When I first started [the business], I thought it would all be okay since I had roughly $10,000 in the bank. But things took longer to get running and I had to buy some expensive equipment.... I saw the money disappearing every month and knew I had to do something.... If things got really bad, I planned to stop paying rent and live in my car to save on that expense and shower at the gym. I can't imagine doing that if I had a family or kids to support, but because it was only me, I knew I could do it for a short while. Lucky for me, it didn't come to that.

Household, Gender, and Race

Wealth is not color-blind. Our country has a long history of racial discrimination that has had a profound and long-lasting impact on racial differences in wealth.[16] For example, in his book *The Hidden Cost of Being African American*, sociologist Thomas Shapiro demonstrates just how large the wealth gap is between blacks and whites: in 1999, the typical white family had $81,000 in wealth, whereas the typical black family had only $8,000.

Consistent with findings by other experts, my own research finds that black and Hispanic households hold significantly less wealth than white households (see figure 2.10).[17] But there are some important differences between groups in the contours of wealth inequality. Among married households, those belonging to the classification "Asian and

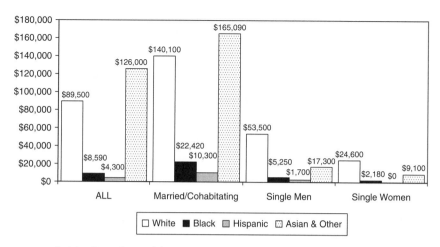

FIGURE 2.10. Racial Wealth Gap by Household Type and Gender, 2004.
Source: Author's calculations of the 2004 Survey of Consumer Finances for persons ages 18–64.

other racial groups" have the highest median wealth,[18] with white married and cohabiting households a close second. Among single men and women, whites have the most wealth and Hispanics have the least. The wealth disadvantage of being black has received much attention, but the wealth disadvantage of being Hispanic appears to be even greater. Research indicates that the wealth disadvantage for Hispanics as a group is related primarily to their larger families, their younger ages at marriage or childbearing, their lower levels of educational attainment and lower earnings, and the influence of a large immigrant population whose general economic profile tends to fall at the lower end of the spectrum.[19]

The gender wealth ratio varies across different racial groups, as illustrated in figure 2.11. Women in the category of "Asian and other" fare best overall, with 53 cents for every dollar of wealth held by their male counterparts. White women and black women are not too far behind, with gender wealth ratios of 46 cents and 42 cents for each dollar earned by white men and by black men, respectively. Hispanic women are particularly wealth poor, with a median wealth of zero. In other words, more than half of single Hispanic women have no wealth at all.

For women as for men, the wealth advantage of being white is tremendous; the wealth disadvantage of being Hispanic is equally severe. But race and gender are entwined. It appears that the more severe the racial wealth disadvantage is, the more severe the gender wealth

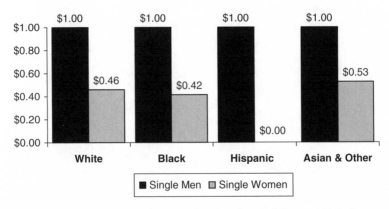

FIGURE 2.11. Dollars to Cents Ratio by Gender and Race, 2004. *Source*: Author's calculations of the 2004 Survey of Consumer Finances for persons ages 18–64.

ratio is within that racial group. For instance, Hispanics experience the most severe wealth disadvantage of the different racial groups presented here, and the gender wealth ratio for Hispanics is also the most dramatic. Conversely, Asian and other races as a group have the highest median household wealth and the highest gender wealth ratio. When there is less wealth overall within a racial group, that wealth appears to be distributed most unevenly between men and women. The women's wealth gap therefore widens within racial groups as the total wealth resources of that racial group decline.

These data underscore the existence of a tremendous racial wealth gap. But racial wealth gaps are magnified for women. While the wealth gap is not experienced uniformly by women of different races, it persists in varying degrees across all racial groups. Of all single women, Hispanics fare worst. The huge wealth gap experienced by Hispanic women is likely caused by a complex set of interrelated factors, including job and residential segregation, discrimination, fertility rates, educational attainment, and an immigration history that limits the ability of Hispanic women to generate wealth[20] (these factors will be discussed in greater detail in chapter 4).

Historical Trends

During the 40 years since Betty Friedan's *The Feminine Mystique* was first published, women have made significant inroads into prestigious, traditionally male occupations, they have surpassed men in their rates of college enrollment and completion,[21] and they have made key inroads into political office. In his book *Destined for Equality*, sociologist Robert Max Jackson documents the progress that women have made toward equality and perhaps too optimistically suggests that "continued progress toward equality is inevitable."[22]

Yet despite improvements in women's access to jobs, incomes, education, and political office since the 1960s, a substantial wage ratio of 78% remains.[23] The wage gap seems stubbornly resistant to the dramatic advances that women have realized in other areas. What about wealth?

Figure 2.12 presents the median wealth for single men and women from 1989 to 2004 in constant 2004 dollars.[24] This overview allows us to examine how well single women and men have fared relative to each other and relative to how they were doing in 2004.[25] From 1989 to 1998, the median wealth of both women and men rose, and the gap between the two actually appeared to be narrowing slightly during the 1990s. However, from 1998 to 2004, two distressing trends emerged. First, in relative terms, the median wealth of single women actually declined. In 2004 dollars, single women were faring better in 1998 than in 2004: in 1998, their median wealth was $12,748, whereas in 2004, it was $10,400. Second, the median wealth of single men improved dramatically between 1998 and 2004, from $19,238 to $28,610. The consequence of the divergent trends of men's and women's wealth is that the wealth gap between single men and women actually worsened from 1998 to 2004.[26] In other words, the women's wealth gap, which

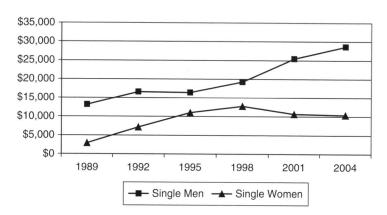

FIGURE 2.12. Trends in Median Wealth for Single Women and Men, 1989–2004 (in 2004 dollars). *Source*: Author's calculations of the 1989, 1992, 1995, 1998, 2001, and 2004 Survey of Consumer Finances for persons ages 18–64.

had been declining through the 1990s, has been increasing in the first decade of our new millennium.[27]

While the reversal after 1998 of what had been a declining women's wealth gap is no doubt the result of many factors, a divergence in debt between single men and women likely plays a critical role.[28] The proportion of single men with any debt declined from 1998 to 2004, whereas the proportion of single women with any debt increased by 8% over this time period. Moreover, types of debt differed for men and women. Between 1998 and 2004, median levels of mortgage debt increased by 33% for men and 23% for women, but men's median credit card debt increased by only 1.5%, whereas women's median credit card debt increased by 17%. During this period, debt levels for car loans and education loans declined for men, but increased for women, who also experienced higher increases in levels of debt for goods and services.[29] Women were falling into debt more quickly than men and were acquiring the types of debt (credit cards, car loans, goods and services) that act like financial quicksand, taking money out of the household without providing a durable benefit.[30] In contrast, men were acquiring mostly mortgage debt, which has several wealth-building advantages (more detail on the differences between productive and destructive debt is provided in chapter 3).

Women's Income vs. Women's Wealth

Income is related to wealth, but the women's wealth gap cannot be attributed solely to lower earnings, nor is it simply a reflection of the more general gender inequalities in American society. A comparison of the gender income and wealth ratios provides a glimpse into just how complicated the women's wealth gap is.

Like the gender wealth ratio, the gender income ratio varies significantly depending on whether one compares men and women who are married, divorced, widowed, or never married (table 2.3). Data from the U.S. Census Bureau reveal that never-married women working full-time earn 95% of what their male counterparts earn. This very small gap in the gender wage ratio is likely a result of the typically younger ages of never-married women, who are likely to have reaped the largest benefits from the advances of the feminist movement, including higher educational attainment, legislation prohibiting sex discrimination in the workplace, and changing norms about women's role in society. In addition, wage differences between men and women tend to be smaller

TABLE 2.3. Gender income and wealth ratios for full-time workers (ages 18–64)

Household type	Median income	Gender ratio	Median wealth	Gender ratio
Never-married		95.2%		15.8%
Women	$27,999		$3,150	
Men	$29,402		$20,000	
Divorced[a]		83.9%		69.3%
Women	$33,897		$30,500	
Men	$40,407		$44,000	
Widowed		77.2%		420.5%
Women	$31,149		$132,750	
Men	$40,331		$31,570	
Married		68.9%		
Women	$32,216			
Men	$46,773			

[a]The "Divorced" category contains separated individuals with distinguishable assets for the data on wealth but only divorced people for the data on income.

Sources: Income data are from the U.S. Census Bureau. 2004. Current Population Survey, Annual Social and Economic Supplement. http://pubdb3.census.gov/macro/032004/perinc/new02_062 .htm. Wealth data are from author's calculations from the 2004 Survey of Consumer Finances.

at younger ages,[31] when people are relatively new to the labor market and working disproportionately in lower-paying entry-level positions. In stark contrast to the data on earnings, never-married women working full-time own only 16 cents of wealth for every dollar of wealth owned by men. One possible explanation for the lack of wealth for never-married women is the financial disadvantage posed by single parenthood (see table 2.1), which I will explore further in chapter 4.

Even if a woman does not have children, a small initial difference in income can add up to a tremendous wealth disadvantage over the long term: women who have no margin for savings lose out on compounding interest and the appreciation of assets. For a simple illustration, consider the hypothetical typical never-married male and female working full-time. As suggested by the median incomes in table 2.3, the typical woman earns $1,403 less than the typical man. Now suppose that this man took his extra $1,403 and invested it. If he never added a dime to this initial amount and simply let this money grow over the next 20 years at a very modest 5% return, he would accumulate $3,723 in wealth (i.e., the original amount plus the compounded interest). Now suppose that during each of these 20 years, he added the initial male income bonus of $1,403 and subjected it to the same savings/interest regime: he would have a total of $50,114.[32] (If he simply put the extra money under his mattress, earning no interest or capital gains, he would have only $28,060.) This simple example reveals how even a small gender gap in earnings can result in a substantial wealth gap over time.

In comparison with that of never-married people, the situation of widows is complicated. Women tend to lose their spouses at younger ages than men do, as women tend to marry men who are older than they are and men have a shorter average life expectancy. Consequently, there are many more widowed women than men among those under 65 years old. When we examine the wealth of men and women under age 65 who are working full-time, widowed women appear to be doing exceptionally well, with the typical widowed woman owning more than four times as much wealth as the typical widowed man. But when we expand that category to include persons younger than 65 who are not working full-time, we see the opposite, with the typical widowed woman owning only 60% of the wealth of the typical widowed man (figure 2.5). The favorable result for widows working full-time is likely being driven in part by differences in *who* is working full-time. It appears that widowed men under age 65 who have enough wealth are not working full-time, most likely because they can afford to retire or to work part-time.

Comparisons of the gender wealth and income ratios for full-time workers have important implications. First and most simply, the gender wealth ratio is smaller than the gender income ratio. For example, divorced women working full-time earn 84% of the income and own 70% of the wealth of divorced men their own age. The income and wealth contrast is even more striking for never-married women who are working full-time: they earn 95% of their male counterparts' income but own only 16% as much wealth. Relying on income to represent women's economic situation has painted a much rosier picture of how women are faring financially.

Second, income and wealth give us contradictory information regarding where the gender gaps are greatest. With respect to income, single women, whether they are divorced, widowed, or simply never married, fare better than married women (the gender income ratio is smaller for married women than for divorced, widowed, or never-married women). Although the wealth of married couples is not broken down by gender, if we assume that married women have access to approximately half of the total household wealth during marriage, their economic situation is far superior to that of single women. (The assumption that marital wealth is controlled equally will be discussed in detail in chapter 6.) Therefore, in contrast to what the data on income show, when it comes to wealth, nonmarried women appear to fare more poorly than married women.

To summarize, examining the wealth ratio reveals that economic inequality between men and women is much greater than the income ratio suggests. Furthermore, the gender income and wealth ratios reveal sharp differences in the relative economic situations of married and single women. Nonmarried women fare better than their married counterparts with respect to the gender income ratio, but if we assume that partners in a household share their wealth equally, the gender wealth ratio is much smaller for nonmarried women than it is for married women. Comparisons of the gender income and wealth ratios reveal that the gender wealth ratio is not merely an exaggeration of the gender income ratio; it is a unique dimension of women's economic status. An accurate measurement of women's financial well-being cannot be obtained without attention to the women's wealth gap.

Conclusion

For every dollar of wealth owned by single men, single women own only 36 cents. The reliance on income to depict women's economic status has painted a much rosier picture of how well women are doing financially. In spite of better incomes, women's economic disadvantage is not disappearing or becoming a relic of prior generations. We know this because the gender wealth gap persists even for women in their 20s and 30s, who have had access to the most lucrative occupations and have benefited from the economic advancements of the feminist movement. Furthermore, since 1998, the gender wealth ratio has been on the rise, suggesting that this problem will continue to plague women and the people—children, older parents, disabled spouses, and others—who depend on them.

Until women can accrue enough wealth to keep them out of debt and to provide them with the ability to endure periodic unemployment or ill health, they will be living on a financial fault line, at the mercy of the women's wealth gap. And while nearly all women, regardless of their incomes, suffer from this lack of wealth, clearly some are more vulnerable than others. Close to one out of three single women is wealth poor—she has no wealth at all or has negative wealth. The women's wealth gap persists across all racial groups, but according to the data examined here, single Hispanic women fare the worst, with more than half being wealth poor.

It is important to remember that the women's wealth gap varies by marital status. Never-married women fare worse overall, as they hold only 6% of the wealth of never-married men. Their lack of wealth is particularly surprising given that never-married women working full-time have almost closed the earnings gap. But single parenthood is an important factor in understanding this seeming paradox (see chapter 4). The extreme financial vulnerability of never-married women has been hidden by their ability to reduce the income gap.

Married women are by far the wealthiest, with a median net worth of $113,000. If one assumes that this wealth is shared equally, then married women are doing well economically. We might anticipate some problems here, though, if we look ahead to chapter 6. While couples do share wealth, they may not necessarily do so as a 50/50 proposition. It turns out that women's struggles to sustain themselves economically as single persons have implications for the experiences and power dynamics of women who are married or living with a partner.

Success in reducing the women's wealth gap lies not in making sure that more women can exercise their role as consumers in the economy, but in improving women's financial stability and their ability to control their own futures. The persistence of the women's wealth gap is a problem at the heart of women's struggle for economic, political, and social equality. Given that women are so much more likely to have custody of children, the wealth gap affects the development of the nation's next generation as well. Now that we have explored who owns what, we turn our attention to how wealth grows or dissipates and how both of those actions affect the women's wealth gap.

THREE

The Wealth Escalator and the Debt Anchor

WHEN ASKED "DO you think that men and women have the same chances of becoming wealthy if they wanted to?" most of those interviewed responded by making reference to earnings.

I'll believe that when women earn a dollar the way men earn a dollar. Not when we're earning 79 cents.

Yes, but there still may be a bit of a double standard where it might be a little harder for women.... Men are being paid a bit more.... But things are much better. I think it's possible.

No. I think the workplace isn't fair to women. They still earn less than men...

Somehow, I think not.... certainly there are women out there... I mean, look at Oprah Winfrey.... [but] what about all the young women in my office who are trying to move up and move ahead? Why can't they? They're all bright.... Why are they just in the mid- to low-level positions?...They're in these dead-end jobs.

Unfortunately, no...if only because there's still a lot of gender bias in society in terms of income. I think as that disappears—I hope the odds are still good.

While income plays an important role in a person's ability to build wealth, in this chapter I argue that the *wealth escalator* and the *debt anchor* are the true mechanisms underlying the women's wealth gap. The *wealth escalator* is a term I use to describe the variety of legal, institutional, and societal mechanisms that help some convert income into wealth at a much faster pace than is possible by savings alone. Given the components of the wealth escalator, women would continue to have less wealth even if they had the same income as men because of the types of jobs women tend to hold and because women are less likely to work full-time continuously during their lifetime.

The debt anchor acts to prevent aspiring savers from accessing many of the components of the wealth escalator. Women are particularly affected by the debt anchor because they are likely to have higher interest rates on their debts and are more likely to fall victim to predatory lending practices. Women are more likely to have credit card debt and consumer debt, the two most destructive forms of debt. When the debt anchor is accompanied by restricted access to the wealth escalator, women are at a severe disadvantage in their ability to build wealth.

What If Men and Women Had the Same Incomes?

The gender income ratio for women working full-time is 78%. What if women had the same incomes as men? Would this close the women's wealth gap? A quick way of investigating this question is to examine the wealth gap for people with similar incomes. At all income levels, women have less wealth than men (see figure 3.1). For example, women earning $20,000 or less have a median wealth of only $60, which is $240 less than the wealth of the typical male earner in the same income range. Although neither the typical man nor the typical woman in this lowest income category has much of a financial safety net, even the small difference of $240 in resources for low-income households can have a big impact.[1] With only $60 in savings, a person could probably not afford to repair a broken refrigerator or to forgo the earnings of a day's work in order to visit the dentist or care for a sick child.

In general, wealth increases as income increases, for both men and women. But men's wealth increases considerably faster. Men earning more than $80,000 per year have a median wealth of $415,000 whereas women have $297,050—a wealth gap of $117,950. The amount of additional wealth that men have in comparison to women by income category (figure 3.2) reveals just how dramatically men's wealth advantage

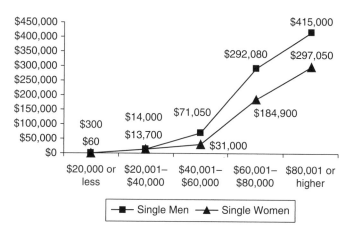

FIGURE 3.1. Median Wealth for Men and Women by Income, 2004. *Source*: Author's calculations from the 2004 Survey of Consumer Finances for persons ages 18–64.

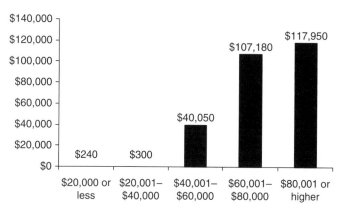

FIGURE 3.2. Amount of Additional Wealth Available to the Typical Single Man by Income, 2004. *Source*: Author's calculations from the 2004 Survey of Consumer Finances for persons ages 18–64.

increases with income. The higher the income, the larger the women's wealth gap.

To further investigate whether men and women would have the same wealth if they had similar incomes, I conducted multivariate analyses[2] to predict wealth based on income and other factors that affect wealth; I found that women would still have less wealth even if they had the same incomes as men (see the appendix, table A2). While income no doubt plays an important role in an individual's ability to build wealth, men's larger incomes alone cannot explain why there is a gender wealth ratio of 36%.

Even when we take into account age, years of employment, level of education, inheritance, and other factors that affect wealth, for every dollar of income men receive, their wealth increases by an average of $5.73 (see the appendix, table A3). In contrast, for every dollar of income women receive, their wealth increases by an average of only $3.85. At a $30,000 income, this difference amounts to an average wealth gap of $56,400. Men's earnings are translated into wealth more effectively than women's. To truly understand the ways that gender, income, and wealth interact, we must understand how income is converted to wealth.

The Wealth Escalator

Unless one is born rich or wins the lottery, wealth is created over a lifetime of earning, saving, and spending. When it comes to building wealth, the key is not just how much you earn, but how well you can tap into the wealth escalator. The *wealth escalator* is a term intended to represent a variety of financial benefits that fall to some—but not all—in our society. These consist of fringe benefits (employer pensions, paid sick days and vacation days, health insurance, stock options, etc.), favorable tax codes (capital gains taxes, tax credits, etc.), and the structure of government benefits (Social Security, unemployment insurance, welfare, etc.) that are tied to employment, income, and marital status, all of which allow people to generate wealth at a much faster rate than can be obtained by collecting income alone.

Mechanisms of the wealth escalator often reinforce each other. Some mechanisms convert income into wealth directly (e.g., pension plans, stock options), while others indirectly help people build wealth by providing things they would otherwise have to pay for (e.g., contributions to health insurance, life insurance, tuition matching grants). Thus, some mechanisms increase a person's disposable income, which can then be saved and invested and translated into wealth. Yet other mechanisms help people hold on to the wealth they have already acquired (e.g., favorable tax rates). When all the possible mechanisms are working in concert, the wealth escalator moves at a faster pace. But even the ability to tap only one of the wealth escalator's mechanisms boosts one's wealth above and beyond what could be created by receiving income alone.

Wealth building is often a mysterious process; most people do not share the intimate details of their financial lives with even their closest friends or family,[3] and despite the multitude of books and infomercials on how to get rich, acquiring great wealth is typically an elusive process. Because we know so little about how those around us are (or are not) acquiring wealth, the wealth escalator is nearly invisible. It might be helpful to imagine the process of wealth building as ascending upward, either on an escalator or on a staircase. Even if the two risers are placed side by side, those taking the stairs may not realize that their upward route requires them to work harder than their neighbor on the escalator and thus is likely to leave them at a lower level. Indeed, so many components of the wealth escalator are hidden that a person on the stairs might not even realize that the escalator exists at all.

Fringe Benefits

Fringe benefits include a variety of forms of compensation received by employees in addition to their regular pay. Common fringe benefits are medical insurance, life insurance, paid vacation time, and pension or retirement programs. Sociologist Angela O'Rand calls fringe benefits "hidden rewards for work."[4] Whether one receives fringe benefits can vary not only across companies, but among employees within the same firm. Fringe benefits can cost employers more than 25% of their total labor compensation expenditures,[5] and that expense reveals how valuable such benefits are. Some fringe benefits increase wealth directly, whereas other types have indirect effects on wealth by defraying expenses and thus making income go further or by providing a safety net for interruptions in earnings. In either case, the recipient of the benefit is left with more disposable income that can be used to save or invest.

Fringe benefits such as employer-sponsored retirement plans put wealth directly in people's hands. Tax benefits, matching contributions from employers, and the power of compounding interest allow people to build more wealth than they could from earnings alone. There are several varieties of employer-sponsored retirement plans, and they all magnify the gender earnings gap into a huge women's wealth gap because men are typically more likely to receive these benefits.

The more traditional pension plans, known as defined benefit plans, often use formulas that include length of employment with the company, age, and past earnings history to calculate the eventual payout. In defined benefit plans, employees do not have to make contributions on their own behalf, nor do they bear the risks associated with the investment of pension funds. When they do happen to be covered by a traditional pension plan, women are often at a disadvantage: their history of lower earnings and their interrupted patterns of labor force participation (i.e., fewer total years of employment) result in a lower payout. Because of these and other factors, economists Weller and Wolff report that single women over age 46 had only 35%–59% of the average pension wealth of their male counterparts of similar ages.[6]

Traditional defined benefit pension plans, in which the employer bears the responsibility for providing retirement income to workers, have been declining since 1974, with the passage of the Employee Retirement Income Security Act. The traditional plans are being replaced with plans that are funded partially or exclusively with employee contributions (called defined contribution plans).[7] Among the best known of these are 401(k) plans. Once again, women are often at a disadvantage in the employee participation plans: the double deficit of lower earnings and fewer years of labor force participation reduces the number of years as well as the dollar amount that they are able to contribute to the plan. Furthermore, access to these plans is often restricted to full-time workers, and so the millions of people who work part-time (disproportionately women) are usually ineligible (table 3.1). Women are also less likely to have union jobs and tend to be employed in occupations or industries that do not offer pensions or retirement benefits. Since retirement programs are a fundamental component of the wealth escalator, women once again lose out.[8]

However, when women do have retirement savings, they often have a hard time holding on to those gains. As they change jobs more frequently than men, these savings tend to "leak" away in transitions from one job to another. Switching employers gives workers the opportunity to choose between receiving a lump sum payment of their retirement assets and rolling them over into another retirement plan.[9] Women are less likely than men to roll over their retirement assets into another investment vehicle, deciding to use their lump sum payment to pay off loans or bills or even to cover everyday expenses.[10] Divorce also increases the likelihood that women will cash out their retirement plans.[11] Women's greater tendency to cash out retirement assets is most likely due to the fact that women have less money accumulated in their accounts and those with less in their accounts are more likely to cash out.[12] In addition, until 2005 employers could cash out vested retirement funds without the employee's permission when an employee left the company if the balance was less than $5,000.[13] The immediate need for the income provided by lump sum payments—a need that we can tie to women's lower income levels—and the ability to cash out retirement wealth further limit women's retirement wealth.

TABLE 3.1. Percentage of employees with access to fringe benefits directly linked to the wealth escalator, by worker and establishment characteristics

	Retirement benefits[a]	Stock options
Worker characteristics		
Occupational group:		
Management	83%	14%[b]
Professional	80%	
Service	44%	2%
Sales and office	67%	10%
Natural resources, construction & maintenance	65%	5%
Production, transportation & material moving	66%	8%
Full-time	75%	10%
Part-time	33%	4%
Union	90%	9%
Nonunion	61%	8%
Establishment characteristics		
Size of establishment		
1–99 workers	47%	4%
100 workers or more	82%	13%
Industry		
Goods-producing	72%	8%
Service-producing	64%	8%
All workers	66%	8%

[a]Includes defined benefit pension plans and defined contribution retirement plans.
[b]Data are for management and professional workers combined.

Source: Data from the U.S. Department of Labor, "Employee Benefits in the United States, March 2008," and additional tables on the Bureau of Labor Statistics Web site (www.bls.gov/ncs/ebs/benefits/2008/benefits.htm#health). All data except for stock options refer to workers in the private nonfarm economy (except those in private households) and workers in the public sector (except the federal government). Stock options data refer to employees in private industry in 2007 and are derived from the U.S. Department of Labor, "National Compensation Survey: Employee Benefits in Private Industry in the United States, March 2007."

Stock options and profit sharing plans are other lucrative fringe benefits. They put wealth directly in the hands of those lucky enough to receive them—and men are more likely to receive them than women.[14] The cumulative effects of these benefits can be substantial.

Bob, an electrician in his 30s, describes the experiences of his neighbor who receives stock options yearly:

He works for [Company X] and they have a great stock option. You don't even need any money for their stock options. They give you a thousand shares in May or something every year and he goes to the phone on the day that he's supposed to get the shares and calls Schwab and says, "All right, dude, here's my thousand shares. Buy me those thousand shares and then turn around and sell them when the price gets to $110." And he buys them through [Company X] for like 40 bucks a share and so last year he made like $32,000 in ten minutes. Just because he works for the company. And his check came in a week. $32,000, whatever, he didn't put out a penny to buy anything. They just send him free money.

Other types of fringe benefits—such as employer-sponsored health insurance, life insurance, paid time off, and flexible spending plans—are indirectly linked with the wealth escalator, making income go further by providing benefits that one would ordinarily need to pay for, replacing earnings if one is sick, or providing tax benefits. Employer-sponsored health insurance, for example, typically costs much less than insurance obtained privately. Women have less access to employer-sponsored health insurance, again because they are less likely to work full-time and less likely to work in jobs or industries that offer this benefit.[15] More than half of all employed women work in service, sales, and office occupations,[16] the jobs least likely to offer medical care benefits. Moreover, only one-fourth of part-time workers (another category dominated by women) have access to employer-sponsored medical benefits (table 3.2). Without employer-sponsored health insurance, women must pay more to obtain private insurance or go without. Either choice puts them at greater financial risk.

Paid time off also indirectly contributes to the wealth escalator by providing income that one would otherwise lose when not working. The lack of paid sick leave is particularly detrimental to single parents, who lose wages not only for their own illnesses but also when their children are ill. According to the National Partnership for Women and Families, "Nearly half (48%) of private-sector workers—and nearly 80% of low-wage workers—do not have paid sick days to care for their own health. And nearly 100 million workers don't have paid sick days to care for a sick child."[17]

The monetary value of some fringe benefits is larger than it appears because they are not taxed. As explained by law professor Edward McCaffery in his book *Taxing Women*,

> Consider Tom Traditional in a 40 percent marginal tax bracket. If his employer offers him a $10,000 raise and Tom takes it in cash, the Traditionals [employees or households in the hypothetical 40 percent tax bracket] will only see $6,000 of the money after they pay their $4,000

TABLE 3.2. Percentage of employees with access to fringe benefits indirectly linked to the wealth, escalator by worker and establishment characteristics

	Medical care benefits	Life insurance benefits	Paid sick leave	Paid holidays	Paid vacation	Paid personal leave	Paid family leave	Dependent care reimb. account	Health care reimb. account
Worker characteristics									
Occupational group:									
Management	94%	85%	80%[a]	94%	94%	55%	17%	56%	59%
Professional	84%	74%		74%	67%	59%	14%	52%	57%
Service	52%	42%	39%	56%	63%	30%	7%	20%	24%
Sales and office	73%	61%	63%	82%	81%	40%	9%	36%	38%
Natural resources, construction & maintenance	78%	58%	44%	78%	77%	28%	7%	21%	23%
Production, transportation & material moving	78%	67%	47%	85%	82%	33%	5%	26%	27%
Full-time	88%	75%	68%	86%	86%	46%	10%	39%	43%
Part-time	25%	17%	23%	39%	37%	22%	5%	19%	19%
Union	91%	82%	61%	79%	73%	57%	12%	44%	48%
Nonunion	70%	58%	57%	75%	76%	38%	9%	33%	35%

(*continued*)

TABLE 3.2. (continued)

	Medical care benefits	Life insurance benefits	Paid sick leave	Paid holidays	Paid vacation	Paid personal leave	Paid family leave	Dependent care reimb. account	Health care reimb. account
Establishment characteristics									
Size of establishment									
1–99 workers	60%	44%	48%	69%	71%	27%	7%	16%	18%
100 workers or more	85%	78%	67%	81%	79%	53%	12%	50%	54%
Industry									
Goods-producing	85%	71%	47%	86%	86%	33%	6%	28%	32%
Service-producing	71%	60%	60%	74%	73%	42%	10%	36%	38%
All workers	74%	62%	57%	76%	75%	41%	9%	34%	37%

[a]Data are for management and professional workers combined.

Source: Data from the U.S. Department of Labor, "Employee Benefits in the United States, March 2008," and additional tables on the Bureau of Labor Statistics Web site (www.bls.gov/ncs/ebs/benefits/2008/benefits.htm#health). All data except for paid sick leave refer to workers in the private nonfarm economy (except those in private households) and workers in the public sector (except the federal government). Paid sick leave data refer to employees in private industry in 2007 and are derived from the U.S. Department of Labor, "National Compensation Survey: Employee Benefits in Private Industry in the United States, March 2007."

in taxes. But if the employer pays $10,000 for a life insurance policy that is not taxable, Tom gets the entire policy....Getting something tax-free is like getting it at a 40 percent discount.[18]

Flexible spending plans that reimburse employees for dependent care expenses and health care costs allow participants to withhold money from their paycheck before it is taxed and then to use those pre-tax dollars to pay for qualified expenses. This program, another feature of the wealth escalator, thus lowers the recipient's taxable income and reduces his (or her) Social Security and Medicare taxes. For example, someone in the 25% federal tax bracket will save about $33 for every $100 spent when Social Security and Medicare taxes are taken into account.[19] Within the 25% tax bracket, spending $5,000 on dependent care (or medical care) expenses within a flexible spending plan amounts to a savings of $1,650. If that $1,650 savings from one year were invested and earned a return of 5% per year, at the end of 10 years it would have grown to $2,688. Women are less likely to have access to the tax advantages of flexible spending plans because they are more likely to work part-time and in service occupations (table 3.2).

Tax Code

The tax code mediates access to the wealth escalator by providing preferential lower tax rates on certain forms of income and wealth. The tax code often works in concert with fringe benefits, since many fringe benefits are not taxed or result in tax savings. The inherent gender disparity lies in the fact that men are more likely to receive fringe benefits and the tax advantages that accompany them. In effect, the initial imbalance between men and women in the receipt of fringe benefits is magnified by how these benefits are treated by the tax code.

Employer-sponsored retirement benefits are worth more simply because they are not taxed as ordinary income.[20] When an employer matches a worker's 401(k) contributions, for instance, or makes contributions on behalf of an employee, the beneficiary does not pay any income taxes on this money until he or she begins to draw on the income in retirement. And as a retiree, the pensioner is likely to be in a lower tax bracket, thus reducing the tax burden of money set aside earlier.

The government also provides some people more opportunities to tap into the wealth escalator via tax-advantaged retirement savings mechanisms, such as Individual Retirement Accounts (IRAs). And historically, Uncle Sam has provided more favorable terms to those with income. For example, until 1997, a nonworking spouse (more likely to be a woman) could contribute only $250 toward a tax-deductible IRA, whereas a spouse with earnings could contribute $2,000.[21] Current law permits nonworking spouses to contribute the same amount to a tax-deductible IRA, to a maximum of $5,000 per year in 2008. While this is a good start, the $5,000 maximum IRA contribution pales in comparison to the maximum contribution of $15,500 for 401(k) and 403(b) plans (which also have tax advantages) that are available to working spouses—again, by and large male workers.[22]

The phrase "long-term capital gains"[23] sounds gender neutral, but the treatment of capital gains by the tax code disproportionately benefits men because men are more likely to have the types of assets that allow them to take advantage of the lower long-term capital gains tax rate.[24] For example, those lucky enough to receive stock options (disproportionately men) as one of their fringe benefits are then often fortunate enough to be taxed at a lower rate on these earnings than on ordinary earnings if the options are held for a year or longer and the profits are classified as long-term capital gains. As of 2008, lower-earning taxpayers in the 10%–15% tax bracket pay no taxes on long-term capital gains. (To qualify for the zero tax rate in 2008, those filing federal taxes as married couples could have a maximum of $65,100 in taxable income, and single filers could have a maximum of $32,550.)[25] Taxpayers in the 25%–35% tax bracket pay only 15% on long-term capital gains.[26] Those with income in the form of long-term capital gains keep more of their money than they would if they had earned it from employment (considered ordinary earned income). Because of the way the tax code is structured, it helps men get onto the wealth escalator by providing tax advantages to assets that men are traditionally more likely to own.

Even the home mortgage deduction disproportionately benefits male homeowners because they generally own houses that are worth more money and have higher mortgages. They are able to deduct their mortgage interest from their taxes, which in effect provides them with a larger tax break as they build up greater home equity. The higher one's earnings, the more the deduction is worth. To illustrate: for a taxpayer in the 10% tax bracket, a $10,000 mortgage interest deduction is worth $1,000; but if the taxpayer is in the 35% tax bracket, the deduction on $10,000 in mortgage interest is worth $3,500.[27] Since men are more likely to be in higher tax brackets because of their higher earnings, they are receiving larger tax deductions, all else being equal.

According to Citizens for Tax Justice, "Who could imagine a direct government spending program that paid an increasing share of, say, mortgage costs as people's incomes rose? But that's exactly the effect of the current deduction for mortgage interest."[28]

In his book *The Hidden Welfare State*, Christopher Howard points out that we do not typically think of employer pensions and home mortgage tax credits as "welfare" and yet these programs redistribute money to citizens in the form of tax deductions and retirement wealth. He estimates that in 1995 the tax breaks associated with employer retirement plans resulted in a revenue loss to the government of $69.4 billion and home mortgage interest deductions cost the government another $53.5 billion in lost revenue. In contrast, the means-tested programs that we typically think of as welfare are much less costly. For example, food stamps cost the government $26.6 billion, and Aid to Families with Dependent Children (AFDC) cost $17.3 billion. Women are more likely to receive welfare as recipients of food stamps or AFDC benefits and less likely to receive what Howard points to as *hidden* welfare because of that double deficit of lower earnings and less continuous labor force participation. And because they own houses that on average are worth much less than houses owned by men, they receive lower mortgage interest tax deductions. The hidden welfare state, which benefits men to a greater degree than it benefits women, certainly plays an important role in maintaining the women's wealth gap. In fact, given the way the tax code is structured, one could argue that the government spends more money subsidizing men's wealth than women's.

Government Benefits

Government benefits take several forms and tend to be structured according to a two-tiered system. The top tier provides financial incentives for individuals or behaviors that are deemed worthy of support (such as working full-time), while the bottom tier provides a financial safety net of last resort for those whose behaviors or circumstances place them at risk of poverty (so-called needs-tested programs). Because of the ways that the government benefits are structured, it is more difficult for women to "earn" the top tier of benefits; instead, women are particularly susceptible to the lower tier of benefits, which could be characterized more as a trap than as a safety net.

At a basic level, society provides a safety net for those members who are most vulnerable. One safety net is unemployment insurance, which provides temporary assistance to those who lose their jobs through downsizing, reorganization, or some other action beyond the worker's control. But low-wage and part-time workers, who, as mentioned above, are disproportionately women and minorities, are often ineligible to receive unemployment benefits.[29] While rules vary, most states have a minimum earnings threshold, which in effect means that low-wage workers must work more hours than high-wage workers in order to qualify for benefits.[30] Part-time workers are also ineligible to receive benefits in most states. In addition, unemployment insurance does not cover job losses that originate in family crises: if one's child becomes disabled, if one refuses to change shifts because one cannot find child care, or if one cannot go to work because of domestic violence or stalking, there is no safety net. And when women do qualify for unemployment benefits, they generally receive less because they have lower earnings to begin with.

The safety net of last resort for women and their children consists of means-tested transfer programs such as the Temporary Assistance to Needy Families (TANF), which replaced Aid to Families with Dependent Children (AFDC) following the welfare reform of 1996. Programs such as TANF tend to discourage asset accumulation because people lose benefits if they have managed to save or if they own an automobile whose value surpasses the vehicle asset limit.[31] For example, in fifteen states, owning a vehicle worth more than $5,000 disqualifies a person from being eligible for benefits.[32] Yet many recipients need a reliable vehicle to apply for jobs or get to their place of employment, and research indicates that owning a vehicle increases the probability of employment, hours worked, and earnings.[33] And all states except Ohio have strict limits on countable assets (such as "cash on hand," the value of savings and checking accounts, bonds, etc.) to ensure that funds are not being allocated to those with adequate personal resources. Thirty-one states have countable asset limits of $2,000 or less.[34] While these limits may seem reasonable, they do not distinguish between money held in a checking account and money held in a retirement account; hence, some recipients must completely drain any retirement savings (and any accompanying benefits from the wealth escalator) in order to qualify for temporary assistance. This requirement means that people must surrender any future security they have already worked to build, simply because they are going through a period of hardship. And once a person has been rendered utterly wealth poor to qualify for assistance, the resulting lack of assets serves as a further barrier to the return to economic self-sufficiency. Hence, the means-tested safety net often functions more like financial quicksand than a support system. Receiving TANF aid, therefore, often costs participants a great deal. These qualifying rules can be particularly hard on single mothers, who often have to support several dependents on one salary, making their road to financial recovery arduous and further limiting their ability to access the wealth escalator.

In contrast to the benefits provided by unemployment insurance and the Personal Responsibility and Work Opportunities Reconciliation Act of 1996, the top tier of government benefits is geared toward those who do not need a safety net. Perhaps the most significant way that the government links earnings with wealth is by the structure of Social Security benefits,[35] which are computed based on a worker's highest 35 years of taxable earnings, with zeros calculated in for those years without taxable earnings. Again we see how women are at a disadvantage with the income/hours double deficit: First, because women generally have lower earnings, their Social Security benefits are lower. Second, because women are more likely to leave the labor force to care for children or elderly relatives, they tend to have more years of zero earnings. In 1993, for instance, 62-year-old males had a median of 4 years with zero earnings, while 62-year-old females had a median of 15 years with zero earnings.[36] In a different but telling example, in 2001 the average single woman approaching retirement (i.e., between ages 56 and 64) had only 71% of the expected Social Security benefits of the average single man of the same age.[37]

To summarize, the wealth escalator—the accelerated upward path composed of fringe benefits, tax code advantages, and government benefits—allows some to convert income into wealth at a much faster rate. The components of the wealth escalator seem gender neutral, but their structure and eligibility requirements put them beyond the reach of many women. Lower earnings, interruptions in full-time labor force participation, and the types of jobs women tend to have limit women's ability to ride the wealth escalator. Because men are much more often the recipients of its benefits, the wealth escalator takes any gender gap in income and then magnifies it into a larger wealth gap. And even when a woman and a man have the same earnings and an identical number of years of continuous full-time labor force participation, the man is still more likely than the woman to have the types of fringe benefits that put him securely on the wealth escalator simply because he has a different job. But such differences are very hard to see, because the compensation circumstances—salary, benefits, tax incentives, and so on—of most workers are private matters. This means that the wealth escalator is often hidden, and that many women are likely not even to be aware of its existence, let alone whether or not they are on it.

The Debt Anchor: Sinking into Financial Quicksand

Debt can prevent people from accessing the wealth escalator or, at a minimum, slow the speed of their ascent. To fully understand wealth, one must also understand its counterforce, debt. Americans are sinking into debt like never before. Between 1989 and 2004, median levels of debt increased by 133% (from $23,721 to $55,300 in constant 2004 dollars), and the median ratio of income to debt increased by 56%. In contrast, median wealth increased by only 16%.[38]

Debt is not always bad. Financial advisors generally agree that mortgage debt is "good," or constructive, debt because it helps to build wealth over the long run. In a similar vein, investing in one's education could be considered a form of good debt because the investment is likely to pay off in terms of higher lifetime wages. In contrast, debt that is used to purchase goods that are consumed or that do not provide any wealth or income is considered "bad," or destructive, debt. Most credit card debt falls into this category, as does any debt that is used to fund consumption. The most common forms of debt are mortgage debt, student loans, credit card debt, and installment debt. Installment debt consists of loans with a fixed payment and a fixed term, as opposed to credit card debt, in which both payments and interest rates may fluctuate from month to month. Automobile loans are a common type of installment debt, but this category includes other items such as loans for furniture, appliances, and other durable goods.[39]

Married couples have the most debt, with 88% reporting that they have debt of some kind (table 3.3). Married couples also have higher median debt and higher debt-to-income ratios than single females or single males. The bulk of married couples' debt is what they owe for their own home, which is considered to be constructive debt and provides access to the wealth escalator via the economic benefits of home mortgage tax deductions. In addition, monthly payments made toward a mortgage not only achieve the goal of "renting" living space; they also provide couples with the opportunity to become property owners, another form of wealth.

Single men and women have similar profiles when it comes to their likelihood of having mortgage debt. However, the Consumer Federation of America[40] has revealed that although men and women have

TABLE 3.3. Debt by household type and gender

	Married/ cohabitating	Single female	Single male
% with any debt	88%	77%	76%
Median value	$96,600	$25,500	$28,900
Median debt-to-income ratio	1.22	0.97	0.91
"Good" debt			
% with home debt	65%	37%	36%
Median value	$112,000	$80,000	$83,000
Median debt-to-income ratio	1.31	2.02	2.05
% with education debt	17%	16%	16%
Median value	$9,700	$9,200	$7,500
Median debt-to-income ratio	0.13	0.41	0.36
"Bad" debt			
% with credit card debt	55%	50%	39%
Median value	$2,500	$1,900	$2,000
Median debt-to-income ratio	0.04	0.06	0.06
% with installment debt	53%	36%	33%
Median value	$12,000	$8,200	$7,600
Median debt-to-income ratio	0.16	0.23	0.22

Source: Author's calculations from the 2004 Survey of Consumer Finances for persons ages 18–64.

similar credit profiles, women are 32% more likely to receive sub-prime mortgages than men.[41] Women of color are particularly likely to receive subprime loans: African-American women were 6% more likely than African-American men to have subprime mortgages[42] and 256% more likely than white men to have subprime mortgages. Latino women were 13% more likely than Latino men to have subprime mortgages and 177% more likely than white men to have subprime mortgages. White women were 26% more likely than white men to have subprime mortgages. Income differences and risk factors do not explain the gender difference in subprime loans. At all income levels, women were more likely to have subprime loans. In fact, the gender gap in subprime loans actually increased as income increased (meaning that the gender gap in subprime mortgages is greater for men and women with the highest incomes). Among borrowers with the highest incomes (people earning twice the median income), women were 50% more likely to receive subprime loans than men.

The higher interest rates of subprime mortgages typically add somewhere between $85,000 and $186,000 in interest over the life of the loan. The larger monthly payments associated with these loans also leave less money in the pockets of women and other borrowers to spend on other budget items. Moreover, subprime rates prevent borrowers from building wealth as quickly as persons with standard rates because a greater proportion of the monthly payment goes to interest instead of home equity. Now that the housing market is in a downward "adjustment," homeowners with subprime loans—who, as noted above, are more likely to be women—are particularly vulnerable to foreclosure. The end result is that women are less likely than men to attain housing wealth or to build it as quickly, because of the cumulative disadvantage of higher interest rates on their mortgages.

Single men and women are equally likely to have education debt, but women report higher debt levels than men (table 3.3). The skyrocketing cost of college has been identified as one of the primary reasons that today's young adults are drowning in debt.[43] Of those who graduated from college in 2000, 65% borrowed money to finance their undergraduate education, borrowing an average of $19,300.[44] Women are slightly more likely to have student loan debt, have slightly higher levels of student loan debt, and face a heavier debt burden (i.e., monthly loan payment as a percentage of monthly income).[45] Because women contribute a larger percentage of their monthly incomes to pay off student loans, they have less money for other living expenses or for savings. As the cost of college continues to soar, the anchor of education debt is likely to become an even larger impediment to wealth building for all young adults, but particularly for women. Women are now surpassing men in rates of college enrollment and completion,[46] but they face a corresponding burden of debt. In *Up to Our Eyeballs: How Shady Lenders and Failed Economic Policies Are Drowning Americans in Debt*, the authors comment that "it's getting harder and harder to say where good debt leaves off and bad debt begins."[47]

Of the two remaining types of debt listed in table 3.3, single women are slightly more likely than men to have installment debt, but they are much more likely to have credit card debt. Whereas 39% of single men have credit card debt, half of all single women report having credit card debt. There are two possible explanations for the higher percentage of single women with credit card debt. The first explanation is that women simply make too many unwise or unnecessary purchases. While this may be true for some individuals, studies have concluded that, in general, men and women are just as likely to overspend on nonessential items.[48]

The second explanation for the higher percentage of single women with credit card debt is that women are using their credit cards to meet living expenses. Already financially vulnerable because of their generally lower incomes, the rising costs of necessities, predatory lending practices, and, for some, the financial burden of single parenthood, many women have nowhere to turn to meet basic expenses except credit cards.[49] For many people struggling to make ends meet, credit cards provide the only financial lifeboat. Like all lifeboats, they sink quickly if overloaded.

Bankruptcy experts have found that it's not primarily credit cards that are driving single women into bankruptcy, but rather the negative economic consequences of divorce.[50] The bankruptcy data suggest that it is not women's poor spending habits that are at the root of their financial distress, but the other way around. Women—particularly middle-class women—are relying on their credit cards to meet expenses *because* they are in financial distress.

Dorothy has lived with her partner, Anna, for two decades and is the primary breadwinner. Anna is disabled and receives a small amount of Social Security every month, which pays about half of the rent. Dorothy pays all other living expenses, including Anna's expensive medical bills not covered by insurance. Dorothy describes the series of events that led her to declare bankruptcy over a decade ago:

> Anna and I, when we first started our living situation we didn't have any furniture, we didn't have any of these things and because we couldn't get *married* and get all these things in showers and stuff. We had to buy our own refrigerator, our own stuff for our apartment. Not that we got a bunch of expensive stuff either, but credit cards were used for all of these things. And then the credit card payments were what I was paying all the time....Utilities, rent, and credit card payments. I would have to pay the credit cards and then use the credit card once the payment went through to get food....it was a vicious cycle. And they kept offering them to me, even above my salary. I thought, why are they doing this?...I tried to get a loan from a credit union to pay off all these bills and stuff and they wouldn't give it to me....It was at the point where I was having a really hard time. Anxiety-wise, it was a mess. To me it was like a failure to declare bankruptcy, it was a real failure. I was very ashamed. For me, money and shame are linked in my life. It's funny— you could ask me questions about my sexuality, what I read, all these other things, but the shame has to do with money....I must say that I feel extremely grateful to the system...to be forgiven of that debt because it was so huge in my mind. I never could see my way out of it. It was about $45,000 and my salary at the time was in the 30s....It was way more than I made....I didn't have any collateral. I didn't have a

car. I didn't have a house or anything.... Of course I was getting credit card offers immediately after I declared bankruptcy...only it was worse ones with terribly high interest.

Kelly is also drowning in credit card debt. She is a single mother, raising a 16-year-old daughter with only minimal financial assistance from her former husband. For a while they lived with Kelly's mother, which allowed them to barely make ends meet on her salary. When that living situation became infeasible, she needed to find her own apartment, and like many other single parents, she had expenses that were much higher than her income. Credit cards provided the means by which she could bridge the gap: "You get to the end of the month and 'Hmm. We need food.' Credit card. And this went on for a while." She acknowledges also purchasing items that were not necessities out of guilt arising from the divorce. She explains:

> When you're raising a child from a broken relationship, you tend to—you try to make up sometimes with material things. Even though you know that buying another Barbie really isn't a smart thing. Or remember when scooters were all the rage? When they first came out they were like $85 and...of course she didn't really need one, she had a bike. But you know, she's [from a] broken home. Fine, I'll buy it. I'm still paying for that damn scooter!

Kelly has not reached the point where she has considered declaring bankruptcy, but she is currently looking for a second job to pay down her credit card debt. She is hopeful because she has risen several pay grades since she started working for her current employer 7 years ago. She has no savings for emergencies, though, and is in a perilous financial situation that could potentially spiral downward if she loses her job or faces other unanticipated expenses.

Attitudes toward Borrowing Money

One way of helping to disentangle the reasons behind credit card debt is to examine men's and women's attitudes toward credit. Looking at single men's and women's attitudes toward borrowing money for different purposes suggests that women are less likely to approve of using credit to pay for luxury items, such as fur coats or jewelry or even an automobile (table 3.4). Women are more likely to say that it is okay to borrow to meet living expenses when income is cut.

TABLE 3.4.   Percentages of single men and women who agree that it is all right to borrow money for different types of expenses

It is all right for someone like yourself to borrow money...	Women	Men
to cover the expenses of a vacation trip	18.4%	20.3%
to cover living expenses when income is cut	54.7%	48.9%
to finance the purchase of a fur coat or jewelry	4.4%	11.7%
to finance the purchase of a car	79.2%	82.3%
to finance educational expenses	84.4%	87.6%

Source: Author's calculations from the 2004 Survey of Consumer Finances for persons ages 18–64.

Another factor that may be contributing to women's greater indebtedness to credit cards is the fact that the credit cards held by women have higher annual percentage rates than those held by men. Eleven percent of single women have credit card interest rates of 20% or higher, whereas only 6% of single men face such high interest rates.[51] The average interest rate women paid on the credit cards where they had the largest balance was 13.64%, whereas men's was 12.31%[52]— that difference can amount to a large sum of money over time. Clearly, women face disadvantages in the arena of debt. Their difficulty in obtaining the benefits represented by the wealth escalator is compounded by the pernicious effects of the debt anchor.

Conclusion

In this chapter, I have shown that wealth building is not just about income, but is powerfully affected by the way that a variety of benefits might be deployed, as well as the ability to avoid the consequences of destructive debt. Women are less likely to have access to wealth-building mechanisms in society—that is, the wealth escalator. They are more likely to be impeded by the debt anchor, as they tend to use credit to compensate for lower incomes and a greater vulnerability to financial crisis.

The fringe benefits, tax code, and government benefits that comprise the wealth escalator help men build wealth more easily and at a faster rate because men are more likely to (1) work full-time throughout their adult lives, (2) work in jobs and industries whose benefits are compatible with the escalator, (3) have higher incomes that allow them to save more and also help them ride the escalator more quickly because many benefits increase with income, and (4) have the types of assets that receive preferential tax treatment.

Because of men's greater access to the wealth escalator, men and women have different amounts of wealth even when they have similar incomes. Women may be working just as hard as men, but given the way that the wealth escalator is structured, they cannot turn their incomes into wealth as efficiently.

Women are not only less likely to have access to the wealth escalator, but also more likely to be weighed down by the debt anchor. They are more likely to be targeted by predatory lending practices, and what may seem like small differences in interest rates on loans cumulate over time and cost women a great deal of money. Women are therefore at a double disadvantage. Their ability to ride the wealth escalator is restricted, and they are climbing the stairs while loaded down with a heavy debt anchor.

The testimony featured at the opening of this chapter demonstrates that we tend to think of wealth as deriving primarily from income. But income is only one aspect of financial well-being. Looking from the outside, we can see that those climbing the staircase of wealth attainment must work harder than those riding the escalator; yet because wealth building is complicated and enigmatic, those lacking access to the wealth escalator may not even have considered that they are excluded, while those who are on the wealth escalator may not even realize the advantage they have. Educating ourselves about the invisible mechanisms that can accelerate and impede wealth is an essential first step toward understanding and overcoming the women's wealth gap.

FOUR

How the Deck Is Stacked
Against Mothers

If a man gets a woman pregnant he can walk away from a financial standpoint to a large degree...whereas a woman...would incur that financial responsibility.

—*28-year-old married woman*

CHILDREN MAY BE priceless, but they sure are expensive. The U.S. Department of Agriculture estimates that currently it will cost between $176,890 and $353,410 to raise a child from birth to age 17,[1] and this does not even include the costs of college.[2] But the hefty price tag of raising a child is not shared equally by mothers and fathers. Children play a tremendous role in the women's wealth gap. The evidence shows that raising children has a larger negative financial impact on women than on men.

In this chapter, I investigate the motherhood wealth tax, which is borne by all mothers, whether married or single. The motherhood wealth tax includes a motherhood wage penalty, restricted access to the wealth escalator, and, for single mothers, the financial burden of being a sole custodial parent.[3] Until men and women share equal financial responsibility for raising their children, the gender wealth gap will persist.

Although fathers are increasingly seeking and being granted custody of children, 84% of custodial parents are mothers.[4] As long as women are more likely than men to have custody of children, they will inevitably shoulder more of the economic burden of parenthood.[5] Never-married single mothers experience the most difficult situation, with 50% living in poverty. In comparison, 29% of never-married single fathers, 25% of divorced single mothers, and 14% of divorced single fathers live in poverty.[6] Without a doubt, the economic costs of single parenthood are typically shouldered mostly by women.

The burden of single parenthood is magnified by the fact that most custodial parents do not receive adequate child support. Less than half of all single parents receive the full child support due to them, and almost one-fourth of those awarded child support receive nothing.[7] And even when parents do receive child support, it often does not rise adequately with inflation and usually does not equalize the heavier financial burden placed on the custodial parent. Since women are more likely to have custody of children, they typically find that they must make ends meet without adequate financial support.

Denise is the never-married mother of a grown son and 5-year-old Luke. She lives with Tony, Luke's father, and has been able to purchase a home, in spite of a lack of financial support from Tony. When it comes to the household expenses, Denise explains,

> I do everything. If he doesn't give me money, I still do everything because everything is in my name. The house is solely in my name because he didn't contribute. So therefore if he gives me money, he gives me money; if he doesn't, I don't lose sleep over it because that's the way I went into purchasing the house, solely on my income alone. That way, if he walks out tomorrow, I'm financially straight. I won't have no problems; I could still make my own living. I don't count on his money. His money is extra good. But I don't count on it....I like to keep it separate, and if he contributes he contributes and if he don't I can still survive....my biggest reason for not marrying him is financial....It is the greatest tension....He's all over the place with his finances....He likes to party and hang out with his money. As opposed to me—I think of me and my children—where we're going to live, what I have to do, they have to have day care....You can't teach a man to be a father. If he wants to provide for his child, so be it; if he don't, don't chase him and track him down to do it. Just leave him be.

Unlike Denise, Vicky has not been able to purchase a home and is in a more precarious financial situation. Vicky has been divorced twice and is a single mother of two children: a grown son and a 16-year-old daughter, each from a different marriage. She married for the first time when she was 17 and was married for only a couple of years. Like many divorced women, she never received any child support from the father of her son. She hasn't seen him since her son was 4 years old and "wouldn't recognize him if I fell over him…[financially] he was pretty useless." Her second marriage lasted for about a decade. For her daughter, she receives only $80 a week in child support, which was based on a family court judgment made more than 8 years ago. She hasn't gone back to court to request an increase in the amount he is required to pay because

> If I took him to court, he would have been a real jerk about it....he's pretty generous with our daughter most of the time *if she plays the game.* If I did the whole legal thing, he would be just a real jerk about it so it's best to do it this way....Every once in a while he'll come up with a good chunk of cash or he'll call her and say, "Hey, you want to go shopping?" You never know when the mood's going to strike, when the stars are aligned or something.

She explains that he is more generous when he considers the support to be given of his own free will. His willingness to pay support is also influenced by his assessment of his daughter's emotional debt to him. For example, one birthday he sent her a check for much less than he would typically give her, and he did not take her out to celebrate. Later, he explained that he had not been as generous as usual because he felt that she had not given him adequate attention on Father's Day. She had spent part of the day at a basketball tournament rather than offering to spend the entire day with him. For Vicky and her daughter, adequate financial support is contingent on the father's feelings and cannot be counted on. His economic support comes with a hefty emotional price tag, but Vicky believes that accommodating his views is the best strategy for obtaining financial support from him.

For single mothers like Vicky, the financial toll of motherhood does not end when the children are grown. Not only did she raise her son without any child support, but she also recently helped pay for part of his wedding:

> I paid for the rehearsal dinner and there were like 40-something people there. And my daughter was a bridesmaid....Having the alterations done cost almost as much as the dress did in the first place. It was just one thing after another. And then we needed a hotel for the night after the wedding....Charge it, charge it....Now I'm even deeper in debt.

Vicky's continued financial support of her adult son is fairly typical of single mothers, who are more likely than single fathers to provide economic support to children over age 18.[8] Besides money for college and weddings, adult children often need financial assistance as they transition to self-sufficiency, seeking help with security deposits, the expense of setting up an independent household, and other necessities. As a result, the financial costs of single parenthood often continue to burden single parents long after their children have reached adulthood.

Single Mothers Are Wealth-Poor

Comparing the wealth of unmarried childless people with that of mothers and fathers reveals just how steep the wealth penalty is for mothers (table 4.1). The wealth ratio between single mothers and fathers is 22%, which means that for every dollar of wealth owned by fathers, mothers own only 22 cents. The wealth tax is the steepest for never-married mothers, who have a median wealth of only $40 (table 4.2). To put it a different way, *half* of all never-married mothers have $40 or less in wealth. In comparison, the typical never-married father has $24,300 in wealth. The dire financial situation of never-married mothers is underscored by the fact that 46% of never-married mothers have zero—or negative—wealth (table 4.3).

Divorced mothers fare better overall than never-married mothers, most likely because they are older, may have benefited from the wealth-enhancing effects of marriage, and are more likely to receive economic assistance from their child's father.[9] Nevertheless, a women's wealth gap exists for this group as well: divorced mothers still have only about half of the wealth of divorced fathers. And more than one-quarter of divorced mothers have no wealth at all.

TABLE 4.1. Median wealth for single men and women by parental status, 2004

	Childless	Have children of any age	Have children under age 18
Men	$19,500	$40,000	$21,920
Women	$16,300	$8,600	$1,650
Gender gap	$3,200	$31,400	$20,270
Gender ratio	84%	22%	8%

Source: Author's calculations from the 2004 Survey of Consumer Finances for persons ages 18–64.

TABLE 4.2.   Median wealth for never-married, divorced, and widowed men and women with children, 2004

Household type	Have children of any age	Have children under age 18
Never-married		
Men	$24,300	$16,450
Women	$40	$0
Gender gap	$24,260	$16,450
Gender ratio	0.2%	0%
Divorced[a]		
Men	$45,000	$23,900
Women	$15,100	$10,400
Gender gap	$29,900	$13,500
Gender ratio	34%	44%
Widowed		
Men	$69,400	n/a[b]
Women	$70,400	$57,760
Gender gap	+ $1,000	
Gender ratio	101%	

[a]The "Divorced" category contains people who are legally separated if they own most or all of the assets.
[b]Unweighted sample size in this category contains fewer than 10 households.
Source: Author's calculations from the 2004 Survey of Consumer Finances for persons ages 18–64.

TABLE 4.3.   Percentages of never-married, divorced, and widowed fathers and mothers with zero or negative wealth, 2004

Household type	Have children of any age	Have children under age 18
Never-married		
Men	24%	24%
Women	46%	50%
Divorced[a]		
Men	16%	20%
Women	29%	32%
Widowed		
Men	6%	n/a[b]
Women	21%	20%
Total		
Men	17%	20%
Women	32%	39%

[a]The "Divorced" category contains people who are legally separated if they own most or all of the assets.
[b]Unweighted sample size in this category contains fewer than 10 households.
Source: Author's calculations from the 2004 Survey of Consumer Finances for persons ages 18–64.

When we limit our discussion to the parents in the data set whose children are under age 18 (table 4.2), women's financial situation is even worse. Although divorced women have only 44 cents of wealth for every dollar of wealth owned by divorced men, never-married women with minor children are even more disadvantaged. The typical never-married mother with children under age 18 has zero or even negative wealth. In comparison, the typical never-married father with children under age 18 has $16,450 in wealth. Being wealth poor and being a mother go hand in hand if a woman is not married.

The price of single parenthood is felt by women of all racial and ethnic groups, but the price is heaviest for nonwhite or Hispanic women (table 4.4).[10] Nonwhite or Hispanic mothers with children under age 18 have a median wealth of $250, which amounts to only 2% of the median wealth of their male counterparts. The financial vulnerability of nonwhite or Hispanic women likely results from a combination of factors, including lower levels of education and income, higher fertility rates in general, and higher birth rates for unmarried women more specifically.[11] In 2002, the fertility rate (total births per 1,000 women ages 15–44 years) was 94.4 for Hispanic women, 57.4 for non-Hispanic white women, and 67.4 for non-Hispanic black women.[12] In that same year, the birth rate for unmarried women was 87.9 for Hispanics, 66.2 for blacks, and 38.9 for whites. The motherhood wealth penalty for nonwhite or Hispanic women is likely to be magnified even further because they become mothers at younger ages: the mean age of mothers at first birth is 28 for non-Hispanic white women and 25 for non-Hispanic black women, Mexican women, and Puerto Rican women.[13]

TABLE 4.4.   Gender differences in median wealth for single men and women with children by race, 2004

Race	Have children of any age	Have children under age 18
White, non-Hispanic		
Men	$58,500	$25,500
Women	$27,250	$10,400
Gender gap	$31,250	$15,100
Gender ratio	47%	41%
Nonwhite or Hispanic		
Men	$13,300	$10,080
Women	$1,000	$250
Gender gap	$12,300	$9,830
Gender ratio	8%	2%

Source: Author's calculations from the 2004 Survey of Consumer Finances for persons ages 18–64.

The women's wealth gap is central to understanding the black-white wealth gap because more than two-thirds of black children are born to unmarried mothers.[14] The black-white wealth gap will not disappear unless the cost of being a single mother is addressed, since so many black mothers are not married.

Motherhood Is a Financial Liability for Married Women, Too

The costs of motherhood affect not only single women, but also married women. Motherhood within marriage often means lower earnings through reduced participation in full-time employment, especially in the types of jobs that would put women on the wealth escalator.

Many married women take breaks from full-time employment when they have children. Some women decide to leave their jobs because they want to be a stay-at-home parent, but many others choose to stop working or to reduce their work schedule in response to the difficulties of combining work and motherhood.[15] While part-time work might alleviate some of the tension between work and motherhood, it costs women and their families a lot of money—through lost income and reduced access to the wealth escalator. In a study comparing the earnings of men and women over a 15-year time period during their prime working years (ages 26–59), researchers found that when they took into consideration women's part-time work and years out of the labor force to engage in caregiving, over the 15-year period, men earned a total of $722,693 whereas women earned only $273,592—a difference of $449,101.[16] Based on what we know about the wealth escalator, this earnings disadvantage is likely to be magnified into a tremendous wealth gap as well.

The Motherhood Wage Penalty

Even women who continue to work full-time after becoming mothers are at an economic disadvantage. Women experience a motherhood wage penalty that cannot be explained by work experience, education, and other factors that are typically associated with one's earnings.[17] When researchers take into account differences related to earnings such as job experience, educational attainment, and previous part-time employment, they find that mothers receive a 4% wage penalty for the first child and a 12% penalty for each additional child.[18]

Why should mothers earn less, even after differences in work histories and educational attainment are taken into account? Research suggests that mothers earn less because the stereotypes associated with motherhood cause them to be perceived as less capable in the workplace and less worthy of raises and promotions.[19] Good mothers are considered to be nurturing, always available for their children, willing to place their children's welfare above their own, and continually directing their time and attention to their children. Although research shows that employed mothers are no less committed to their work than are other employees,[20] they suffer economic losses because of the expectation that mothers cannot be fully committed to both work and family. In other words, their performance, contributions, and effort are less favorably perceived simply because the role of mother is viewed as incompatible with the role of the ideal worker (in which one is expected to be available at all times for work). In her book *Opting Out?*,[21] sociologist Pamela Stone reveals that many women are "pushed" out when they are given less challenging work or fewer opportunities because of the perception that having children rendered them less committed to career advancement or made them "flight risks."

In contrast, fatherhood is typically perceived as increasing a man's commitment to work because *his* family responsibilities indicate he will be more devoted to work in order to fulfill his duties as a "good provider."[22] In fact, in contrast to the motherhood wage penalty, research indicates men's wages increase by 9% with the birth of their first child.[23] Moreover, in comparison to childless men, fathers are viewed as more committed to their work and are offered higher starting salaries.[24]

Mothers Are Thrown Off the Wealth Escalator

Lost earnings are just the tip of the iceberg: the most powerful and possibly longest lasting financial impact of motherhood comes from losing the opportunity to save for retirement. As we explored in chapter 3, the wealth escalator magnifies income differences at one point in time into a tremendous wealth gap later. Social Security benefits, for example, are based on the highest 35 years of taxable earnings, and even a few years of part-time work or time spent as a stay-at-home parent can have a large negative impact. If even one of the years over that averaging period was spent working part-time or engaging in full-time caregiving, a person's average earnings will be penalized. To make up for low-earning years, a woman needs to either work full-time for additional years, have higher average earnings for those years when she did work in order to compensate for the low-earning years, or save even larger sums of money for retirement.

Michelle stayed home for about 6 years when her son and daughter were young. While she feels fortunate to have had the extra time with her children, she recognizes her Social Security benefits will be lower because of it: "I got that Social Security thing in the mail…and I have all these blank lines [zeroes]…oh, that's so sad. It's *sad*. I'll *never* be able to make up for all the blank lines."

While Social Security is a broad program, open to almost all American earners, it is not the only type of retirement income. Traditional pensions and defined contribution pension plans are tied directly to labor force participation and earnings. As a result, women often acquire lower benefits because of their generally lower earnings histories and interruptions in employment to pursue caregiving responsibilities.[25] Women with children are less likely to participate in defined contribution employer pension plans, and this is true for mothers across all occupations and earnings levels[26]—which may suggest that mothers cannot afford to make pension contributions that reduce their take-home incomes. Also, these benefits are often unavailable to part-time workers, again a group made up disproportionately of women workers. Only 21% of part-time workers in the United States are included in their employers' pension plans.[27] And most part-time workers are excluded from participating in company-sponsored defined contribution retirement plans that would provide access to the wealth escalator.

Other employment-related benefits are also denied to most part-time employees. For example, many part-time employees are not covered by the Family and Medical Leave Act of 1993. This exclusion occurs because employees must have worked at least 1,250 hours during the previous 12 months to be eligible (a full-time job generally calls for 2,080 work hours a year, so a "half-time" job would fall well below this standard). In addition, part-time employees are often ineligible for unemployment insurance.[28]

When it comes to earnings and wealth, mothers who reduce their work hours to engage in caregiving lose far more than the income they surrender. They also have fewer benefits available for saving for retirement and are more vulnerable to the negative economic impact of unemployment or of family or medical emergencies. Consequently, they bear long-term financial penalties with respect to their wealth—particularly their retirement wealth.

Greater household wealth actually makes it more financially feasible for married mothers to stay home with their children, thereby limiting women's own ability to accumulate wealth independently. Claudia was a financial executive and Todd was a corporate attorney when they married. Both jobs required long hours and frequent business travel. They continued to work at a hectic pace when they had children, relying on nannies and juggling work schedules as much as they could. Claudia describes the toll that it took on their family lives:

> All of the travel, long hours, dinners with clients, and pressure really got to us after a while. When the kids were babies and in preschool… I think we were just on autopilot, but the stress of it all got to be too much. We went back and forth about it for almost a year, but finally decided that we could do it differently.…I was more burned out from work than Todd was and we could afford to live on his salary and savings, so I gave the company three months' notice and never looked back.

Because people are more likely to marry others with similar levels of education and of similar class backgrounds, women with well-paying jobs are more likely to marry men with well-paying jobs.[29] As a result, the very women who could potentially tap into the wealth escalator most easily are more likely to be able to afford to quit working to take care of children because of the high incomes of their spouses.[30]

Adding Insult to Injury: Women Help Men Ride the Wealth Escalator

The irony of mothers' lack of access to the top-tier employment benefits is that women who are mothers often increase their husbands' ability to attain top-tier benefits. Besides having the traditional good worker traits, such as being punctual, trustworthy, and hard-working, today's ideal employee is one who can work when, how, for how long, and where the employer deems necessary. Depending on the type of job, this may mean that the employee can work off hours, work overtime, travel extensively, or relocate. In other words, the ideal employee does not have any obligations that interfere with work. Career success often dictates that the employee adhere to the new nearly 24-hour work day, or at least appear to be adhering to it. Children often interfere with one's ability to work constantly because they require supervision, get sick, and place demands on their parents' time. Going to a school conference or taking a child to the doctor can interfere with travel, with working overtime, with job-related socializing, and with any other obligations that must be fulfilled in the pursuit of success at work.

As the demands of the workplace have increased, so have the demands of parenthood.[31] Today's parents experience an increased need to supervise children in light of fears fueled by real or perceived dangers from gangs, drugs, and violence. It is no longer culturally acceptable to let a 6-year-old wander around the neighborhood unsupervised until dinner time. In addition, as a result of the growing awareness of the importance of early childhood learning, parents face rising pressure and desire to provide stimulating environments to their children, which inevitably brings on the scheduling and carpooling duties associated with those enrichment activities. Furthermore, the increasing competition to get into a "good" college has trickled down, affecting children at younger and younger ages. Parents of elementary school children often feel pressure to make their children as competitive as possible for admission to the college of their choice. These parents feel pressured to devote even greater time and energy arranging for tutors, helping with homework, and otherwise managing the educational experience of their children.

Paradoxically, the increasing demands of parenthood, which require greater physical availability of parents (for quality time, carpooling, supervision) than ever before, make it even more difficult for adults with children to live up to the new 24/7 workplace. At the same time, the pursuit of excellence in education, the desire to provide children with sports and extracurricular opportunities, the pressure to eventually pay for an expensive postsecondary education—all are costly in financial terms as well as in time: it is now even more necessary that both parents work.

The increasing demands of parenthood are overwhelming for single parents who must earn a living at the same time that they try to negotiate schedules and activities for their children. But the demands are challenging for married parents as well—particularly if both spouses are working full-time and in a manner that is consistent with being an "ideal worker," free from family responsibilities and available for work at all times.[32]

Steve has been married 14 years and has two children, Katie (age 9) and Zack (age 12):

When I was growing up, after-school sports meant playing baseball at the end of the street. Now kids have to be in *organized* sports. [They] have uniforms and coaches and play against other teams. Zack does soccer and has to be driven to practice and games. We try to arrange work schedules to get him there but they don't post the schedule far in advance....Katie's on the swim team and takes piano lessons. All of the driving...plus it costs us an arm and a leg. When I took piano, I rode my bike a few blocks away to a lady in the neighborhood. I don't remember my mom needing to drive me everywhere....My wife complains that she's working to pay for kids' lessons and the like, but then can't drive them to all the lessons because she has to work.

Confronted with the growing conflict between the constant demands of the workplace and the never-ending demands of child care, mothers and fathers do their best to fill the impossibly large shoes of the perfect parent. To cope with the competing demands of work and family, it is usually one parent who endangers her status as an ideal worker or relegates her work role to secondary to the care and nurturance of children. If men and women shared the responsibility for tending to and nurturing children equally, then both men and women would experience the attendant economic vulnerability and financial responsibility of parenthood. Parenthood alone then is not the cause of the women's wealth gap; instead, we should understand that social norms and structures encourage women to assume the primary responsibility for caregiving and men to focus on careers. This division of labor has implications for women's ability to attain financial well-being.

In most households, men strive to be the ideal worker and women take on the responsibility of being the primary caregiver. Men preserve their ideal worker status, and they get the benefit of knowing that their children are being cared for and nurtured by a parent. Women gain the ability to be more attentive to their children, but it comes at the price of their ideal worker status.

Wives are economic assets. Researchers have verified that being married is a financial advantage for men. Married men earn more than men who are not married; this difference persists even if we take into account factors that typically explain differences in earnings. And men with stay-at-home wives have greater wage growth than men whose wives are in the labor force.[33] Stay-at-home wives most likely contribute to the growth in their husbands' earnings by meeting family and social responsibilities, allowing their husbands to devote more time and energy to work.[34]

Given that roughly half of all marriages end in divorce, putting caregiving ahead of a career is a financially risky choice for women. As law professor Joan Williams eloquently pointed out,

> The real cause of women's impoverishment upon divorce is not the level of child-support payments, but a double application of the ideal worker norm: women first are marginalized at work because of their inability to perform as ideal workers, and then upon divorce are cut off from the ideal worker wage they helped create.[35]

Danielle divorced Brad 4 years ago, after 8 years of marriage. She recalls:

> A year after we got married, Brad was offered a promotion and we had to move [to another state]. At that time, I was working in corporate events and really liked my job, but when he was offered the promotion, I was pregnant, and it seemed to make sense to follow his career for a while until our daughter Isabelle was a bit older.... Then he got another promotion and such and was traveling all the time.... I thought about going back to work, but with his schedule, I thought going back full-time would be too much on the family—by then Jack was born—and so I went back part-time at the kids' school as an aide.... We thought it was the best solution, to focus on his career.... Well, now that we're divorced, his career is doing great and I'm back at square one. My skills are obsolete and I don't know anyone in the business anymore.

Closing the Income Gap Will Not Eliminate the Women's Wealth Gap

Some argue that women are more likely to place caregiving over full-time work because they earn less than their husbands. For instance, although Paula and Dan do not yet have children, she describes their preference for managing the demands of caring for children and how income differences would shape those choices:

> In the ideal world, if we could financially afford to have one of us stay home we'd like to do that...at least for the first 3 years.... I'd like for myself or my husband to be part of that early development. In all like-lihood, it would be me because of what I make in comparison to what he makes. We could manage on his salary more than we could manage on mine.

While it makes sense financially for the lower-earning spouse to leave the labor force or reduce her working hours, deciding who stays home with the children is not based solely on economic considerations. Whether because of biological or cultural factors, women are more likely to become full-time parents—even when they earn as much as or more than their partners. In her study of successful women financial executives, sociologist Mary Blair-Loy found that two-thirds of women who left prestigious careers to become the primary caretaker actually earned *as much as or more than* their husbands.[36] Blair-Loy explains that the pressure women feel to be the primary caretaker is prevalent in even the most career-oriented women:

> If unexpected crises require that family members need more nurturing than paid caregivers can provide, even the most intensely career-committed and successful women are likely to abandon the career track to provide that nurturing while their lower-paid husbands continue working.

Men's reluctance to decrease their work hours to assume greater caregiving responsibilities may be influenced by cultural pressures of traditional gender roles: men should be the breadwinners and should successfully climb the corporate ladder. It is much more socially acceptable for a woman to put caregiving ahead of her job than it is for a man to do so. Although this is changing, men's sense of accomplishment, identity, and status are much more closely tied to their role as wage earner than is the case for women.

Eliminating the gender wage gap will not erase the wealth gap for two reasons. First, even when married women earn as much as or more than their husbands, they are more likely to reduce their working hours for caregiving. Working part-time or leaving the labor force for even a short period of time to be a caregiver will have a negative impact on a woman's ability to benefit from the wealth escalator. Second, single women with children are more likely than men to have custody of those children. Even if men's and women's earnings were identical, the custodial parent would have greater expenses and less money left over for investing in wealth-creating assets.

To further explore the effects of custodial parenthood on wealth, I conducted quantile regression analysis (see table A4 in the appendix) that separates custodial parenthood (having children under age 18 in the household) from parenthood per se. The analysis indicates that being a custodial parent has additional negative effects on wealth that go beyond the effects of simply being a parent. Until the financial costs of parenthood are distributed equally between men and women, the women's wealth gap will persist.

Conclusion

Whether mothers follow the "career path," the "mommy path," or some combination of the two, they are financially penalized. Mothers who stay home or work part-time experience lower earnings and have restricted opportunities for building retirement wealth because many components of the wealth escalator are available only to those who work full-time. Mothers who continue working full-time suffer from the "mommy effect," a gap in income that cannot be explained either by women's labor force history in general or by the specific types of jobs these women have had.

Single and married mothers both bear the economic price of motherhood. The price paid by married women comes primarily in the form of lower earnings and lower wealth linked with labor force participation, such as 401(k) or pension benefits. Women who remain married will have some protection from the worst aspects of the wealth penalty of motherhood. But for many women, the economic perils of divorce or widowhood derail their plans for well-being later in life.

Single mothers experience heavy financial burdens because they are more likely to bear a disproportionate share of the financial costs of raising children. The economic consequences of single motherhood are so grim that bankruptcy experts Elizabeth Warren and Amelia Warren Tyagi claim that "in the world of financial devastation, there are two groups of people: single mothers and others....Motherhood is now the single best indicator that an unmarried middle-class woman will end up bankrupt."[37] About one out of every thirty-eight single mothers files for bankruptcy each year. Warren and Tyagi point out that it's not teen mothers or welfare recipients who are declaring bankruptcy, but middle-class women with college educations.

Indeed, statistics comparing the wealth gap between single mothers and single fathers reveal the hefty wealth tax that mothers pay. Single women with children have dramatically less wealth than their male counterparts. For example, never-married mothers have a median wealth of only $40, and 46% of never-married mothers have no wealth at all. In contrast, never-married fathers have a median wealth of $24,300. The financial toll of having a child but never being married is certainly not gender blind.

The wealth penalties associated with motherhood outside marriage play an important role in the racial wealth gap as well. A large percentage of unmarried mothers are black or Hispanic. Even if other factors that contribute to the racial wealth gap—such as racial differences in inheritance and earnings—are eliminated, the racial wealth gap will continue unless the motherhood wealth penalty disappears.

Single parents, the vast majority of whom are women, must provide for their children's needs, leaving them with less money with which to build wealth. *A women's wealth gap would continue to exist even if men and women had the same incomes* because women are more likely to have custody of children and of the expenses that children accrue. Child support can help ease the burden, but custodial parents are more likely to have their careers affected by the demands of parenthood, which leaves them with less time to travel, may make it difficult to relocate, and sometimes causes more absences from work, all of which may adversely affect their career opportunities, wages, and, subsequently, wealth. Women may blame themselves, their ex-husbands, their financial advisors, or the economy for their financial situation, but most fail to recognize that the deck has been stacked against them by the ways that social policies, employers, and society have not resolved the inherent economic liabilities of motherhood. Clearly, if we seek to eliminate the women's wealth gap, we must move beyond the notion that equality in earnings will put financial well-being within the grasp of all Americans. The women's wealth gap cannot be closed until the costs of parenthood are shared by fathers and mothers equally.

FIVE

Saving and Investing

Do Men and Women Do It Differently?

A Penny Saved Is a Penny Earned. A Penny Invested Is Someday a Quarter.[1]

ALTHOUGH THE FORTUNATE few may inherit huge sums of money or win a fortune in the lottery, most people create wealth by saving and investing. *Saving* involves having cash available to fund future purchases and having a safety net in case one's income fluctuates. *Investing* involves a commitment of money in the hopes of eventual profit. Both are important for financial stability, and saving typically precedes investing. This chapter investigates differences in how men and women save and invest their money, focusing on five common assets—cash accounts, homes, stocks, investment real estate, and business assets—and their implications for the women's wealth gap.

Reasons for Saving

Even if men and women had the same earnings, had the same amount of disposable income, and benefited equally from the wealth escalator, gender differences in wealth could still occur if women and men made

TABLE 5.1. Most common reasons for saving, 2004

	Retirement, old age	Emergencies	Child's education	Purchases	Own education[a]	Family, children	Own home[b]
Married/cohabitating	55%	32%	21%	14%	11%	7%	4% (13%)
Single male	42%	34%	5%	19%	4%	6%	2% (3%)
Single female	39%	35%	14%	17%	8%	6%	5% (8%)
Total	49%	33%	17%	15%	9%	6%	4% (9%)

Note: Percentages are based on answers to the following question: "People have different reasons for saving, even though they may not be saving all the time. What are your (family's) most important reasons for saving? What else?" Up to six reasons for saving were reported by the interviewers. Answers reported in this table do not distinguish based on whether the respondent listed this reason as the only reason or one of several reasons for saving.

[a] Includes saving for one's own education or education not specified.

[b] Numbers in parentheses refer to those who do not yet own a home.

Source: Author's calculations from the 2004 Survey of Consumer Finances for persons ages 18–64.

different financial decisions. Both men and women make bad invest-ments on occasion and spend money that they shouldn't. Research suggests that men and women at similar income levels spend similar amounts of money on nonessential items.[2]

For the most part, men and women report very similar reasons for saving: retirement is given as the primary motivation for saving, fol-lowed by the desire to have a safety net in the event of emergencies (table 5.1). The next question is, therefore, *how* do men and women invest their savings and, if there are differences by gender, how do these differences affect their ability to build wealth?

All Wealth Is Not Equal: Why Forms of Wealth Are Important

Not only do the richest Americans own most of the wealth, but the composition of their wealth differs in fundamental ways from that of the rest of the population (table 5.2). While home equity accounts for 66% of the total wealth for the middle class,[3] it represents only 11% of the total wealth for the wealthiest 1% of the population. In con-trast, corporate stock, financial securities, mutual funds, and personal

TABLE 5.2. Composition of household wealth by wealth class, 2004 (percent of gross assets)

Asset	Top 1%	Next 19%	Middle 3 quintiles	All households
Principal residence	10.9%	32.2%	66.1%	33.5%
Liquid assets[a]	5.1%	8.6%	8.5%	7.3%
Pension accounts	5.3%	16.0%	12.0%	11.8%
Corporate stock, financial securities, mutual funds, and personal trusts	26.9%	16.3%	4.2%	17.0%
Unincorporated business equity and other real estate	49.3%	25.4%	7.9%	28.6%
Miscellaneous assets	2.6%	1.5%	1.4%	1.8%
Total assets	100%	100%	100%	100%

Note: Top 1%: net worth of $6,191,501 or more; next 19%: net worth between $406,451 and $6,191,500; middle 3 quintiles: net worth between $500 and $406,450.
[a]Includes bank deposits, money market funds, and cash surrender value of life insurance.

Source: Table 6 in Wolff, Edward N. 2007. "Recent Trends in Household Wealth in the United States: Rising Debt and the Middle-Class Squeeze." Levy Economics Institute Working Paper No. 502. www.levy.org/pubs/wp_502.pdf

trusts combined make up 27% of the total wealth for the richest 1% of U.S. households, but only 4% of the total wealth for middle-class households.

Understanding the differences in the composition of wealth across households is essential for grasping the dynamics of wealth inequality. Since the wealthy are more likely not only to own stock, but to own large amounts of stock, the stock market plays an important role in the distribution of wealth along class lines.[4] All else being equal, when the stock market booms, the rich become richer. When the stock market loses value, the rich become less rich, and wealth inequality declines. In a similar fashion, if men generally own more stock than women, the gender gap in wealth should increase when the stock market rises and decrease when the stock market declines in value.

Differences in portfolio composition are also important because asset classes have different average rates of return (table 5.3). Average historical rates of return vary substantially between stocks and cash, but consequential differences in rates of return also exist among low-risk assets such as bank accounts, money market deposit accounts, and certificates of deposit (CDs). Analyses of Federal Reserve data reveal that, on an aggregate level, the American public is losing $30 to $50 billion every year in interest by relying heavily on bank accounts for saving money instead of other vehicles—such as CDs or money market deposit accounts—that are just as safe.[5]

A few percentage point differences in rates of return may seem inconsequential; however, small differences can have long-term implications for wealth—even for a modest investment of $5 per week. For example, if a person saved $5 a week beginning at age 25 and earned 5% interest, he or she would have accumulated almost $35,000 by age

TABLE 5.3.   Average historical annual rates of return by asset type

Asset	Average annual rate of return	
	1926–1996	1993–2003
Cash (30-day T-bills)	3.7%	4.41%
Bonds	5.2%	6.95%
Real estate	11.1%	10.06%
Stocks (S&P 500)	10.5%	11.07%

Source: Data for 1926–1996 from Dorfman, John R. 1996. "Dow Diary—A Weekly Look at the Average in Its 100th Year." *Wall Street Journal* September 30, p. C.1. Data for 1993–2003 from http://www.nd.gov/rio/SIB/Publications/Your%20 Vested%20Interest/2004-03.htm.

65. And at 7% interest, this same $5 per week would amount to more than $59,000—a difference of more than $24,000.[6] With larger percentage point differences in rates of return or with larger investment amounts, disparities are even greater over the long run.

Gender and Types of Wealth

Because different types of investments are subject to varying amounts of financial risk and average rates of return, a first step in untangling gender wealth inequality is to investigate whether men and women own different types of assets. Wealth comes in a variety of forms that can be roughly construed as layers of a financial pyramid. Cash reserves form the base of the pyramid, and experts advise building the base before adding additional assets or investments.

Cash Reserves: "Money in the Bank"

Having money saved for a rainy day is the foundation of economic security. Savings help people meet short-term fluctuations in income and unexpected costs such as car repairs or medical bills. Full participation in today's financial marketplace often involves having a savings or checking account to help establish credit and pay bills. Those without a savings or checking account may need to rely on cashing outlets that are four to six times as expensive as banks.[7]

Almost all households have a cash account of some form,[8] most commonly a checking or savings account (table 5.4). Single men and women are about equally likely to have cash accounts, but the typical

TABLE 5.4.   Cash accounts by household type and gender

Household type	% with cash accounts	Median value, if owned	Gender gap (in median value)	Gender ratio
Married/cohabitating	93%	$5,800		
Single male	87%	$2,800		
Single female	86%	$1,200	$1,600	0.43

Note: Cash accounts include money held in savings accounts, checking accounts (including money market accounts), and certificates of deposit (CDs).

Source: Author's calculations from the 2004 Survey of Consumer Finances for persons ages 18–64.

single woman has only 43% as much in her account as the typical single man, a difference of $1,600.

Gender differences in the ownership of cash accounts exist within all racial groups except for blacks (table 5.5). Black women are much more likely to own cash accounts than black men, and blacks have the highest gender ratio of all racial groups. In fact, black men and Hispanic women are the most likely of all groups to operate outside basic mainstream financial institutions (only 68% of black men and 68% of Hispanic women have cash accounts).

As the recent economic crisis has demonstrated, it is desirable to have at least a few months of income in savings, even if one has other assets. Yet close to 40% of households managed by persons between the ages of 25 and 54 do not have enough savings to cover one month's living expenses in the event of a loss of income.[9] Those with inadequate savings are living paycheck to paycheck, continually at risk of being unable to cover basic expenses like food, housing, electricity, or medical care.

TABLE 5.5. Cash accounts by household type, gender, and race

Household type	% with cash accounts	Median value, if owned	Gender gap (in median value)	Gender ratio
White				
Married/cohabitating	96%	$7,000		
Single male	92%	$3,000		
Single female	93%	$1,605	$1,395	0.54
Black				
Married/cohabitating	85%	$2,300		
Single male	68%	$1,580		
Single female	76%	$1,000	$580	0.63
Hispanic				
Married/cohabitating	77%	$1,900		
Single male	79%	$1,700		
Single female	68%	$400	$1,300	0.24
Asian and other				
Married/cohabitating	97%	$7,500		
Single male	96%	$5,000		
Single female	86%	$365	$4,635	0.07

Note: Cash accounts include money held in savings accounts, checking accounts (including money market accounts), and certificates of deposit (CDs).

Source: Author's calculations from the 2004 Survey of Consumer Finances for persons ages 18–64.

Home Ownership

Home ownership is a central component of the American Dream, and Americans place it above many other goals. For instance, a 1996 survey found that 67% of Americans would delay retirement for 10 years in order to own a home.[10]

Home ownership has several financial advantages. Perhaps most important, owning a home provides access to the wealth escalator. Mortgage interest, property taxes, and home equity loans and lines of credit often have tax advantages that help build wealth. Furthermore, if one's home increases in value, so does home equity. Increases in home equity not only provide homeowners with a larger financial reserve, but are a source of wealth if the home is sold. Capital gains from the sale of one's home are taxed differently than other capital gains. For instance, single people can make up to $250,000 and married couples can make up to $500,000[11] in profit from the sale of their home, *tax free*.

Home equity can also serve as a financial reserve. Home equity loans and lines of credit provide people with cash to make home improvements, finance a new car, pay college tuition, start a business, or pay off credit card debt. In addition to serving as a potential financial reserve, homes can also create income. Rooms can be rented out, and home equity can sometimes be converted into a reliable income stream known as a reverse mortgage.

Home equity is the single most important asset for the majority of Americans. In the United States, homeowners account for 69% of all households.[12] Further, home equity accounts for 66% of the wealth of middle-class households.[13]

For those who cannot amass enough money for a down payment, becoming a homeowner remains only a dream. Diane, currently in her 50s, has never owned a home, in spite of her strongest desires. Home ownership always seemed out of reach given the income she made working in the low-wage food services industry and the additional financial toll she faced in taking care of her dying mother. When talking about her desire to own a home one day, her eyes tear up as she explains why it is so important to her:

> To have the control, the comfort, the happiness—knowing that you're the owner and not someone else. That you won't get a slip or a letter in the mail that your rent is $800 now but as of January 1st, it will

TABLE 5.6. Home ownership by household type and gender

Household type	% who own homes	Median equity, if owned	Gender gap (in median value)	Gender ratio
Married/ cohabitating	77%	$83,000		
Single male	49%	$61,000		
Single female	47%	$47,000	$14,000	0.77

Note: Home ownership includes single-family and multiple-family residences, condominiums, town houses, and mobile homes. Equity represents the current market value minus the mortgage and any loans against the property, such as home equity lines of credit.

Source: Author's calculations from the 2004 Survey of Consumer Finances for persons ages 18–64.

TABLE 5.7. Home ownership by household type, gender, and race

Household type	% who own homes	Median equity, if owned	Gender gap (in median value)	Gender ratio
White				
Married/ cohabitating	83%	$85,000		
Single male	55%	$67,000		
Single female	52%	$52,000	$15,000	0.78
Black				
Married/ cohabitating	56%	$50,000		
Single male	36%	$39,000		
Single female	42%	$28,000	$11,000	0.72
Hispanic				
Married/ cohabitating	54%	$60,000		
Single male	33%	$44,000		
Single female	23%	$45,000	+$1,000	1.02
Asian and other				
Married/ cohabitating	70%	$163,000		
Single male	26%	*		
Single female	34%	*	*	*

*Unweighted sample size is too small; fewer than 10 men and/or women in this category have home equity.

Note: Home ownership includes single-family and multiple-family residences, condominiums, town houses, and mobile homes. Equity represents the current market value minus the mortgage and any loans against the property, such as home equity lines of credit.

Source: Author's calculations from the 2004 Survey of Consumer Finances for persons ages 18–64.

increase by \$250....Owning your own home comes with some peace of mind, knowing that it's yours....I think it would be a very comfortable feeling....*I would be so happy.* I would be so happy to be able to own a house, to have the keys to the front door in my hand. That would be such a blessing.

Single men are only slightly more likely to own homes than single women, but female homeowners have only 77% as much equity in their homes as their male counterparts (table 5.6). Within each racial group, with the exception of blacks, gender gaps in home ownership favor single males (table 5.7). As in ownership of cash accounts, black women have an ownership advantage that is not seen in other racial groups. Although in both instances the median value of the asset is lower for women, blacks clearly stand out as the only racial group in which women have higher ownership rates than men. Although single black women are still not as likely as single white women to own cash accounts and homes, they do have an advantage over single black men when it comes to building a financial base.

Capital-Building Assets: Money in Action

Savings and home ownership are the backbone of financial security. However, great wealth does not typically arise from savings alone, nor can it come from home ownership. The acquisition of great wealth usually requires investment. The three most common forms of investment are stocks, investment real estate, and business assets. Clearly, investing in these assets involves risk. For instance, the stock market has made people millionaires in a very short amount of time, but it has also cost some their life savings. Therefore, owning these assets in and of themselves does not necessarily lead to great wealth. Nevertheless, stocks, real estate, and business assets are important because of the role they play in facilitating the acquisition of large amounts of wealth. As this chapter will show, data from the Survey of Consumer Finances reveal that women are less likely than men to own each of these types of assets.

Stocks and investment real estate have an important feature that further magnifies wealth. If they are held for more than one year, they are subject to the long-term capital gains tax rate and thus taxed at a much lower rate than earnings. It is therefore much more efficient to create income and wealth from capital assets than from earnings. And because men are more likely than women to participate in these methods of wealth making, investments such as stocks and real estate have an important role in the women's wealth gap.

Stocks

Once limited to the extremely wealthy, stock ownership and access has been "democratized."[14] In 1962, only 18% of all households owned stocks;[15] by 2003, about half of all households owned stocks—directly or, more commonly, indirectly through mutual funds or retirement accounts.[16] Yet the democratization did not affect men and women equally. Whereas only 36% of single women own any stock at all, almost half of single men are stock owners (table 5.8).[17] Even when single women do own stock, they own only 68 cents for every dollar of stock owned by single men.

Gender gaps in stock ownership persist across racial groups. As shown in table 5.9, white women are more likely to own stock than nonwhite women, and the gender ratio for stock ownership is highest for whites, consistent with research indicating that blacks and other minority groups are underrepresented in this financial marketplace.[18]

Investment Real Estate

Investment real estate includes vacation homes, timeshares, vacant lots, and other commercial or residential properties, excluding one's personal residence. The appeal of investing in real estate has grown in recent years—particularly since the dot.com bust.[19] Frank, a journeyman in his late 50s, grew up in a single-parent family and recalls that his mother had to depend on welfare to support them. He takes pride in his very strong work ethic and dedication to his family. He and his

TABLE 5.8. Stock ownership by household type and gender

Household type	% who own stock	Median value, if owned	Gender gap (in median value)	Gender ratio
Married/cohabitating	59%	$23,450		
Single male	45%	$13,200		
Single female	36%	$9,000	$4,200	0.68

Note: Stock ownership includes direct ownership of stock shares and indirect ownership through mutual funds and retirement accounts (such as 401(k) and IRA accounts).

Source: Author's calculations from the 2004 Survey of Consumer Finances for persons ages 18–64.

TABLE 5.9. Stock ownership by household type, gender, and race

Household type	% who own stock	Median equity, if owned	Gender gap (in median value)	Gender ratio
White				
Married/ cohabitating	67%	$26,020		
Single male	51%	$18,250		
Single female	45%	$12,800	$5,450	0.70
Black				
Married/ cohabitating	36%	$9,400		
Single male	28%	$6,000		
Single female	23%	$3,240	$2,760	0.54
Hispanic				
Married/ cohabitating	23%	$5,100		
Single male	21%	*		
Single female	10%	*	*	*
Asian and other				
Married/ cohabitating	53%	$47,600		
Single male	51%	*		
Single female	28%	*	*	*

*Unweighted sample size is too small; fewer than 10 men and/or women in this category have stock equity.

Note: Stock ownership includes direct ownership of stock shares and indirect ownership through mutual funds and retirement accounts (such as 401(k) and IRA accounts).

Source: Author's calculations from the 2004 Survey of Consumer Finances for persons ages 18–64.

wife investigated different options for saving for retirement, ranging from the retirement plan at his work to investing in the stock market. They decided that investing their extra income in their rental house is the best option because of the favorable rate of appreciation on their rental property over the years and because of the tax advantages. In fact, he *prefers* to put extra income into the rental property rather than into his employer's retirement plan. Frank explains: "Instead of putting $35 a week into a savings account I put it into something that can also keep ahead of inflation....I think that real estate outperforms savings and the stock market....We've looked at it a little differently than others."

Although investment real estate is growing in popularity and accessibility, only a small percentage of households own real estate other than their home (see table 5.10). Married households are the most likely to own investment real estate; single women are the least likely. Even when women do own investment real estate, the median value of their investment is only 37% of the median value owned by single men. The gender gap in ownership of investment real estate is consistent across racial groups, except that black women and black men are equally unlikely to own this asset (table 5.11).

Entrepreneurship and Business Assets

The Reverend Jesse Jackson hails entrepreneurship as a "time-honored road to wealth in America."[20] But entrepreneurship involves risks—about half of all new businesses fail within the first four years. Starting a business is clearly not a guaranteed way to acquire wealth; however, business assets can be some of the most financially lucrative assets to own. As the *Forbes* list of the wealthiest Americans demonstrates, the richest Americans derived most of their wealth from entrepreneurship or inherited their wealth from former entrepreneurs.

Economists Edlund and Kopczuk[21] show that women's representation at the very top of the wealth distribution has been declining since the early 1970s. They attribute the declining numbers of women among the wealthiest Americans to the shifting relative importance of entrepreneurship over inheritance as a source of vast amounts of wealth. Inheritance can potentially help to lessen gender wealth gaps across generations if women are just as likely to inherit wealth as men. Men may have historically had the upper hand with respect to inheriting family fortunes, but most research indicates that there is no longer a gender difference in the receipt of inheritances.[22] Men and women may now inherit roughly equal amounts, but Edlund and Kopczuk found that those who inherit wealth are being eclipsed at the top of the wealth distribution by people who acquire wealth from entrepreneurial activity. They argue that in

TABLE 5.10.   Investment real estate wealth by household type and gender

Household type	% who own investment real estate	Median value, if owned	Gender gap (in median value)	Gender ratio
Married/ cohabitating	21%	$100,000		
Single male	13%	$95,000		
Single female	10%	$35,000	$60,000	0.37

Note: Investment real estate includes any real estate other than one's primary residence. Median value is pro-rated based on the percentage owned by the respondent if ownership is shared.

Source: Author's calculations from the 2004 Survey of Consumer Finances for persons ages 18–64.

TABLE 5.11. Investment real estate wealth by household type, gender, and race

Household type	% who own investment real estate	Median value, if owned	Gender gap (in median value)	Gender ratio
White				
Married/ cohabitating	22%	$110,000		
Single male	14%	$130,000		
Single female	12%	$36,000	$94,000	0.28
Black				
Married/ cohabitating	17%	$40,000		
Single male	9%	*		
Single female	9%	*	*	*
Hispanic				
Married/ cohabitating	16%	$60,000		
Single male	13%	*		
Single female	0%	*	*	*
Asian and other				
Married/ cohabitating	24%	$150,000		
Single male	16%	*		
Single female	8%	*	*	*

*Unweighted sample size is too small; fewer than 10 men and/or women in this category own investment real estate.

Note: Investment real estate includes any real estate other than one's primary residence. Median value is pro-rated based on the percentage owned by the respondent if ownership is shared.

Source: Author's calculations from the 2004 Survey of Consumer Finances for persons ages 18–64.

times of rapid technological change (such as we have currently), when vast fortunes are made quickly, self-made entrepreneurs tend to displace those with inherited wealth at the top of the wealth distribution.

The link between entrepreneurship and wealth holds for those not on the *Forbes* list as well. Sociologist Lisa Keister found that entrepreneurs have higher wealth even when she controlled for other factors that predict wealth. She also found that a person did not have to be rich in order to engage in entrepreneurial activities.[23] In other words, entrepreneurs come from all social backgrounds, and hence entrepreneurship is one of the most accessible avenues to wealth.

Tables 5.12 and 5.13 provide information on gender differences in the ownership of privately held business assets. The Survey of Consumer Finances distinguishes stock in publicly traded companies from other business assets. The SCF's definition of business assets includes any privately held businesses—ranging from sole proprietorships to limited partnerships to S corporations. A wide variety of businesses fall within this category, including family-owned restaurants, farms, and Web-based businesses. The distinguishing feature is that these businesses are privately owned (and hence do not have any publicly traded stock).

Of the various investment assets investigated here, privately owned business assets are owned by the fewest Americans. However, the importance of business assets in creating wealth is likely understated by this statistic because extremely successful privately owned businesses can become publicly traded companies, providing their founders with very generous compensation and valuable stock.

Because of the key role that entrepreneurship plays in the creation of wealth, gender gaps in the ownership of business assets are extremely worrisome. Only 4% of single women have any privately owned business assets, and among those who do, the median value of the business assets is only about half of the median value of business assets owned by single men. As part of a married couple, wives are more likely than single women to own business assets, but any business assets owned during marriage are less likely to be retained by women when the marriage ends, whether by divorce or widowhood.[24]

Yet women are a growing segment of business owners. In 2002, women owned (or co-owned) 28% of nonfarm businesses, a 20% increase since 1997. Nevertheless, female-owned businesses had average receipts of $145,000—$391,000 *less* than the average receipts of male-owned businesses.[25] One of the reasons that women-owned businesses are less profitable is that they tend to be younger and smaller than other businesses. But this is not the only reason. Women-owned businesses

TABLE 5.12. Privately owned business assets by household type and gender

Household type	% with privately owned business assets	Median value, if owned	Gender gap (in median value)	Gender ratio
Married/ cohabitating	17%	$135,000		
Single male	11%	$105,000		
Single female	4%	$57,000	$48,000	0.54

Source: Author's calculations from the 2004 Survey of Consumer Finances for persons ages 18–64.

TABLE 5.13. Privately owned business assets by household type, gender, and race

Household type	% with privately owned business assets	Median value, if owned	Gender gap (in median value)	Gender ratio
White				
Married/cohabitating	19%	$150,000		
Single male	12%	$100,000		
Single female	6%	$60,000	$40,000	0.60
Black				
Married/cohabitating	7%	$50,000		
Single male	9%	*		
Single female	3%	*	*	*
Hispanic				
Married/cohabitating	6%	$62,000		
Single male	2%	*		
Single female	0%	*	*	*
Asian and other				
Married/cohabitating	18%	$100,000		
Single male	15%	*		
Single female	3%	*	*	*

*Unweighted sample size is too small; fewer than 10 men and/or women in this category have privately owned business assets.

Source: Author's calculations from the 2004 Survey of Consumer Finances for persons ages 18–64.

tend to be in the less profitable service industry.[26] As of 2006, 69% of women-owned firms were in the service sector,[27] where businesses are generally labor-intensive and less profitable, experience slower growth, lack assets that can be used as collateral, and are hence less attractive to lenders, which can further limit their ability to grow.[28]

Starting a business requires access to capital. One of the most prestigious and valuable sources of funding for prospective business owners is venture capital. In 1999, women entrepreneurs received $2.4 billion in venture capital, only 5% of the $48 billion of venture capital invested that year.[29] Businesses also rely on loans or funding from banks and other lenders. Until the passage of the Equal Credit Opportunity Act of 1974, women were routinely discriminated against when applying for loans, effectively closing one of the lucrative avenues to building wealth for generations of women. Although it is now illegal to discriminate against women loan applicants, there are still gender inequities in access to credit because women generally have less wealth that can be used as collateral, which may help to explain why women-owned firms are more likely to use credit cards to finance start-up costs.[30]

The gender gap in business assets is most likely one of the reasons that we find so few women listed among the wealthiest Americans. Although women are now becoming business owners in record numbers, they have a long way to go before their businesses receive the same amount of start-up funding or enjoy the same level of profitability as male-owned businesses.

Understanding Gender Differences in Asset Ownership and Portfolio Composition

While it is true that men are more likely to own riskier investments and hold a larger percentage of their wealth in high-risk ventures, gender differences in portfolio composition could be due to a variety of possible factors that may have different implications. Are women inherently more risk averse, or are women less likely to own riskier assets for other reasons?

Research indicates that men take more risks generally.[31] When it comes to financial risks specifically, most studies have found that women are more risk averse—even when one controls for income and other relevant factors.[32] Explanations for women's generally lower financial risk tolerance include gender differences in access to financial information, confidence in economic matters, gender socialization that discourages women from engaging in risk taking, and differences between men and women in levels of testosterone.[33]

The conventional understanding of women and risk taking was echoed in the responses of the people I interviewed. For instance, when asked whether she thought that men or women would be better at investing in the stock market, one woman in her 50s explained:

> Men, I think would be more willing to take risks.... Men do, you know, men do goofy sports.... I just think that men in the culture are taught to take risks in ways that women aren't. I also think that men are more likely to be more aggressive.

Other women reported that they did not feel comfortable undertaking the financial risks of investing in the stock market:

> I'd rather get no return and have the money safely put aside somewhere than take the chance of losing it. You couldn't replace it... [the

stock market] would be very risky for me because I have no clue how it works. I know people who do very well in it; I can't imagine it....I'm not a gambling sort.

Yet there were also men who reported that they were financially risk averse, and women who were willing to invest in the stock market. The men and women who were most willing to invest in the stock market pointed out that the stock market fluctuated, but that over time it has produced favorable returns on average. Often, the men and women who were least willing to consider investing in the stock market explained that they thought that it was like gambling or that investing in the stock market would involve extensive investments of time or knowledge that they could not make to follow the market.

Men were more likely to say that they would invest in the stock market, despite the risks involved, because they perceived that they could take *calculated* risks, which in a sense disqualified them from falling into the category of being financial risk takers. For example, Michael, a successful account manager, explained:

> I'm actually fundamentally very conservative....I buy to hold. I'm not a day trader. I don't flip stocks—to my benefit in some cases and to my detriment in other cases. I tend to be a buy and hold person. I tend to be a measured risk taker, when I think it's appropriate, but not a real risk taker. I wish I were more of a risk taker actually. I'd follow the stocks more carefully, I'd consider investing in other stocks. If that were something that I was interested in, I'm sure I could make a lot more money, but I'm not interested in it that much.

Like Michael, other men reported that, despite owning stocks, they would not consider their decisions financially risky. For example, Andrew explains his choice to invest a large percentage of his retirement account in foreign stocks this way:

> I don't enjoy or seek risks, but some people might feel that the distribution of my portfolio in equities around the world with very little bonds and very little cash equivalents was in some way a very risky portfolio and that at age 36 it might be time to have a higher percentage of non-equity assets. My sense is that because I'm so spread out in different markets around the globe, including index funds in developing markets, that some of these areas will flourish so to some extent that might lessen the risk. I also have a certain amount of an index fund in real estate investment trusts and that tends to be on a somewhat different

cycle than other financial markets. So the answer would be that I don't think of my portfolio as that risky, but some people might.

The interviews suggest that men and women hold different perceptions about what financial risk entails. Both men and women generally said that they were quite conservative and not much of a financial risk taker, but men were less likely to think that the stock market was risky. When it came to financial risk taking generally, men and women held different perceptions about the consequences of losing money as a result of a bad investment. Women were more likely to explain that if they lost money, it would be gone and irreplaceable, whereas men were more likely to report that they could make up for money that they lost. For example, when talking about financial risk, Dan, a media technician with a newborn son, reported, "I've never worried about not having enough money. I've always felt confident that I could do *something* to make money." Another respondent echoed, "Men are more free with their money because it's easier for them to make." Statements such as these suggest that men are less likely to question their ability to make money and that they seem to have a greater sense of confidence that they can replace money that is lost, should an investment go south or fail completely.

Despite some women's reservations about investing in the stock market, research shows that women often perform better than men when making investment decisions. For example, a study of a large discount brokerage firm revealed that female investors had better returns than male investors.[34] Researchers speculate that women who do invest are more likely to research investments thoroughly, to be bargain hunters, to seek professional advice, and to trade less often.[35] So the good news is that when women do invest in the stock market, they are just as good as or better than men.

Explaining Gender Differences in Types of Wealth

Why is it that women are less likely to own certain assets? Answering this question is important if we are to understand the underlying causes of the women's wealth gap. Is financial risk tolerance the reason that there are gender differences in types of assets owned? Is the gender income gap responsible? Or perhaps there are other factors that explain gender differences in wealth portfolios.

To answer these questions empirically, I employed a statistical technique called multivariate logistic regression to determine whether women are less likely to own each of the different types of assets discussed—cash accounts, homes, stock, investment real estate, and business assets (see the appendix, table A5)—when one controls for other important variables that influence wealth. The results reveal that *if* men and women were identical with respect to key factors that affect wealth building—such as income, risk tolerance, age, years of full-time labor force participation, and education—there would be no gender differences in the ownership of homes, stock, or investment real estate. This is a big "if" because we know that women and men do not have the same incomes or years of full-time labor force participation, for instance. It would be wrong to conclude that gender differences in asset ownership are not important if they can be rendered statistically nonsignificant by controlling for important wealth-building factors that differ between men and women; on the contrary, the findings indicate that differences in wealth-building behavior between men and women tend to be structural—that is, they arise from the different societal and cultural opportunities and constraints experienced by men and women, rather than an innate lack of financial competence on the part of women.

Women are found to be more likely than men to own cash accounts and less likely to own business assets when we look closely at their wealth-building practices (appendix, table A5). In other words, even when men and women have the same incomes, levels of financial risk tolerance, and employment characteristics and match in other ways that are likely to influence wealth, women remain more likely to own cash accounts and less likely to own business assets. Consequently, there are likely other factors that affect the decision or opportunity to own cash and business assets; perhaps social norms or gender roles encourage women to save conservatively (in cash accounts) or encourage men to start their own businesses. Further research is needed to address this issue, but the persistence of the gender gap in business asset ownership is particularly discouraging given the strong link between business assets and wealth.

Conclusion

Those with the least financial means are caught in a financial Catch-22. Those with the lowest incomes are able to save the least and therefore need a higher return on their money in order to catch up to the accumulated savings of someone who is able to save more. At the same time, those with the least savings are the ones who most need liquidity because they have no financial safety net. But needing liquidity means that they are likely to receive a much lower return on their money. The end result is that those who earn more are able to save more and can therefore better afford the risk and the longer time frame associated with investing in assets that have historically had the highest rates of return. In other words, it takes money to make money.

When it comes to saving and investing, women and men do have different portfolios. Women are less likely to own all asset types, and women have less wealth in each type of asset when they do own it. In particular, the largest gender gaps exist for those assets that are considered more financially risky but that also have historically higher average rates of return—stocks, investment real estate, and business assets. Women are more likely to engage in *saving* rather than *investing*.

Research suggests that women and men probably do have different tolerances for taking risks overall, including financial risks. It would be premature, however, to conclude that the gender wealth gap is purely a result of gender differences in willingness to take financial risks. Financial risk tolerance is no doubt related to how financially vulnerable one would feel if the investment were to fail. Given men's overall better position in the labor market and men's higher earnings trajectories, they are more likely to feel confident of their ability to land on their feet financially if a risk does not pay off. In other words, men may perceive that they have a bigger financial safety net, should they need it. It is very difficult to separate gender differences in financial risk tolerance from the broader conditions that men and women face in society, such as the glass ceiling at work, the gender wage gap, and gender norms that place financial matters in the realm of male expertise.

Women's lack of business assets is also a serious concern. Although women are starting businesses in record numbers, they are starting businesses in the least profitable industries. Women's overrepresentation in business ownership in the service industry is likely to be a result of the heavy concentration of women in the occupations within the service industry (child care worker, hairdresser, etc.) because this is where their work experience lies. Women need to increase their participation in the more lucrative segments of the economy if they are to increase their access to wealth through business assets. Furthermore, women's lack of wealth is likely an important impediment to business growth because of the important role that collateral plays in securing business financing.

For the most part, gender differences in patterns of asset ownership are similar across racial groups, with men more likely than women to own most assets. However, single black women stand out because they are much more likely to own cash accounts and homes than single black men. Black women may be doing much better than their single male counterparts, but black women still do not have rates of ownership equal to those of white women. While black women have indeed made tremendous economic progress, their accomplishments should not be taken to imply that the playing field is completely level. They do not have the same wealth as white women and fall far behind white men in economic measures. The fact that single black women are more likely to own cash accounts and homes than single black men may be evidence that black men also experience barriers to the wealth escalator. Many components of the wealth escalator are unavailable to black men as a result of their lower educational attainment, higher rates of unemployment, and smaller presence in professional and managerial occupations.[36] Black men are also more likely than men of other races to be out of the labor force entirely. In 2007, 16.3% of black males ages 25–54 were not in the labor force at all (neither employed nor looking for work), about twice the percentage of men of other races.[37] Improving black men's access to employment, and especially types of employment that provide access to the wealth escalator, is a central component of reducing the racial wealth gap.

Hispanic women as a group face the greatest barriers to the wealth escalator, as reflected in their lack of basic financial assets and extremely low levels of median wealth. For the most part, Hispanic women work in jobs far removed from the kinds of wealth-generating benefits discussed here, such as pension plans, health insurance, and tuition matching. Because race intersects with gender to shape saving and investment opportunities, the wealth escalator has important implications for understanding the racial wealth gap.

The root of the gender wealth gap is most likely not gender differences in financial risk tolerance or the desire to own businesses. Rather, women are more likely to be caught in the financial Catch-22 to which they are the most economically vulnerable, which places them at an additional disadvantage with respect to their ability to invest in riskier assets that are likely to earn higher returns over the long run. The old adage "it takes money to make money" reminds us of how hard it will be to close the women's wealth gap without meaningful change in the structure of women's opportunities.

SIX

Marriage

What's Mine Is Yours?

For me, "for richer or for poorer" meant we shared the riches or shared the poverty.

—*43-year-old married woman*

I N AMERICAN SOCIETY, it is customary to think of the wealth of a married couple as belonging to both the husband and the wife equally. Consequently, many might assume that the women's wealth gap wasn't an issue for married couples; however, research indicates that the reality is much more complicated than we might have imagined. With marriage, the gender difference in wealth is transformed from having less of one's own wealth to a latent inequality in which women often have less control over wealth. The shift is subtle, but it demonstrates that the women's wealth gap exists even in marriage and is therefore salient for all women.

Easily quantifiable gender differences in wealth for single people do not translate directly to marital relationships. Marriage involves its own sets of norms and expectations that shape the ways that gender influences control over wealth in marriage. Married women may experience a wealth gap in terms of control over marital wealth, but this aspect of the gender wealth gap is oftentimes "hidden" within the bounds of marriage. The tendency to view marital wealth as communal has undermined our appreciation of the pervasiveness of the women's wealth gap. In this chapter, I demonstrate that tensions between equality within marriage and traditional gender roles (often strengthened by men's greater access to the wealth escalator) are reconciled in ways that limit women's access to and control over wealth.

The Economics of Marital Power

If money is owned equally by husbands and wives, it shouldn't matter who brings home more. In real life, however, it matters a great deal. When it comes to earnings, inequalities between husbands and wives often translate into power differences in the marriage. For example, research shows that wives who earn less than their husbands do more housework than wives who earn the same amount as their husbands, even when both partners work full-time.[1]

To explain why gender differences in earnings are translated into power differences in marriage, academics draw on the concepts of exchange theory and game theory,[2] explaining that when husbands earn more than wives, the wives are financially dependent and less able to support themselves if the marriage ends.[3] As a consequence of their greater financial dependency, women will be less likely to leave a marriage than men will, a hesitancy that renders them less powerful within the marriage and more likely to capitulate when conflict arises. In exchange for the economic benefits of marriage, women are more likely to do the least desirable household tasks (such as cleaning toilets, changing diapers, etc.), defer financial decisions to their husbands, and put their own career choices second to their husbands'.[4] Even in the realm of philanthropy, couples are more likely to adhere to the husband's wishes regarding charitable giving than the wife's.[5]

While the gender earnings gap affects power between husbands and wives, what about wealth? Gayle, a preschool teacher in her 50s, experienced firsthand the ways that having wealth can transform her own power within marriage. She explains:

> Our youngest son, Kyle, wasn't really thriving at school and I wanted to send him to a private school I thought better suited his personality and style of learning...but my husband didn't agree, and although we could have afforded it, he wouldn't do it. He thought the public school

was just fine. That Kyle just needed to focus more and it was a waste of money to send him there....but when my mother passed away, she left me some money that would more than cover the tuition of the private school for Kyle until he graduated from high school....When I got that money, I told my husband I was going to use it to send Kyle to [the private school]. Even though I know my husband still thought it was a waste of money, he didn't say anything because it was money I got from my mother. Kyle is doing better in school now, and I think in a year or so, my husband will agree it was a good thing to do.

Legal Rules Governing Ownership of Marital Assets

Two systems govern the ownership of marital property in the United States: community property and common law (also called marital property). Nine states (Arizona, California, Idaho, Louisiana, Nevada, New Mexico, Texas, Washington, and Wisconsin) are community property states, in which all assets acquired during marriage are equally co-owned by both spouses.[6] There are important exceptions to the law, including assets owned prior to marriage and gifts or inheritances received during marriage.[7] In contrast, the remaining forty-one states are common law states, where ownership is determined by whose name the asset is held under. Nevertheless, in common law states, each spouse has a right to an "equitable share" of marital assets upon divorce. The "equitable share" is usually determined in divorce court that takes into account a variety of factors which vary across states.

Ownership of marital property takes on a new meaning if one spouse dies. The surviving spouse does not necessarily inherit the entire marital estate. Laws vary by state, but in most states, if there is no will, widows are entitled to one-third of their spouse's estate[8] and the remainder is divided among the children, parents, siblings, or other relatives of the deceased. For example, if someone dies without a will and leaves a spouse and no children, some states divide the assets equally between the spouse and the parents of the deceased person.[9]

Even in community property states, the estate is not necessarily passed along to the surviving spouse. The American Bar Association reports:

> Unlike joint tenancy, community property isn't automatically transferred to the surviving spouse. When your spouse dies, you own only your share of the community property and your spouse must give his

or her share to you (or anyone else) in a will.... What if your spouse assumes his or her life insurance will give you enough money and leaves everything to your grown children? In a community property state that means half of the community property goes to the children. They now own half the house, half the car, half the vacation place on the lake. If there wasn't much cash in the estate or in insurance paid to them, the only way they can really benefit from the will is to sell the property so they can share the proceeds.[10]

Ownership vs. Control over Wealth

In thinking about gender differences in wealth for married couples, it is important to bear in mind that the formal *ownership* of or legal right to wealth is not the same as *control* over wealth, which involves making financial decisions regarding how to spend or save it.[11] While it is important for women to own wealth, it is equally important for women to exert control over wealth. Consequently, the remainder of this chapter focuses on control over wealth. My interviews reveal unique insights into the extent to which wealth is shared by married couples (including any potential gender differences therein), as they navigate the complicated interactions among norms of marital equality, gender, and control over wealth.

Men as Head of the Household

In the not-so-distant past, in the traditional marriage of a male bread-winner and female homemaker, the husband was the head of the household and had sole responsibility for many major decisions. Wives may have had discretion over some household spending decisions, but husbands generally made the major economic decisions regarding expensive purchases, how much to save or invest, and how much discretionary spending the couple could afford.

Vicky describes her first marriage in these terms. She married for the first time when she was 17 and gave birth to a son, who is now grown. During the 2-year marriage, she had almost no say over financial matters:

> At first, I couldn't touch anything—it was a joint checking account— but I couldn't touch the checks.... Later, I was able to *write* the checks,

but he made the financial decisions. When I walked away from the marriage, I had no credit. Everything was in his name.

Although some couples may follow this approach to financial management, no couples I interviewed described their current marriages in these terms. In place of the outdated system of men making all decisions as head of the household, couples adopted one of three distinct methods of financial organization: (1) complete partnership in financial management; (2) voluntary specialization in which one partner assumes the primary responsibility for managing household finances; and (3) voluntary separation, in which couples keep "his" money separate from "hers" and each partner makes contributions to common expenses. Each method of financial organization has significant implications for the financial well-being of the female partner, and interestingly enough, each of the three methods of management was viewed by its practitioners as completely compatible with notions of equality between husbands and wives.

Complete Partnership: "What's Mine Is Yours and What's Yours Is Mine"

Judy and Donald were both born in China and moved to the United States when they were in their mid-20s. Both had master's degrees and began working and saving almost immediately so that they could buy their own home and be financially secure before starting a family. Judy recalls:

> Like a typical Chinese family, we were adamant that we had to keep saving to be prepared for emergencies.... At the beginning we saved even more than 50% [of our income]....we thought that if we wanted to live a quality life, we needed to think about how we can use our money to make money rather than just keep saving...and so my husband and I tried to read a lot of magazines to try to find out what other options were. At the beginning, we invested money in mutual funds because we tried to be conservative—we didn't want to take risks.... Then after several years, we started investing in stocks. My husband was tracking the investments, and because we got better returns in stocks we started to invest more money there.

Over the years, they actively monitored their investments and worked together to build their export business. They also began their family and were blessed with two sons, now teenagers. As their export business expanded and became more successful, Donald traveled more and more. As a result, Judy took over the management of the mutual fund and stock investments (while working part-time and raising their children), and Donald focused on building their export business. Although they divided the financial tasks, they keep each other abreast of the status of the business and the investments and consider all assets to be collectively owned. In fact, when I asked whether they keep their finances pooled or separate, Judy looked quite puzzled and replied: "What do you mean 'separate'?" When I explained that some couples keep their money or their income separate and then decide how to meet joint expenses, she then replied:

> No, we always put it together. For *me*, I feel that doing it separately means that your marriage isn't that secure. I really don't know.... Some families do separate accounts, but I don't know the advantage of that. Maybe one person wants to be independent? I really don't know.

In many ways, Judy and Donald are the quintessential example of the complete partnership method of managing marital finances. They do not distinguish his money from hers, and when she explains their decisions, she uses the word "we." Both work together toward their financial goals and consider all assets to belong to both husband and wife equally.

Joe and Becky have few marital assets other than their own home and some savings for retirement, but they also embody the complete partnership method of financial management. They have been married for 26 years and have two grown children. Joe is currently retired from his job in sales, and Becky hopes to retire soon from her job as an administrative assistant. She explains their approach to managing money:

> We've always had one checking account....We always talk over our purchases. Anything over $50 we talk about it....Everything goes in the pot. We don't keep anything separate. When we first started dating, he had a lot more money than I did. I had zero. I was in debt. Over the years, things have gone back and forth. Some years I made more money, some years he made more money. But everything goes into the pot.

These couples embody the conception that wealth is owned and controlled equally by both spouses. In these situations, both partners take an active role in managing household finances and making financial decisions. With similar financial goals and objectives, these couples can successfully pool their resources and their efforts to increase their joint financial well-being. Although these couples did sometimes divide the financial tasks, they actively co-managed their assets and coordinated their activities to focus on mutual financial goals. A key distinguishing feature of this method of financial management is the communication about tasks and information so that each partner has the same amount of knowledge about marital assets and financial strategies. Both partners have an intimate knowledge of how finances are being managed, and both view marital assets as truly collective.

In the complete partnership model, women have an equal voice and an equal role in managing marital wealth. But there are obstacles that prevent couples from adopting this approach. First of all, in order for the complete partnership method to work successfully, both partners must have similar financial goals and similar approaches to spending and saving money. Second, couples must truly view their own and their spouse's economic resources as collective. This may be more difficult when couples enter marriage with vastly different resources or when one earns much more than the other. It is also difficult for couples who are remarried because of the greater tendency to acknowledge the implications and difficulties of dividing assets in the event of divorce. Couples with children from a prior relationship may also be hesitant to combine all assets in order to keep financial obligations to children distinct from marital assets.

Given the obstacles to successful implementation of the complete partnership model, it is not surprising that only a minority of couples interviewed adopted this model. When it came to managing wealth, most couples adopted one of the following two strategies: voluntary specialization or voluntary separation.

Voluntary Specialization: He/She Is Better at It or More Interested in Financial Matters

For couples engaged in voluntary specialization, financial resources are perceived as collective, but one person has the primary responsibility for making the types of investment decisions that are most directly linked to the acquisition of and control over wealth.[12] Yet, unlike couples in the outdated arrangement in which men are *automatically* assumed to be the financial decision makers, couples who engage in voluntary specialization decide who will be the primary financial decision maker based on differences in individual preferences, abilities, or premarital resources that are, in theory at least, gender blind.

Sometimes, differences in financial resources prior to marriage determine who assumes this role. Audrey is a newlywed and is very sensitive to the fact that she entered the marriage with far less wealth than her husband. She feels that it is appropriate that he make the major financial decisions, such as those related to purchasing their first home, because he brought almost all of the financial assets to their marriage:

> I feel a huge responsibility towards my husband to be very responsible and to be very much like "Yes, you are making substantially more money than I. I'm not just going to take that extra money and *just go crazy*." He certainly consults with me and we'll talk about things. But generally, I pretty much defer to him because he makes a lot more money than I do....He has the money for the house. Every time we've been looking at houses, he asks, "Do you like this house?" and if I don't like it, I'll say so and then it won't really be considered. But other times when I've said, "I really love this house; I really want us to try to get this," he'll say we can't afford it and that puts the kibosh on it....I'll defer to that. If he says we can't afford it, then I believe him.

Men are more likely to have greater wealth before getting married because of their typically higher earnings and their greater access to the wealth escalator and because women are likely to marry men who are older than they are.[13] Even a modest age difference means that, all else being equal, men have had more years prior to marriage to benefit from the wealth escalator.

For most couples who adopted the voluntary specialization method, the decision as to who should take on the role of financial manager was not based on economic resources, but was explained in terms of individual differences in levels of expertise or interest. However, preferences and abilities are often shaped by deep-rooted cultural ideals about which sex is better suited to or expected to handle particular tasks. Heather, a married woman in her late 30s, explains:

> I don't remember my parents sitting down and teaching my brother and not teaching me, but he just picked up on it. I don't know if it's a personality thing or if it's part of the expectations that men have for themselves and think "I have to know how to do this"....I never had that sense that "I have to learn to manage my money." I just didn't learn it and it just wasn't something in my little internal toolbox. My gut feeling is that a lot of men really do have that internal toolbox. I think they get it from expectations from society...somehow my brother ended up

with all of this canny financial—he has a house—he's 4 years younger than I am and he's owned a house for 10 years and has stocks and bonds and everything else. I think on some level he must have felt—and my husband feels this way too—that he needs to be responsible for money because he's a man and he makes more money and he needs to be on top of it.

In the interviews that I conducted, I saw some cases in which the husband took on the role of financial manager reluctantly and sought greater input from his wife. Yet even women who describe themselves as feminists sometimes resisted their husbands' attempts to involve them more in the family's financial planning. For Carol, the situation is extreme:

My eyes glaze over when my husband talks to me about financial matters. He always says things like "Don't you want to see the financial statements or look at the mutual fund prospectus?" But I don't. Once we went to a financial planner and I noticed a Mozart clarinet concerto was playing in the background and so I couldn't concentrate on the conversation with the financial planner. I asked whether the concerto was a CD or on the radio and they looked at me like I was in a totally different world. My husband asked if I would come to the second visit with the financial planner, but I said no. I feel guilty and very conflicted about not being more interested in financial affairs. Although I'm a feminist, my attitude toward letting my husband control the finances is straight from the 1950s. My sisters, husband, and some friends are always telling me to become more knowledgeable. But I just don't want to know.

Although most of the women I interviewed did not hold such extreme views of financial matters, the majority of women whose husbands took the role of main financial decision maker mentioned that they were not very interested in these matters. They were content to let their husbands take the lead.

It also seems that men's taking responsibility for financial matters is associated with romantic ideals of chivalry. Even some women who in all other ways would consider themselves feminists revealed that they enjoyed it when their husbands paid for things because doing so represented deeply held ideals about romance. Fay, a very successful professional with a PhD, explains:

I like it when [my husband] pays the bill when we go out for a nice dinner or a show.... This doesn't sound very feminist, *which I am*—but it is more romantic if he pays. It's weird that I consider myself a feminist and still feel this way.[14]

Sociologists point out that couples "do gender," meaning that they expect themselves and others to act in ways that exemplify traditional masculine and feminine behavior and continually reinforce these expectations in their everyday interactions.[15] Handling financial matters is one of the ways that men "do gender." For example, in her book *Earning More and Getting Less*, sociologist Veronica Jaris Tichenor found that even women who earn more than their husbands often defer control over financial decisions as a way of "doing gender," demonstrating that they are appropriately feminine and are not trying to dominate their husbands.[16] Given the links among cultural expectations that men should be good providers, romantic notions of chivalry, and deep-rooted notions that financial matters are within the "male" realm of expertise, it's no wonder that men are more likely to assume the role of being the main financial manager within the marriage.

In direct conflict with couples' cultural notions about men handling financial tasks and being good providers are marital ideals about partnership and equality. Women were quick to point out that their delegation of financial tasks to their husbands was at odds with their own beliefs regarding gender equality. But most of these women framed the husband-as-money-manager choice in terms of individual abilities and preferences—not notions about the man being the head of the household. By adopting this rationale, couples were able to reconcile their more traditional gender practices with their gender-egalitarian beliefs.

In the voluntary specialization model of organizing financial decision making, men were usually the ones to assume the lead role. Yet there were several instances in which women functioned as the primary money manager, and this choice, too, was always explained in reference to individual differences in interest or experience. One married woman in her late 50s explains:

> I think I'm better at numbers than he is. He never did very well in math. And he got married late—he was 44—and he had lived a very simple bachelor's life. He didn't own a car. He didn't have health insurance. I don't think he even had a credit card. I was more used to dealing with money and papers and loans.

Interestingly, women were more likely to take the role of financial manager when they had higher levels of education than their husbands. Education appears to be closely coupled with financial proficiency in ways that can contradict current gender norms that say men should assume the role of financial manager and decision maker.

Implications of Voluntary Specialization

Couples who have adopted the voluntary specialization method of managing marital assets may never perceive that one partner has more or less power than the other. After all, if both partners freely enjoy discretionary income or benefit from the wealth created by one partner's management of the finances, does it really matter which partner is managing the assets? In a worst-case scenario, it matters a great deal. If one partner retains complete control over assets, it is possible for him or her to hide assets or mask a bad financial situation. The dissipation of marital assets (for example, wasting assets or transferring them to a third party) can influence divorce settlements, but in order to demonstrate that marital assets were dissipated, one must have knowledge about the types and the extent of marital assets over the duration of the marriage.

Even in a best-case scenario, in which both partners enjoy marital assets equally and the balance of marital power is in no way affected by who is making the economic decisions, the voluntary specialization method contains a hidden disadvantage that is structurally more likely to harm women. Half of all marriages end in divorce, and even if the couple never divorce, most married women will outlive their husbands.[17] At some point in their lives, the majority of women will experience life as a single woman. Women are often thrown into the financial "deep end" at a time when they are already stressed and vulnerable—at the time of divorce or widowhood. If women are left in the dark with respect to finances or do not gain financial knowledge or the confidence that comes with experience, they are at a disadvantage when they must manage their assets to make ends meet as a single woman.

Several people I interviewed mentioned that they knew someone who suddenly had to take over handling finances when a spouse died. For example, Evelyn mentions:

> My neighbor's husband got up one morning and had a massive heart attack, fell on the floor and died. She had no idea at all what to do with the money they had and lost $10,000 before she was able to get in touch with someone to help her.

Although women are usually the ones left in the dark about financial matters, men can also face this situation. Ben recounts:

My mother was the brighter one. She wrote the checks, she did all their finances. My mother developed diabetes which led to Alzheimer's. She lived 10 years with Alzheimer's. She went from being brilliant to walking around with socks on her head. My brother and I had to take over a lot of stuff because my father didn't know how to write a check. He didn't know how to do anything. My mother always took care of it— bills, taxes, everything. Bills would come in and he'd forget.... Finally my brother and I took over paying everything.

When either spouse does not understand or participate in financial decision making, the other is likely to suffer if he or she must suddenly assume fiscal responsibility. Because women have longer life expectancies and are likely to marry men who are older than they are, women are much more likely to be in the unenviable position of grieving the loss of a spouse as they assume a major responsibility that they are unprepared for.

Voluntary Separation as the New Equality: Separate Checks, Please

Other couples solved the problem of managing marital assets by adopting a method with distinct "his," "hers," and "ours" pots of money, devising strategies to meet joint expenses while at the same time controlling their own money. The most common arrangement was for both to contribute to common expenses and then use their remaining money as they see fit. Some couples split all joint expenses so that each pays a roughly equal amount:

> We usually share the mortgage and usually my husband pays most of the other bills and I pay everything that comes directly out of my paycheck—the medical insurance, the cars......it kind of evens out. When my son was in day care, the cost of the day care just almost exactly equaled the cost of the mortgage and so my husband paid the mortgage and I paid the day care.

Another strategy was for each spouse to contribute to joint expenses in proportion to income. Newlyweds Audrey and Brent have vastly different incomes and have allocated their contributions accordingly. Audrey explains:

> Before we got married, I paid a certain percentage of the rent and he paid the larger percentage of the rent and the same went for bills. Our rent at that time was about $1,100. I think I paid $400 and he took care

of the rest. Then, when we got married and moved to a much bigger place, he pays substantially more than I do. Our rent is close to $2,000 and I pay $500 and he takes care of the rest....For the new place, he asked me, "What is a comfortable amount for you to pay?" I told him what I thought a comfortable amount would be and he said that would be fine....If we buy [a house] later we'll probably figure the breakdown [in mortgage payments] that way.

Couples who adopted this approach to managing their finances explained that keeping separate pools of money is one way of minimizing conflict over how money should be spent. As Audrey explains,

My husband has hobbies and things that he likes to buy and I feel that he should be able to do that without my knowing...and I have mine as well. I want to be able to have my own little pocket of money that I can say I'm going to do with this what I want.

Keeping separate pools of money was also perceived as a *fair* way to manage resources so that each partner did not have to contribute to items that didn't pertain directly to him or her.[18] For example, in pondering the benefits of keeping finances separate, one woman explained that, on some occasions, "I want to give gifts to my god-child who he's never even met. Is it *fair* that I pull that out of our *joint* account?"

Couples who choose to separate marital assets into "his," "hers," and "ours" are guided by the goals of equality, fairness, and simplification. These couples are trying to balance individuality and collectivity as they navigate the ever-changing norms of gender equality and women's economic role in society.

Sometimes, the separate checks framework is taken to an extreme, challenging the basic notion that economic resources are shared by married couples. Glen and Nora have been married for 14 years and have each contributed half to common expenses. Last year, Nora's mother became ill with Alzheimer's, and she decided to cut back her work schedule to part-time to assist with the daily care her mother now required. She feels very fortunate to be able to care for her mother; however, the shift from full-time to part-time work cut her income in half. Yet Nora continued to contribute half to all joint expenses and, as a result, incurred quite a bit of credit card debt. Her husband, however, continued to pay off his credit cards every month and continued to contribute half to the common household expenses. Nora explains their situation this way:

I did get into a jam with credit cards. Not to the point that I couldn't use them any longer, but my payments on a monthly basis were so much for so many different credit cards that it was ridiculous.... To make a long story short, I just went and got a consolidation loan and because I was part-time I had to get someone to co-sign and so my husband did co-sign and he was fine with that.

Nora didn't want to ask Glen for the money to pay off her credit card debt or to modify the amount that she contributes to common expenses because she felt that it wouldn't be fair. Some may perceive that she is being taken advantage of because the division of expenses is clearly in her husband's favor. But Nora doesn't see it that way at all. She acknowledges that he could afford to "lend" her the money she needs, but notions of fairness and equality prevent her from taking this route. She wants to continue to participate as a financial equal rather than being dependent on her spouse.

The Hidden Inequality of the "New Equality"

Separating financial resources into "his," "hers," and "ours" may seem at first glance to be a fairly good method of minimizing conflict over how money is spent while at the same time injecting fairness into marital finances. Indeed, there are definitely benefits to this system—most notably the ability for each spouse to have some degree of financial independence. It also formally recognizes women's financial contributions to joint expenses. Yet, as the situation of Nora and Glen demonstrates, if it is taken to an extreme, the partner with a lower income, usually the wife, ends up with little or no access to the assets of the spouse.

Even in less extreme cases, where couples have tried to recognize inequalities in earnings, the solution often leaves women with less discretionary money and less control over assets. Hypothetically, if the husband earns 60% of their joint income, they may decide that he should contribute 60% to joint expenses and she should contribute 40%. Let's say that the husband has a salary of $6,000 per month and the wife has a salary of $4,000 per month. Their monthly mortgage payment is $1,000. He contributes $600 and she contributes $400. The remainder of their joint expenses comes to another $2,000 per month. According to their agreement, he pays $1,200 and she pays $800. So, with mortgage and other joint expenses, he is paying a total of $1,800 and she is paying a total of $1,200. He is indeed paying $600 more per month than she is, but he also has $4,200 left over at the end of the month to spend as he chooses and she has $2,800 left over to spend as she chooses. This arrangement may be *proportional* but it is not *equal*, and it illustrates how mistaken we may be when we assume marital wealth is equally accessible to each spouse. Because of the gender earnings gap, women are more likely to find themselves in the position of being the lower-earning spouse and hence the one with fewer financial resources at her disposal.

Differences in discretionary funds are often exacerbated by the distinction between "his" expenses and "her" expenses and the resulting decision about who should pay for what. In theory, the strategy of each paying for his or her own expenses sounds like a fair and reasonable strategy. The decision about what types of expenses are considered joint can be far from straightforward, though.

In the bestselling book *The Joy Luck Club*, Amy Tam chronicles the financial arrangements of Lena and Harold:

> My mother and I are alone in the house.... She is standing on her tiptoes, peering at a list stuck on our refrigerator door....

Lena	Harold
chicken, veg., bread,	Garage stuff $25.35
broccoli, shampoo,	Bathroom stuff $5.41
beer $19.63	Car stuff $6.57
Maria (clean + tip) $65	Light Fixtures $87.26
Groceries	Road gravel $19.99
(see shop list) $55.15	Gas $22.00
petunias, potting soil	Car Smog Check $35
$14.11	Movies & Dinner $65
Photo developing	Ice Cream $4.50
$13.83	

> ...
>
> I feel embarrassed, knowing what she's seeing. I'm relieved that she doesn't see the other half of it, the discussions. Through countless talks, Harold and I reached an understanding about not including personal things like "mascara," and "shaving lotion"...

And we've had philosophical arguments over things that have gray borders, like my birth control pills, or dinners at home when we entertain people who are really his clients or my old friends from college, or food magazines that I subscribe to but he also reads only because he's bored, not because he would have chosen them for himself.

And we still argue about Mirugai, *the* cat—not our cat, or my cat, but *the* cat that was his gift to me for my birthday last year....

"Why you do this?"

My mother has a wounded sound in her voice, as if I had put the list up to hurt her. I think how to explain this, recalling the words Harold and I have used with each other in the past: "So we can eliminate false dependencies...be equals...love without obligation...." But these are words she could never understand.

So instead I tell my mother this: "I don't really know. It's something we started before we got married. And for some reason we never stopped."[19]

Like the fictional characters Lena and Harold, couples adopting the separate checks strategy often have to negotiate whose column expenses belong in. In one interview, Jay, a married man in his 30s, illustrates how tricky it can be to decide who should pay for various expenses:

> My wife wanted to buy a new therapeutic bed...and I actually preferred the regular mattress—I was actually more comfortable on that—but she wanted this because it helps her back and everything so I didn't really want to get it but she really wanted to get it and so I said as long as you pay for it.

The purchase is payment- and interest-free for one year, so he is collecting money from her every month and putting it into his account so he can pay the bill when it comes due. Although they both use the new bed, he didn't really want it and therefore it was considered "her" purchase.

Even when couples were more liberal about categorizing items as joint expenses, the ways that the joint expenses were divvied up often reflected subtle biases about the roles played by her income and his. Sociologist Viviana Zelizer documents how throughout history women's earnings were often treated as "pin money"—used to pay for extras, but not considered to be of equal importance in supporting the household.[20] Treating women's earnings as "pin money" devalued women's economic contributions and supported the notion that the man was the head of the household.

Although economic realities today force married couples to depend heavily on women's earnings for basic household expenses,[21] many couples continue to organize the paying of joint household expenses in ways that subtly devalue women's contributions. For example, in explaining how he and his wife divvy up the bills, here's what one married man I interviewed said:

> I take care of the mortgage and then she takes care of all of the other expenses, which aren't too much...stuff like all of the little monthly bills like phone, electricity, oil, and gas for the cars, and their insurance, and so on and so forth. I kind of take care of the big whopper and then she takes care of all of the little bills.

While it may not be intentional, characterizing her contribution as paying the "little bills" could be perceived as implying that her contributions are less important to the household budget.

Another feature of the "separate but equal" financial approach is that people often did not know much about the financial assets of their spouses. When I asked one married woman in her 50s whether her husband was saving for retirement, she responded, "I don't know. I *really* don't know. I *hope* he is!"

We also can't assume that financial decisions regarding debt are collective. Julie and Frank have been married for more than a decade and are in their late 40s. However, they are finding that his use of credit cards is increasingly the topic of arguments:

> [We] argue that I'm paying more and that he doesn't save and he's reckless with his credit card. Because we're refinancing again. We both racked up some credit card debt and I was assuming that he was going to help me pay mine off, only to learn that he had racked up his own credit card debt without telling me....Everything I used mine for I told him—like for our vacation, and stuff for the house...we had an electrical emergency...that ended up costing $2,500....Sometimes you need a good chunk of change for like the electrical thing....These were all things that I told him about and was expecting him to help me pay off and it didn't happen....The other thing was—he got another credit card without me knowing....I was pretty upset when I found out that he had gotten this card without me knowing. He said he wanted it in case of an emergency or something....He's impulsive...he's gone

on these impulsive spending sprees. For instance the car. He bought the car without even telling me and that's like *huge*.

The debts that are incurred by one spouse can continue to haunt the other even after the marriage ends. Bob divorced his wife several years ago, only to find she was deep in debt. He explains:

> I had to go bankrupt because my ex-wife left me so much debt. I had credit cards I didn't even know I had....I looked down and was $20,000 in debt. We had a timeshare and she left it 8 months behind and credit card debt of $20 grand. It was to the point where I had no choice.

These couples' experiences illustrate that we cannot assume that all household wealth is owned equally, nor can we assume that both spouses are making financial decisions collectively. As these couples show, it matters a great deal how assets are owned and managed. Some spouses are like financial islands, some marriages are like financial despotism, and others are more like partnerships. The adage "what's mine is yours and what's yours is mine" sounds great in theory, but for many married couples, the adage should be rephrased to "part of what's mine is yours, but the rest is mine."

The Paradox of Women, Marriage, and Wealth

Married women and men are wealthier, all else being equal. If marital assets are shared, women generally end up with much greater financial resources than if they had remained single. The statistics on the wealth of married couples and single women could be taken to argue that the solution to women's lack of wealth is to get married and stay married.

Marriage is potentially the biggest financial safety net for women, but paradoxically, it also masks the latent vulnerability that women experience if their marriage ends in divorce, as roughly half of all marriages do. The solution to the gender wealth gap is not to encourage women to get married and stay married. First of all, when women's primary access to wealth is through marriage, they end up having less power than men in the marriage because they are less likely to be able to support themselves outside of marriage. As Rhona Mahony explains in her book *Kidding Ourselves: Breadwinning, Babies, and Bargaining Power*, "In a society in which separated or divorced men get on much better than separated or divorced women, men can threaten to walk out of the relationship and be believed by their spouses more easily than women can."[22] Having children makes a woman more vulnerable to her husband's demands because of the increased financial difficulty of supporting a family on her own. Furthermore, if a divorce does occur, she is more likely to have custody of children, generally lowering her chances of remarrying,[23] while at the same time her ex-husband's ability to find a new wife is likely to remain promising, given his financial means. As a result, women have a greater financial incentive to ensure their marriages remain intact and are hence more likely to give in when conflicts arise and to give primacy to their husbands' needs and wishes.[24] Ironically, then, unless women have access to wealth independent of marriage, they are likely to have less power within marriage.

A second reason that marriage is not the answer to eliminating the wealth gap is that the marriage safety net leaves many women out—especially less-educated women and black women, as they are less likely to marry. To begin with, women with a college degree are more likely to marry than women without a college degree.[25] If marriage were women's primary avenue to wealth, less-educated women would be less likely to benefit. Also, about 36% of black women are forecasted to never marry, in contrast to 7% of white women.[26] Furthermore, marriage itself provides less of a financial safety net for black and Hispanic women because they are more often widowed and at younger ages.[27] Widowhood for minority women "is the continuation or worsening of an already vulnerable situation"[28] because the death of their husbands worsens their already precarious economic situation as they lose the income of their husbands and have little wealth to draw on.[29] If women's access to wealth remains contingent on marriage, racial wealth gaps between women will continue to grow.[30]

Third, access to the potential wealth effects of marriage is not equal for all women. Because people often marry others with the same class background, low-income women may face a smaller pool of "eligible men" who have stable employment and who can achieve the standard of living they desire in order to marry.[31] College-educated women earn more than those without a college degree, and when college-educated women marry, they are likely to marry college-educated men, who also have higher earnings and better access to the wealth escalator than men without a college degree.[32] The result is that higher-income (and higher-wealth) men and women are marrying each other and creating wealth in ways that lower-income couples cannot, increasing overall class-based inequality.

A fourth reason that marriage is not the answer is that, in contrast to prior generations, Americans now spend more of their adult lives unmarried than married.[33] They marry later and take longer to remarry (if they remarry at all) if marriages end in divorce or widowhood.[34] Also, because of their longer life expectancy, in later life women outnumber older men and have fewer potential marriage partners. At ages 55 and older, unmarried women outnumber unmarried men by more than 2.5 to 1, and the gender imbalance increases with age.[35] Hence, women face a demographic challenge in remaining married throughout their lives.

Conclusion

Even before the feminist movement of the 1960s, women realized the importance of having control over economic resources. Now, at the beginning of the twenty-first century, with increasing numbers of married women working full-time and the ever-growing economic contributions women make to household income, couples are experiencing a much stronger financial *inter*dependence, with the earnings of both spouses needed to meet basic expenses. The growing financial interdependence has weakened the old cultural norm of the man of the house being the sole provider and making all the financial decisions. In its place, new patterns have emerged, ranging from complete co-builders of wealth to voluntary specialization to complete separation of assets.

Some may view the new pattern of voluntary specialization as the old traditional division of labor disguised as a decision based solely on interest or ability. This conclusion, however, would be incorrect because with voluntary specialization, women can become more active in managing the household finances if they wish. In fact, many women have become the primary financial decision maker and exert a tremendous amount of control over household wealth. Yet among those I interviewed, these women remain in the minority.

Conventional belief once indicated that couples with separate assets were less committed to the marriage.[36] But the interviews I conducted suggest that couples often separate assets in an attempt to inject fairness into financial decision making. The increasing economic participation of women as earners and the growing financial interdependence of couples have helped to foster a new approach to couples' financial decision making. In these new models, people are attempting to reconcile the communal aspects of marriage with an individualistic approach to managing one's own financial destiny, while at the same time promoting equity between financial partners. Ironically, an approach born out of women's financial agency and the desire for equality between partners often leaves women at a financial disadvantage with respect to discretionary income and access to wealth.

Although there are no doubt still some marriages where traditional assumptions that exclude women from financial matters exist, my interviews suggest that ideals of equality between partners have fundamentally changed the ways that couples organize financial decision making. Yet ideals of equality do not manifest as one uniform approach to managing marital assets. Rather, couples have adopted different strategies that are at least in part justified by strongly held beliefs in the innate equality between husbands and wives.

Despite idealistic norms of equality and couples' increasing financial interdependence, cultural assumptions about men being good providers and structural factors such as men's generally higher earnings often tip the scale in the direction of husbands having more control over marital assets. Yet the interviews suggest that when women have their own wealth, they are likely to assert more control over the way wealth is used (as Gayle did when she inherited money and used it to send her son to a private school). This finding is consistent with research that demonstrates that women's bargaining power within marriage increases when they have their own source of wealth.[37]

The experiences of the couples highlighted in this chapter challenge the implicit assumption that husbands and wives have equal control over household wealth. Gender differences in wealth do not disappear when a woman marries; they are transformed from measurable differences in men's and women's wealth to more subtle differences in control of marital wealth. Thus, when we are thinking about women's access to wealth, we must move beyond the approach that the women's wealth gap matters only for unmarried women. The women's wealth gap is often present for married women as well—it is just much more difficult to assign it a dollar value. Often women do not realize how little ownership and authority they have over marital assets until the marriage ends through death or divorce.

SEVEN

Public Solutions

*Why Equal Pay and Family-Friendly
Policies Aren't Enough and What Should
Be Done Instead*

C URRENT POLICIES THAT have a strong influence on a person's
ability to build wealth are based on an outdated foundation:
Social Security, pensions, and the government subsidies that
constitute the wealth escalator work best for people employed full-time
and continuously throughout their entire adult lives. As I have shown
in the preceding chapters, this model fits men better than women. Yet
it is also failing to meet the needs of a growing number of men, who
are increasingly likely to experience layoffs and periods of unemployment from the loss of blue-collar and skilled crafts jobs and the recent
economic crisis. Women may be hit hardest and hit first by the failure
of policies to include opportunities for everyone to build wealth, but
many men, particularly minorities and those without a college degree,
are also losing access to opportunities for wealth building.

Before addressing more inclusive wealth-building policy options,
it is useful to examine current policies designed to improve women's
economic well-being so that we can understand why more needs to
be done. Policies to improve women's financial status have focused on
equal pay and on helping women balance full-time employment with

family responsibilities. But equality of earnings and family-friendly policies do not necessarily translate into wealth.

Equal Pay and Family-Friendly Policies

The 1963 Equal Pay Act and Title VII of the 1964 Civil Rights Act were important first steps toward promoting economic equality between women and men. These laws barred employers from firing women for getting married or becoming pregnant and from denying them a job or promotion simply because of their sex, and women were now legally entitled to the same wages when they worked the same job as men. In the more than 40 years since these laws were passed, the wage ratio has improved only 18 percentage points, from 60% to 78%.[1] Why has the wage gap persisted?

First, the 1963 Equal Pay Act applies only to women and men in the same firm, but women and men tend to work in different firms, even when they have identical or similar jobs. And when they do work at the same firm, they usually have different job titles and different pay.[2] For instance, the Census Bureau reports that "firms with 75–90 percent male employees paid wages that, on average, were 40 percent higher than similar firms whose work force was almost entirely female."[3] The persistence of the gender wage gap can be explained primarily by occupational and industrial sex segregation—meaning that men and women are working in different jobs and in different industries.[4] In other words, men are more likely to work in jobs and in industries that pay more. But there is some gender bias built into the wage structure because many jobs traditionally held by women are undervalued—they have lower wages than jobs requiring less skill, training, or responsibility that are held primarily by men.[5] For example, one study revealed that nurses in Denver were paid less than gardeners in that city.[6] Despite legal efforts to achieve pay equity by adjusting wages to reflect the job's requisite qualifications and demands, in practice, comparable worth has been difficult to implement.[7]

Other efforts to improve women's financial status focused on encouraging women to play by the same rules as men. Women were encouraged to work full-time, to climb the corporate ladder, and to enter high-paying occupations that were traditionally dominated by men, such as doctor, lawyer, and corporate executive. The underlying premise was that if women started working in the same jobs as men and with the same attachment to the workplace—meaning full-time and continuously for their entire adult lives until retirement age—economic inequality between women and men would disappear.

Although many women did climb the corporate ladder and raised their earnings substantially, they encountered barriers to progress—a so-called glass ceiling that was difficult to break through. Upon returning home from their successful careers, they faced a "second shift" of child care, housework, and household management.[8] Women found it extremely difficult to combine full-time employment with this second shift, and, as a result, many successful and highly paid women sought part-time employment, switched to less demanding jobs, or dropped out of paid employment when the demands of caregiving were most time-consuming.

Employers increasingly sought to make the workplace more "family friendly." On-site day care, flexible scheduling, telecommuting, and job sharing were touted as remedies that would allow women to balance their responsibilities as workers and as caregivers. Lists like *Working Mother* magazine's "Best 100 Companies to Work For" reflected growing acceptance of this approach and also helped to convince employers that making the workplace more family friendly permitted them to retain valuable employees and improved, or at least didn't hurt, their bottom line. Likewise, the Family and Medical Leave Act of 1993 allowed many workers the right to 12 weeks off from work for certain family or health-related reasons without the risk of losing their jobs.

Why Current Policies Can't Eliminate the Gender Wealth Gap

So what went wrong? Why, despite anti-discrimination legislation, women's increasing accomplishments in the workplace, and the growth of family-friendly workplace policies, do women earn only 78% of what men do and own only 36% as much wealth?

The first problem with existing policies is that they fail to place women on the wealth escalator, where earnings are more rapidly and reliably translated into wealth. "Family-friendly" policies like job sharing and part-time employment are often not compensated proportionately to their full-time equivalents, and part-time employees are often denied access to wealth-enhancing benefits such as 401(k) plans and pensions.

Second, existing policies simply don't encourage or provide adequate financial compensation. For example, the Family Medical Leave

Act of 1993 is definitely a step in the right direction, but the leave is unpaid.[9] Most people don't have enough in savings to take a month off from work, let alone 12 weeks; four-fifths of middle-class families do not have sufficient assets to go for 3 months without income.[10] Furthermore, only employers with fifty or more employees are obligated to follow this law,[11] and it does not apply to employees who have worked for the particular employer for less than a year or who have worked fewer than 1,250 hours during the preceding 12 months. This effectively excludes part-time employees who work fewer than 25 hours per week. Ironically, women are less likely than men to be eligible for the Family and Medical Leave Act of 1993 because women are more likely to be employed in part-time work.

The third problem with existing policies is that they uphold the "ideal worker norm," in which employees are expected to be constantly available. Work-family policies may help people find more balance between work and family, but pursuing this balance often has a price. Many men and women alike fear that taking advantage of these benefits will signal that they are less work-oriented than others and that this perception will negatively influence their earnings and their chances for promotion. Apparently, there is reason to worry. Research by sociologist Jennifer Glass reveals that even when employee productivity and other related factors are controlled, women who took advantage of work-family policies experienced slower earnings growth than women who did not.[12] She found that women in managerial and professional occupations were heavily penalized when they took advantage of policies like telecommuting or working part-time, which limited the hours they spent at the office. It is possible that higher-paid managerial and professional occupations share more rigid norms of what it means to be dedicated to one's career; if that is the case, it would explain why women in these positions were penalized for not putting in the "face time" required by those norms.

Women are not the only ones disadvantaged by the ideal worker norm. Many men also desire more family time but are unwilling to risk marginalization in the work force, which could jeopardize their role as the family's primary breadwinner. Given that being a breadwinner is so central to our society's definition of what it means to be a man,[13] it would not be surprising if men were penalized even more than women for engaging in full-time caregiving, making their re-entry into the labor market even more precarious.

A fourth problem in current policies that seek gender equity is their failure to challenge the underlying assumption that matters relating to family life (e.g., parenting, caring for sick relatives, and divorce) are *private* matters. Decisions about how family resources should be organized—whether for the care of small children, an injured person, or an elder—are viewed as arising solely from personal choices and preferences, and the government, the workplace, and the law are not seen as having any responsibility for addressing economic penalties that arise from such private (i.e., family-related) decisions.

Society benefits, however, when caregiving is done well. As economist Nancy Folbre points out,

> High-quality care creates benefits that extend well beyond the immediate recipients.…happy, healthy, and successful children create an especially important public good. Children themselves are not the only beneficiaries. Employers profit from access to productive workers. The elderly benefit from Social Security taxes paid by the younger generation.…Fellow citizens gain from having productive and law-abiding neighbors.[14]

Caregiving also fills an important social function. Not only does everyone need care as a child, but most people will again require care themselves at some point due either to a health problem or to old age. Or they may find themselves responsible for providing care to a spouse, parent, or other relative. Caregiving is not only about children and hence is not only about the needs of people with children. The provision of care is a social good and should be formally recognized as something that benefits society as a whole.

Moreover, defining work-family decisions as an *individual* matter does not reflect the fact that the accommodations one partner makes in response to caregiving are almost always the result of a *joint* decision. For instance, husbands and wives usually decide together that one person will take time off to care for children. We must rethink the current rationale that if a couple divorces, they make a clean break, retaining their own current and future earnings and going their separate ways. If joint economic decisions disproportionately penalize caregivers after divorce, one parent is unfairly required to shoulder the financial burden of a joint decision.

Fifth, existing solutions to work-family conflicts and the gender wage gap have failed to promote economic equity because they neglect the important role that men should play in caregiving. Quite apart from the third point made above, about economic penalties to persons who pursue work-family policies, are the cultural barriers that men face in seeking a greater connection to their families. Many men do want to devote more time to their children, but they are discouraged from doing so because of cultural pressures that define men's family role as primarily one of breadwinner. But men as well as women are enriched by a life with their children and spouses. And unless men move back into the household at the same rate that women are moving into the labor market, a work-family balance can never be achieved for anyone. Until then, women will remain burdened by greater caregiving responsibilities, which will keep them at the mercy of the double deficit of lower earnings and limited access to full-time employment, preventing women from accessing the wealth escalator to the same extent as men.

Finally, existing solutions have failed because they have not addressed the true needs and desires of most individuals and families. Policies that focus on encouraging women (and men) to maintain full-time and uninterrupted work histories leave out caregiving as a necessary social good. If improved access to the labor market is the only solution that business and government can offer for overcoming the women's wealth gap, it is an incomplete solution at best. In fact, this is not necessarily the solution that today's men, women, or children want or need. And I would argue that it is not the solution that our society needs, either.

The Elephant in the Room

When it comes to discussions of gender equality, one of the most difficult issues to address is the fact that *some women prefer* to work part-time or be stay-at-home mothers in order to spend more time with their children. Women's views on caregiving are hardly uniform. Whether it is a result of biology, psychology, socialization, tradition, patriarchy, or economics, women are more likely than men to assume the role of full-time or part-time caregiver than the role of full-time employee.

In discussing her plans to start a family, one recently married woman commented, "At least the first couple years, I would really prefer to be at home. It's how I was raised and I think it's very valuable....*one of us*—one of the parents, I feel, has to stay home." Another unmarried woman speculated, "If I had children I think I would want to work less. I don't think it would be practical to leave the house at 7:30 or 8 in the morning and come home at 7:30 at night."

Marina is a single mother of a 10-year-old son. At one time, she was on the career fast-track, climbing the corporate ladder and earning a comfortable six-figure salary. Then, when her son was 2, she was laid off. She eventually found a part-time job she thought would be temporary until she was able to find something full-time in her field. She decided, however, to keep her part-time work in order to spend more time with her son:

> This was the perfect answer...and I decided not to go back to the corporate atmosphere. I'm very happy here....It's the perfect job...I used to be a very Type A personality—very, you know, climb the corporate ladder—and now, I have all kinds of time to spend with my son...I'm home when he gets home from school. It really is perfect. Financially it's a drain. But that's the only downfall. But...we're making it work. I'm making less than half of what I made in the corporate arena and so, I fought it for a while. Then when I saw how wonderful it was outside of work, it's like this light went on and I realized that I'd rather be there for my son. I'm not sure that a man who had lost his job would have said, "Oh, I'll just take a part-time job and stay here because I want to watch my son grow up." I think men are less inclined to do that than women are. I think it's maternal instincts....this is what I was meant to do....This is my CEO job.

Of course, some men would also prefer to work part-time to spend more time parenting, and some women prefer (or need) to work full-time while raising children. The problem is that people, primarily women, who do choose to leave full-time employment even for a while have not been figured in to most policies that seek to promote gender equality in income or wealth. We need to find ways to recognize the choice to reduce work hours, and the impact it has on wealth must specifically be addressed if the women's wealth gap is to be eliminated. It is clear that after more than 40 years of striving for equality we can no longer operate under the assumption that making women's employment patterns look more like men's will fix the women's wealth gap (or even the wage gap).

Consider the words of law professor and author Joan Williams:

> Instead of defining equality as allowing women into market work on the terms traditionally available to men, we need to redefine equality as changing the relationship of market and family work so that all adults—men as well as women—can meet both family and work ideals.[15]

New Policy Directions

Before discussing policies for reducing the women's wealth gap, it is important to emphasize that existing policies *already* make it easier for some to accumulate more wealth and that tax dollars now supplement the accumulation of assets for some through mechanisms such as tax deductions for mortgage interest, retirement accounts, and long-term capital gains. In an analysis of the tax policy in fiscal year 2003, the Corporation for Enterprise Development revealed that federal asset development policies cost taxpayers $335 billion.[16] The report found that, with respect to mortgage interest and property tax deductions, the wealthiest 5% of taxpayers received 35% of the benefits of these policies, whereas the bottom 80% received only 21% of the benefits. Combining mortgage interest and property tax deductions with preferential tax rates on capital gains and dividends, the report revealed that the average dollar amount of benefits received by taxpayers with incomes in the bottom 20% was $4.24. In contrast, the average benefit received by taxpayers with incomes in the top 5% was $3,060.69, and taxpayers in the top 1% received an average benefit of $38,107.10. The government is already subsidizing asset development, but most of the policies disproportionately benefit the wealthy, who are more likely to be men than women.

Current federal policies need to be adjusted so that more of the benefits generated by these policies go to those at the bottom and less to those who already have substantial wealth. Addressing wider racial and class-based inequality in wealth-building strategies is crucial to building a stronger, more stable, and financially coherent society. Since others have made recommendations to mitigate class- and race-based inequalities in wealth,[17] I focus on roadblocks faced by women that cannot be addressed solely by class- and race-based policies.

No single new policy can solve the problem of the women's wealth gap. The solutions to eliminating the women's wealth gap are multidimensional and interrelated, but future, more effective policies must have several critical components, including providing paid family leave, incorporating caregiving into the wealth escalator, encouraging more caregiving from men, giving women greater access to low-interest loans, changing the definition of assets in divorce laws, helping single parents tap into the wealth escalator, disconnecting benefits like health care and Social Security from full-time employment, and supporting women's entrepreneurship. Some of these components seek to address wealth directly by providing women with greater access to the wealth escalator, while others have more indirect effects on the ability to build wealth by helping women, especially women with parental responsibilities, increase their disposable income, thus giving them more income to generate wealth.

The policies below are designed to address the two primary causes of the gender wealth gap: the caregiving wealth penalty and women's lack of access to the wealth escalator. These causes are not mutually exclusive, but for purposes of simplification, I will address each in turn.

Policies to Reduce the Caregiving Wealth Penalty

Much of the wealth penalty associated with caregiving is a result of women decreasing their labor force participation (and hence losing access to the aspects of the wealth escalator tied to time spent in full-time work and level of earnings) and the heavy financial burden of single parenthood. Policies seeking to reduce the caregiving wealth penalty must include the following aspects: providing paid parental leave, incorporating caregiving into the wealth escalator, increasing men's participation in caregiving, and providing additional avenues for custodial parents to tap into the wealth escalator.

Provide Paid Family Leave

If there is any time at which parents need both financial assistance and time away from work, it would be immediately following the birth or adoption of a child. When it comes to paid maternity leave, the United States stands out as one of only two industrialized countries without a national paid maternity leave (Australia is the other country).[18] Only California, Hawaii, New Jersey, New York, Rhode Island, and Puerto Rico have any type of paid maternity leave, which is covered under temporary disability insurance programs.[19] But most women receive only a fraction of their regular earnings, and benefits are available only for an average of 5–13 weeks.[20] Women in the remaining forty-five states are not legally entitled to any paid leave, and only 8% of workers have access to even partially paid family leave through their employers.[21] In comparison, most other countries have a national system of paid maternity leave.[22] Globally, 128 countries provide paid maternity leave averaging 16 weeks, oftentimes replacing women's full wage.[23] Forty-seven *developing countries* provide at least 12 weeks of paid maternity leave at 100% of wages (table 7.1). In fact, not only do most countries have paid maternity leave, but many also give fathers the option of taking a paid paternity leave as well.

An even better option would be to make a minimal amount of both maternity and paternity leave paid and *compulsory*.[24] Besides the obvious financial benefit of paid leave, the advantage of a period of compulsory leave for mothers and fathers is that it does not stigmatize those who take leave as being less committed to their jobs. Paternity leave also has other important consequences for fathers' bonding and involvement in their children's lives. A study of paternity leave in Sweden revealed that men who took parental leave after the birth of a child were more involved in child care later on as well.[25] Additional research suggests

TABLE 7.1.   List of developing countries with at least 12 weeks of paid maternity leave at 100% of wages

Afghanistan	Guatemala
Algeria	Guinea
Angola	India
Argentina	Indonesia
Bangladesh	Laos
Barbados	Madagascar
Belarus	Mali
Benin	Mauritania
Brazil	Mauritius
Bulgaria	Mexico
Burkina Faso	Morocco
Cameroon	Pakistan
Chile	Panama
China	Peru
Colombia	Senegal
Comoros	Sri Lanka
Congo	Tanzania
Costa Rica	Togo
Cote d'Ivoire	Ukraine
Cuba	Uruguay
Dominican Republic	Venezuela
Ecuador	Vietnam
Gabon	Zambia
The Gambia	

Source: "Maternity Leave Around the World—A Table of Comparisons," www.apesma.asn.au/women/maternity_leave_around_the_world.asp (accessed March 28, 2008). Criteria for categorizing countries as developing countries are from the World Bank: www.worldbank.org/data/countryclass/classgroups.htm (accessed January 12, 2008).

that being involved in child care actually encouraged men to do more housework, thus distributing the "second shift" more equally between men and women.[26]

Paid parental leave has several benefits. First, the income it provides reduces the need for mothers and families to spend down savings or increase debt when a child is born. Second, if fathers are required to take some of the leave, they are more likely to be involved in child care later on, which is critical for helping equalize the costs of parenthood and hence reduce the women's wealth gap.

Some have argued that paid leave should be expanded to encompass those women who are outside of the labor force as well.[27] Many countries provide a "family allowance" or other cash benefit that is available to mothers whether or not they are in the paid labor force, recognizing that investing in children benefits the nation as a whole. Family allowances can be used to offset the lost wages of the parent who is staying home, or they can be used to subsidize child care expenses for those parents who wish or need to return to work.

In her book *No Exit*,[28] Anne Alstott argues for the creation of caretaker resource accounts of $5,000 per year, given to the caretakers of every child under age 13. The grant could be used to pay for child care or to further the education of the caretaker, or it could be placed in the parents' retirement savings. Any money not spent during the year is carried over to the next in an interest-bearing account. The grant acknowledges that children's primary caretakers typically experience lower wages, slower human capital development, and lost retirement wealth and takes steps to remedy these problems while recognizing the important job that caretakers do. The accounts take into consideration that the needs of caretakers are different and allow them to choose to continue working, to work part-time, or to leave the labor force entirely. The plan also recognizes that some caregivers benefit most from economic assistance for child care or funding retirement savings whereas others benefit most from furthering their own education.

Choice is critical. In a study of ten countries that had routinely reported statistics to the Organisation for Economic Cooperation and Development (OECD), sociologists found that mothers (both single and married) fare best economically in countries with policies that provide men and women with an economically supported choice of whether to care for their children at home or to return to work and pay for child care.[29]

The United States lags far behind many other industrialized countries with respect to caregiving benefits. In an examination of twenty high-income countries, Hegewisch and Gornick report that seventeen have statutes allowing parents to adjust or reduce working hours to care for children and six of the twenty countries permit employees to do the same if they are providing care to a spouse or elderly relative.[30] For example, Belgium provides both parents with the option of up to 3 months of full-time leave before a child's fourth birthday (or eighth birthday if the child is disabled). The leave can be taken as 3 months of full-time leave, 6 months of 50%, or half-time, leave, or 15 months of 80% of one's usual work hours. In Switzerland, caregivers for adults or children can refuse overtime or a change in schedule if it conflicts with caregiving responsibilities. Norway provides 4 weeks of "use or lose" paid parental leave for fathers.[31] These types of policies help both parents share the responsibilities of caregiving and keep mothers from losing access to the parts of the wealth escalator linked to employment.

Incorporate Caregiving into the Wealth Escalator

Paid parental leave is only a first step in helping to bring about greater wealth equality. Caregiving responsibilities do not end when a child reaches the age of 6 weeks, 6 months, or 6 years. Furthermore, caregiving involves caring for other adults such as aging parents or ill spouses. Solutions to the women's wealth gap must address the long-term wealth penalties faced by caregivers by incorporating them into the wealth escalator. In other words, we need to restructure access to the hidden wealth escalator so that caregiving becomes equivalent to market work. For example, caregivers should not be penalized with respect to their future Social Security payments. Years spent caring for children or elderly parents should not be cause for reduced benefits. The formula for Social Security benefits could be revised so that years out of the labor force (or years worked part-time) were not included in income averaging if those zero- or low-income years were devoted to caregiving.[32] This simple adjustment could make a tremendous difference to women's retirement income because it would prevent the zero- or low-income years from averaging away the benefits accrued from contributions during more substantial periods of work. Other countries have gone even further to incorporate caregiving into the wealth escalator. For example, Germany subsidizes pension contributions for caregivers who are outside the labor market, as well as those who work part-time.[33]

Another important policy mechanism would be to make part-time jobs a meaningful option for men and women, with equal pay, equal chances for promotion, and the same pension and benefit options currently available primarily to full-time workers. Other countries have been able to achieve this goal. The 1997 European Union Part-Time Work Directive, implemented in 2000, bounds all European Union countries to give part-time workers the same pro rata pay and benefits that are granted to comparable full-time workers. In recognition that women are much less likely to work full-time, case law in some countries has determined that denying part-time workers the same pro rata pay and benefits constitutes indirect sex discrimination (or disparate impact).[34]

It is also important to expand the range of occupations that offer opportunities for part-time work. In the United States, the majority of part-time workers are located in low-skill and low-wage occupations, whereas in Sweden, the option to work part-time is found across many occupations, even professional and managerial jobs. Pay gaps between part-time and full-time workers are larger in the United States than they are in many other countries, even after taking into account other factors that affect earnings, such as age, occupation, and education.[35]

Making part-time work a serious option for men and women has three important benefits. First, it helps men and women balance work and personal responsibilities. Second, if part-time workers are given the same pension and retirement benefits as full-time workers, they can profit from the wealth escalator. Third, it keeps them linked to the labor market, where they can stay abreast of technological changes in their field, keep their skills up to date, and maintain professional networks—thus improving their lifetime job prospects, their earnings, and their wealth accumulation.

To minimize the negative long-term effects that caregiving has on wealth, we also need to improve the mechanisms that help women and men move in and out of the labor force without suffering wage penalties or lost promotional opportunities. Some people will choose full-time caregiving, but this is not a permanent decision for most. Our society seems to assume that caregivers lose human capital when they are not working. On the contrary, many of the skills involved in caregiving (and the volunteer work that many full-time caregivers engage in) carry over into employment.[36] After all, full-time workers often switch careers and are forced to learn new skills and master new technologies. Those re-entering the labor force after a period of full-time caregiving should be given the same opportunity to show that they, too, can switch gears and get up to speed quickly in a new field.

In her book *Off-Ramps and On-Ramps*, economist Sylvia Ann Hewlett documents how providing opportunities for women to move back into professional careers after being out of the labor force for a period of time has benefited companies such as Lehman Brothers and Goldman Sachs. Providing opportunities to women who are seeking to move back into the labor force has also been recommended as one way to help reduce the "brain drain" in science, technology, and engineering fields.[37]

Encourage Caregiving by Men, Too

Encouraging men to engage in caregiving might not have a direct impact on women's wealth, but it provides an important cultural shift that enhances the success of policies seeking to reduce the gender wealth gap.[38] Increasing men's involvement in caregiving will have several important consequences. First of all, because men are more likely to hold positions of power in business and politics, they are in a better position to effectively demand the types of changes to work culture that support caregiving. The more often men in positions of authority take parental leave, work part-time to care for an ill parent, or work flexible hours to help drive the carpool, the sooner these types of policies will become legitimate, permitting both men and women employees to follow suit without worrying about being stigmatized or experiencing negative career ramifications. To alter cultural ideals about the behavior typical of an ideal employee or what constitutes success in the workplace, changes need to be embraced and enacted by those at the top. And there needs to be gender equity in pursuing flexible work arrangements so that they do not continue to be viewed as a "woman's problem." The more that men are involved in caregiving, the more likely it is that caregiving will be valued, helping shift social norms to the belief that caregiving is worthy of incorporation into the wealth escalator.

Children will also benefit if fathers provide an equitable share of caregiving. Fathers play a specific and important role in their children's emotional, psychological, and social development.[39] Clearly, children need fathers as well as mothers. And many fathers are expressing their interest in increasing their involvement in their children's lives,[40] so the call for a more inclusive culture of caregiving is not coming just from women.

Help Single Parents

Single mothers fare worse economically in the United States than in most other industrialized countries because the United States is less generous with respect to anti-poverty programs and because of the lack of high-quality and affordable child care.[41] Policies designed to reduce the women's wealth gap must address the additional barriers that prevent single parents from gaining access to the wealth escalator.

The cost of child care is one of the largest obstacles limiting the ability of single parents to make ends meet. It reduces their already limited disposable income and jeopardizes their ability to engage in saving or investment. Low-income single parents face the greatest difficulties obtaining affordable quality child care. The National Women's Law Center reports that in 2001, 40% of poor, single, working mothers paid at least half of their income for child care and another 25% paid between 40% and 50% of their income on child care expenses.[42] These single parents are also least likely to receive the tax breaks for child care that better-off families receive. For example, low-income parents are less likely to receive the full benefit of the Child and Dependent Care Tax Credit because the amount of tax they owe is often less than the credit. Single mothers are also more likely to work in low-wage jobs that do not provide the tax benefits that are available through Dependent Care Flexible Spending Accounts. As a result, single parents lack access to tax benefits that other parents enjoy through their employers or by virtue of their higher incomes. A few simple changes to the tax law could help low-income parents—who are disproportionately single mothers—access the same tax benefits that wealthier parents do. For instance, the Child and Dependent Care Tax Credit could be made refundable (meaning that when the amount of the credit exceeds taxes owed, families receive the difference).[43]

Because single parents are more likely to be poor, current policies that seek to assist those with low incomes are helpful. But single parents need additional avenues to the wealth escalator because of the heavier financial burdens imposed on them as custodial parents. Programs such as Individual Development Accounts (IDAs) are advocated by many experts as a way for those with extremely low incomes to begin to build wealth.[44] IDAs not only help those with low incomes to deposit money into savings accounts; they also provide financial education and opportunities to have their savings matched. Withdrawals are matched if they are used for certain purchases—usually to buy a home, attend college, or start a business. Some programs allow additional matched withdrawals for other purposes, such as home repair, job training, purchasing a car, or participating in retirement accounts.[45] One possible way to help remedy the financial limitations faced by single parents would be to provide additional matching funds to single parents.

Changing the asset limits for means-tested programs such as Temporary Assistance to Needy Families (TANF) would also support single parents who are especially vulnerable. Although many single parents who qualify for TANF and other programs are already without assets, raising or eliminating the limits on certain types of assets—such as retirement accounts and college savings accounts—could help keep single parents on the wealth escalator, positioning them for much greater success in gaining economic security in the long run and limiting their need for public assistance in the future.

Opportunities to build wealth for retirement are vital for low-income households and single parents. As pension reform experts Orszag and Greenstein point out, "two-thirds of the benefits from existing tax preferences for pensions accrue to those in the top one-fifth of the income scale."[46] To help persons with lower incomes benefit from the tax advantages of retirement savings plans, Orszag and Greenstein propose a progressive government matching formula that provides larger matches to low-income workers. They explain:

> For every $1 that a taxpayer in the 35-percent marginal tax bracket contributes to a tax-preferred pension, for example, the taxpayer receives a tax benefit of 35 cents. A taxpayer in the 15-percent marginal tax bracket, however, receives only a 15-cent tax benefit for the same contribution. To offset the regressivity of the implicit match provided by the tax code, the explicit government match should be *progressive*.[47]

The government subsidy of the higher-paid worker in the 35% tax bracket costs the government more in terms of lost revenue and makes it even more difficult for low-income taxpayers to build wealth. Policies that govern retirement accounts should be revised so that they do not disproportionately favor those with high incomes.

Policies to Increase Women's Ability to Tap into the Wealth Escalator

In addition to the preceding policies that seek to address the caregiving wealth penalty, women need improved access to avenues of building wealth directly. Greater access to low-interest loans would stimulate

opportunities for women to engage in entrepreneurship. It is also critical to expand the definition of marital assets in divorce laws and to
decouple affordable health insurance from full-time employment.

Improve Women's Access to Low-Interest Loans

Only the most wealthy among us are able to afford homes, businesses,
and college educations for themselves or their children without loans.
Those most in need of loans are the very people for whom securing
a loan is most difficult, as the poor, disproportionately women and
minorities, have few assets to offer as collateral.[48] Without access to
low-interest loans, women must either go without or rely on higher-
interest or subprime loans. As discussed in chapter 3, these financial vehicles have significant drawbacks and limit women's ability to
build wealth. Improving consumer education about the drawbacks of
high-interest loans is important, but it is also necessary to improve
regulation and strengthen consumer protection in the lending industry to help remedy this problem. For example, in their report *By a
Thread: The New Experience of America's Middle Class*, policy experts
Wheary, Shapiro, and Draut suggest that foreclosure rates among
subprime borrowers could be reduced by requiring lenders to qualify
borrowers of adjustable rate mortgages based on the fully indexed
rate of the loan (the rate they are likely to face once the initial rate
has ended) instead of the low initial "teaser" rate.[49] Without access to
low-interest loans, women are denied a variety of potentially wealth-
building opportunities, including home ownership and entrepreneurship. Moreover, women may actually lose what wealth they had
already accrued if they become snagged on the debt anchor, which
is particularly likely if a woman gets caught up in the downward spiral of predatory lending practices that often results in foreclosure or
bankruptcy.

Increase Women's Entrepreneurship

If we take the annual *Forbes* list of the richest Americans as an indicator, many of the wealthiest individuals in the United States are entrepreneurs. Entrepreneurs are more likely to be wealthy, even when one
controls for other relevant factors related to wealth, such as level of
education, earnings, and inheritance.[50] As I demonstrated in chapter 4,
women are less likely to have business assets, but the number of female
entrepreneurs is growing. Programs that assist and encourage women

to start their own businesses could be an important factor in helping to bring about a more gender-balanced wealth distribution.

Improving women entrepreneurs' access to credit and financing is critical. Women are much less likely than men to receive lucrative financing through mechanisms such as venture capital funding and angel investors.[51] Lack of financing and access to credit are tremendous obstacles to female entrepreneurs, leaving them to rely more heavily on credit cards and the disadvantages of "the credit card hustle."[52] If women's businesses are to grow and become as profitable as they can be, they must be able to employ the same tools of financing that are currently enjoyed by male entrepreneurs.

In addition to increasing women's access to venture capital and angel investors, we must make available microenterprise loans. These loans have been utilized successfully elsewhere, particularly in the developing world, as they often serve the needs of low-income, minority, and less-educated women, whose opportunities to build wealth are particularly limited.

An additional obstacle to entrepreneurship is losing access to employer-sponsored health insurance.[53] Health insurance is much more expensive if it is purchased by an individual than if it is purchased through an employer-sponsored plan. Whereas married persons may still be able to access employer-sponsored health insurance through their spouses' employment, single people do not have this option. Losing more affordable employer-based health insurance may be a greater obstacle to single women if they are custodial parents. Caring for children adds even more cost to the insurance equation, and while a woman might be willing to incur greater risk by forgoing insurance altogether for herself, a mother may be unlikely to make that choice for her children. Research shows that women would be more likely to engage in entrepreneurship if the cost of private health insurance were lowered.[54]

Women's entrepreneurship also needs to expand out of the service sector into more profitable areas of the economy. Since women are more likely to engage in entrepreneurship in those areas in which they have knowledge or experience, it is essential for women to continue to gain access to traditionally male-typed occupations and fields in which business profits are greatest. An increase in woman-owned businesses reaching the top of corporate America is likely to have other benefits, besides increasing the wealth of individual women business owners. As the ranks of successful businesswomen grow, they are more likely to be on other companies' boards of directors, where their presence has been shown to increase corporate giving.[55] Creating conditions conducive to the success of female entrepreneurs is also likely to increase women's representation among venture capitalists. These female venture capitalists, in turn, could be more likely to have social networks composed of female entrepreneurs in need of financing.[56]

Expand the Definition of Assets in Divorce Laws

When it comes to the economic consequences of divorce, women usually draw the short straw.[57] Studies have found that women's standard of living declines sharply after divorce whereas men's standard of living often improves.[58] The definition of marital assets has changed dramatically over the past 30 years; pensions, future stock options, and even employment termination packages are now more likely to be considered marital assets and taken into account in a settlement. But in many cases, they are still left out of settlement negotiations. Furthermore, including a broader range of assets in divorce settlements is far from straightforward. Laws for dividing marital property vary by state, and loopholes remain that may prevent one spouse from accessing assets she thought she once held with her husband. For example, as pointed out in a report issued by the Institute for Women's Policy Research:

> The right to cash out or roll over a lump sum payment from a defined contribution [pension] plan opens the door to a loss of spousal rights. Once a defined contribution plan is spent or converted into an individual retirement account, a spouse or former spouse no longer has special rights to the lump sum.[59]

Whereas divorce courts are sorting out these difficult issues and generally trying to divide assets fairly, there is another type of asset that is not as easily distributed: future earnings capacity. Since spouses rarely make career decisions independently of each other,[60] people's career choices and earnings trajectories are unavoidably influenced by those of their spouses. Historically, many couples have chosen the path that enhanced the husband's earnings capacity over time. Correspondingly, women are more likely to turn down more lucrative jobs or promotions that require extensive travel, relocating, long hours, or long commutes. In placing these restrictions on their careers, they often dampen their long-run earnings trajectories. As a result, if the couple divorces, the husband retains his more favorable earnings trajectory, while the wife retains her less favorable earnings trajectory. Under such conditions, even if the wealth is divided equally at the time of divorce, the man is more likely to be wealthier over the long run. A woman's economic disadvantage is further magnified if she is a custodial parent. Not only will she generally shoulder a disproportionate financial responsibility, but her earnings trajectory is likely to be further limited by the need to curtail travel, overtime hours, additional training, or other demands that could lead to promotions or new, more lucrative job opportunities.

We need to do a better job of equalizing the short-term and long-term economic consequences of divorce if we wish to reduce the women's wealth gap. Marital assets should be redefined to include not only wealth as traditionally understood, but also assets such as human capital and the ways that both parties may have helped to increase the earnings trajectory of one partner more than that of the other. As an example, economists Burkhauser and Holden advocate earnings sharing, a "system of sharing Social Security earnings records between married partners. Under such a system, total covered earnings of a couple would be shared equally during marriage. Earnings could be split either annually or at divorce, disability, or retirement."[61] With earnings sharing, divorced women would retain access to Social Security benefits based on their former husbands' earnings during the marriage even if they were married less than 10 years (currently, spouses married less than 10 years have no right to Social Security benefits based on their former spouses' earnings).

Decouple Affordable Health Care from Full-Time Employment

The lack of health care coverage is an issue not only for women's health, but also for their wealth. Women pay more for health care, disproportionately shoulder the burden for their children's health care, and as a result are left with less disposable income. Furthermore, health care crises that result in loss of income and extremely high medical bills are one of the primary causes of bankruptcy for the middle class.[62]

Women are more likely to lack health insurance for a number of reasons already raised in this discussion. They are less likely to work in the types of jobs or industries that provide employment-based health care.[63] Women are also more likely to work part-time in jobs that either are not eligible for employer-sponsored health insurance or, if they are eligible, require much higher out-of-pocket premiums. Women who are not eligible for employment-based health insurance pay higher premiums (sometimes up to 48% higher) than men of the same age if they must purchase insurance directly from the individual health insurance market.[64] And in the private insurance market, insurance companies in the District of Columbia and in nine states are allowed to deny coverage to women who, in the past, have been victims of domestic violence.[65]

Even married women, who are often covered as dependents under their husbands' employer-based coverage, face the risk of losing coverage. Being covered as a dependent is problematic, as it leaves women vulnerable if their marriage ends. But even women who stay married are at risk of losing coverage when their husbands reach retirement age. Because many women marry men who are older than they are, when their husband retires at age 65 and loses employment-based health care (in which both had coverage), *he* is eligible for Medicare, but *she* is not. She must find replacement coverage until she, too, reaches the age of Medicare eligibility.[66] To make matters worse, some employers are beginning to eliminate dependent care coverage in response to rising heath care costs.[67]

As single mothers, women are often not only paying the medical bills of children, but also losing income when they have to take time off from work to provide care for them. Women are also more likely to take time off from work or cut back their work hours to take care of spouses, parents, or other family members or friends who are ill or have serious health issues. Keeping everyone healthy by providing good preventative care and treatment for ongoing medical conditions will not only help those affected directly, but also help women avoid the loss of income. Paid sick days are crucial for women, but also for men. Many people do not realize that almost half of all workers do not have paid sick days, resulting not only in loss of income from work, but also in the spread of disease as people return to work while sick because of the potential loss of income or because of the fear of being fired.[68]

Good medical care and insurance is also likely to help women keep any wealth they do have by preventing one of the most common reasons for filing bankruptcy—high medical bills (most likely incurred while either uninsured or underinsured).[69] The broad availability of good medical insurance should also help widows stay out of poverty by eliminating the possibility that extremely high medical bills incurred in the final illness of a spouse will drain their life savings.[70]

It is time to look for new alternatives to health insurance and to expand opportunities to obtain affordable insurance from sources other than full-time employment. The lack of affordable health insurance is becoming increasingly salient for all Americans, now that employment-based health insurance is declining and many companies are less likely to offer this benefit.[71]

Speculation: What If Women Had More Wealth?

Improving women's financial status might have benefits beyond the well-being of the individual. For example, research by sociologist Catherine Kenney has found that children in the United States in two-parent low- to moderate-income households are less likely to experience food insecurity (i.e., having to skip meals because of lack of food) when their mothers control household money.[72] Women are more likely to spend money on food, increasing the likelihood that their children will have enough to eat. Studies in other countries also indicate that when women control money, they are more likely to spend it in ways that benefit children's health and general welfare.[73] If we can extrapolate these findings to women and wealth more broadly, then increasing women's wealth may improve children's well-being generally—especially that of children in low-income households where resources are scarce. Indeed, research reveals that children of single mothers who have some assets are more likely to graduate from high school and have higher grade point averages, even after controlling for income, mother's education, mother's expectations regarding the child's level of education, and other important factors that predict children's outcomes.[74]

Women also give a larger proportion of their money to charity. The Center on Wealth and Philanthropy at Boston College reported that at all income levels unmarried women give more to charity than unmarried men and that the discrepancy increased as income increased. For example, of those earning less than $25,000, unmarried men donated an average of $244, while unmarried women donated an average of $256; of those earning $100,000 to $199,999, unmarried men donated an average of $2,920, and women's average donation was $3,541; and of those earning $200,000 or more, the average donation of unmarried men was $6,526, while unmarried women donated an average of $28,171. When household wealth (rather than income) was examined, unmarried women still gave more than unmarried men at similar levels of wealth. Of those with $5 million or more of wealth, unmarried men donated an average of $13,565, whereas unmarried women donated an average of $50,298.[75]

Contributions to political candidates, issue-oriented organizations, and foundations offer an avenue for those with wealth to shape national priorities. Women's preference for giving money to social service organizations that help others in need[76] implies that women are more willing to distribute economic resources more equally and inclusively. Research on distributive justice (principles for how things should be allocated) reveals that, in general, men are much more likely to allocate rewards on the basis of *equity* (i.e., rewards are given out in proportion to what persons put in) whereas women are more likely to allocate rewards *equally*.[77] Extending these findings to societal resources more broadly, if women had more control over resource distribution (a likely outcome if they had greater wealth and the corresponding influence over political, economic, and social agendas), the country might be more likely to enact policies to more effectively reduce economic inequality.

Reducing economic inequality is likely to have broad effects on society as a whole. Research from several wealthy countries, including the United States, reveals that "among the developed countries it is not the richest societies which have the best health, but those that have the smallest income differences between rich and poor."[78] According to these studies, more egalitarian countries are healthier because they have a stronger community life (which provides greater social support) and because their citizens have less psychosocial stress associated with the ills of extreme economic inequality, such as higher crime rates, violence, and deep social divisions.

Furthermore, in countries with a more equal distribution of economic resources, married couples are more likely to share control over money and have a more equitable division of housework.[79] Collectively, these findings suggest economic inequality is closely linked with other forms of inequality in part because it helps legitimate inequalities. As sociologists Yodanis and Lauer explain,

> Couples in contexts where economic inequality is pervasive and accepted may be more likely to draw on these institutionalized rules and practices and adopt them within their own relationships. Within economically unequal societies, it may seem reasonable and fair that the spouse who earns the most should have the greater financial control and access.... On the other hand, couples in societies where income equality is normative may be less likely to arrange their finances unequally, regardless of how much each individual spouse earns.

The Current Economic Crisis

How will the economic crisis that began in 2007 affect the women's wealth gap? Three features of this economic meltdown with the greatest potential impact on the wealth gap are rising unemployment rates, suspensions in employer 401(k) contributions, and the housing crisis.

Because men have been losing jobs at a faster rate than women, the current economic crisis has been dubbed a "mancession" in the media.[80] As of May 2009, 10.5% of men were unemployed compared to 8% of women. Men are bearing the brunt of layoffs because they are more likely to work in the economic sectors that are being hit the hardest: manufacturing and construction.[81] The loss of these jobs is particularly devastating because many of these jobs were unionized and had pensions and other fringe benefits that helped many men in blue-collar occupations gain access to the wealth escalator.

While men—particularly men in blue-collar jobs—are losing ground, their losses do not necessarily imply women are gaining ground. *BusinessWeek* reported that the pay gap between men and women widened between the first quarter of 2007 and the first quarter of 2008 and that the types of jobs women do have are not good ones: "they're low-wage, they're dead-end, and they don't have any benefits."[82] Women's unemployment is now rising as the economic crisis has spread to retail and service sectors, where women's employment is concentrated. In May 2009, the unemployment rate for women rose faster than that for men, and the unemployment rate for women who head families was 11% (up from 10% in April 2009).[83]

If there is an effect that may potentially alter the magnitude of the women's wealth gap, it is the rapid loss of well-paid unionized blue-collar occupations with fringe benefits. Many less-educated male workers are now finding themselves in the same situation as less-educated female workers. As employment in the trades and the manufacturing sector continues to decline, the jobs available to men are likely to be lower paid (although women's jobs still pay less), unstable, and without fringe benefits. As a result, the wealth gap between men and women at the lower end of the economic spectrum may narrow a bit. However, women will continue to bear the negative wealth effects of custodial parenthood and lower incomes. And because women have less wealth than men generally, they have less to draw on if they lose their jobs.

Another aspect of the economic crisis meaningful for the women's wealth gap is the growing number of employers that are cutting or suspending benefits, particularly matching 401(k) contributions, one of the core components of the wealth escalator. Despite recent cuts, companies state that the changes are likely to be temporary; in past recessions, most companies that suspended contributions reinstated them within 1–3 years.[84] Even without employer matches, 401(k) accounts have tax benefits that will continue to provide access to the wealth escalator for those who can afford to contribute. All else being equal, men are still more likely to be in jobs that offer retirement benefits like 401(k) plans, and men are more likely than women to have the disposable income to invest. Consequently, the suspension of matching employer contributions is likely to slow the speed of the wealth escalator briefly, but the long-term impact on the women's wealth gap is likely to be negligible.

A third aspect of the economic crisis that may affect the women's wealth gap is the property devaluation and foreclosure emergency that comprises the housing crisis. Because they are more likely to have subprime loans, this crisis is hitting women—and especially minority women—very hard. Homeowners with subprime loans are particularly vulnerable to foreclosure.

Taken as a whole, the current economic crisis hits men harder in some ways (unemployment) and women harder in other ways (foreclosure). In the end, it's most likely the poor and working-class men and women who will suffer the worst effects of the bad economy. The current economic crisis is likely to weaken the financial standing of those with the least—whether they are men or women. As Barbara Ehrenreich summarizes in the *New York Times*, "In good times and grim ones, the misery at the bottom just keeps piling up, like a bad debt that will eventually come due."[85] Only time will tell whether the economic crisis affects the wealth gap and how. If there is one thing that we can learn from the economic crisis, it is that *wealth* is what helps people weather financial storms.

Conclusion

Eliminating the gender income gap is important and will improve women's economic status, but it is insufficient for eliminating the gender wealth gap. The underlying causes of the gender wealth gap are (1) that women shoulder the greater financial burden of parenthood and (2) that women are more likely to be excluded from the wealth escalator simply because of the types of jobs they have, their different lifelong patterns of labor force participation, or the types of assets they own.

The financial price that women pay for becoming mothers is much higher than the price that men pay for becoming fathers. Unless the economic costs of parenthood are shouldered equally by men and women, the gap in wealth between them will persist. Unmarried women are actually taxed twice—first as custodial parents and then via the motherhood wage penalty. Married women are also taxed via their decreased earnings and suppressed wealth trajectories, but they may not have to pay this tax until they become divorced or widowed, as most women eventually do.

We need to recognize that motherhood is detrimental to women's access to wealth, and we must take the public debate about mothers, children, and families in a new direction. Rather than argue over why men don't share domestic responsibilities more equitably or whether mothers should work outside the home, we should recognize that, although most people believe that men and women are equal and that children should spend time with both parents, economic and social pressures prevent many from achieving this goal. We need to support policies and social norms that promote women's equality and that point out the social benefits that are created when caregiving is undertaken by both men and women.

Women's ability to build wealth is also blocked by their lack of access to the wealth escalator, which makes earnings go further and efficiently translates employment into wealth. Women are more likely to work in the nonprofit sector, in nonunionized jobs, and in the service industry, where they not only earn less than men on average but also are denied the wealth boost from access to the wealth escalator.

Current policies that give wealth boosts to some but not others are being subsidized by tax dollars or lost tax revenue. Those benefiting from the wealth escalator are not necessarily working harder in order to tap into its benefits; instead, they are working in the types of jobs and at a level of employment that disproportionately provide them the support of wealth-enhancing benefits. Policies that support the wealth escalator need to become more inclusive and provide greater opportunities for tapping into the American Dream.

Increasing women's wealth is not just good for women; it's good for men. It puts more resources into the hands of families, while at the same time making it easier for men to spend more time with children or caring for family members. Closing the women's wealth gap is good for children because it raises their standard of living and gives them more time with both parents. And doing away with the gap is good for society, as it would help women attain a more secure and stable economic life, with a financial safety net for emergencies and the peace of mind that comes with preparing for self-sufficiency in retirement. Now that we have identified the women's wealth gap, explored its causes, and proposed some possible solutions, it is up to us to work to eliminate it.

Appendix: Data and Methods

THROUGHOUT THE BOOK, I draw upon two complementary sources of data. The first is quantitative data from the Survey of Consumer Finances, which is designed to provide an accurate picture of the distribution of wealth in the United States. The second is qualitative data from in-depth interviews, which allow one to understand people's thoughts, beliefs, and actions that are related to making financial decisions. In combination, quantitative and qualitative data allow a much deeper and more thorough understanding than either could provide alone.

The Survey of Consumer Finances

The Survey of Consumer Finances is a triennial national survey that is sponsored by the Board of Governors of the Federal Reserve System with the cooperation of the U.S. Department of the Treasury. The survey is composed of two samples: a standard geographically based random sample and an oversample of high-income households.[1] The oversample of high-income households is one of the distinguishing features of the Survey of Consumer Finances. Random samples are less likely to contain very wealthy households since they form such a small percentage of the population. Because this very small percentage of the population owns most of the wealth, random samples are likely to underrepresent the magnitude of wealth inequality. For this reason, the Survey of Consumer Finances is considered to provide the best data available for examining the extent of wealth inequality.[2]

The Survey of Consumer Finances is also well equipped for examining issues of wealth because of the depth and extent of questions pertaining to assets and debts. The survey asks detailed questions about the ownership of financial assets (ranging from savings accounts to stock to trusts), nonfinancial assets (ranging from vehicles to homes to business assets), and debts (ranging from credit cards to education loans to loans from family and friends). The survey also contains extensive information on pension and retirement assets as well as key demographic characteristics such as employment history, job characteristics, and marital status. The level of detail of the asset and debt questions and the ability of respondents to consult financial records increase the accuracy of the information.

This book draws on the 2004 Survey of Consumer Finances, which contains data for 4,519 households.[3] As explained in chapter 1, most of the data presented in the book are for households headed by people under age 65 (for married or cohabitating households, the age of the older spouse was used). I excluded twenty-six households in which the respondent was separated but assets were shared or owned primarily by the other spouse. With this restriction, the resulting sample size for households headed by people under age 65 is 3,600 households.

At the time the book was being written, the 2004 data were the most recent available; however, as data continue to be released, I will provide updates on the book's Web site: www.mariko-chang.com/shortchanged. In chapter 2, I also present data from the 1989, 1992, 1995, 1998, and 2001 Surveys of Consumer Finances. Although there are data available for some years prior to 1989, the weights and survey design are most consistent from 1989 onward, rendering the data most comparable over time.[4]

In-Depth Interviews

Although the Survey of Consumer Finances can tell us how large the gender wealth gap is in the United States, I also wanted an understanding of the personal experiences behind the numbers that only interviews can provide. Therefore, in addition to data from the Survey of Consumer Finances, I present data from fifty interviews. The sample of people for the interviews was drawn primarily from a large employer in the Northeast with a very diverse work force, including people with a wide range of ages, occupations, and racial and ethnic backgrounds. To obtain as heterogeneous a group as possible, I used the data from the human resources department to stratify people into groups based on gender, age, and broad occupational category (including full-time or part-time status). I then selected a random sample of people within these groups and invited them to be interviewed for the study.

After about thirty-five interviews, I also began asking people to refer me to someone they knew who was not currently employed or who they thought had very different financial experiences from theirs. I was particularly interested in hearing from people who were not currently employed because people without earnings (particularly those being supported by their spouses or partners) may have very different attitudes and experiences regarding saving, spending, and making financial decisions. Five additional interviewees were selected based on referrals. This type of sample selection (often referred to as snowball sampling) is sometimes criticized for not being representative, but this did not concern me for several reasons. First, although friends and co-workers may have similar economic backgrounds, they often have very different financial experiences and attitudes, which were the main focus of the interviews. In fact, because people do not often talk as openly about their financial situation as they do about their sex life, many people really don't know much about the financial experiences and situations of their friends and acquaintances. Second, I was not troubled by the nonrepresentative interview sample because the purpose is to better understand the personal stories and experiences that are not captured by the quantitative, nationally representative survey data. And finally, the additional interviews obtained by snowball sampling comprised such a small proportion of the total number of interviews conducted.

Most of the interviews were conducted by me, but I was grateful for the assistance of three graduate students who conducted some of the interviews: Audrey Alforque-Thomas, Stephanie Howling, and Renee Richardson. Interviews lasted from 45 minutes to more than 2 hours, and most were held in a private office. I had a list of interview questions, but generally asked them in a semistructured way, letting the conversation evolve as naturally as possible. Before concluding the interview, I always double-checked to make sure that all questions had been addressed and also gave people the opportunity to add anything else that they wanted to say or wanted to clarify. The list of interview questions did evolve somewhat over time, as I learned better ways of asking a particular question or expanded (or shortened) certain topical areas based on the quality or direction of the responses they elicited. However, the basic goals of the interview always remained the same: to better understand people's financial attitudes, experiences, and circumstances. Questions covered a broad range of topics, such as the ways that their parents and family affected their financial attitudes, how their household finances are managed (for married and cohabiting respondents), whom they talk with about financial matters, whether women and men have different financial attitudes, their experiences saving, spending, and investing, and their beliefs about the stock market and taking financial risks.

Of the fifty people interviewed, twenty-eight were women and twenty-two were men. The average age of those interviewed was 47. All but one respondent completed high school, and the majority were college graduates, many with advanced degrees. The men and women interviewed were similar with respect to average age, marital status, and level of education. None of the men were stay-at-home parents or homemakers, but one man was currently unemployed. Incomes ranged from $15,000 to more than $100,000 for individuals and from $35,000 to more than $150,000 for couples. Most individuals reported incomes in the $35,000–$55,000 range, and most couples reported incomes in the $65,000–$125,000 range. More than half of the respondents were married, and several were cohabiting. About two-thirds of the respondents had children, and about three-fourths were Caucasian (the majority of nonwhites were Asian or black).

All interviews except two were recorded and transcribed.[5] I took copious notes during and immediately after the two interviews that were not recorded in order to retain as much detail as possible. In order to ensure the confidentiality of all participants, all names have been changed. In a few instances, additional details were altered slightly to protect the identity of the respondents (such as his or her occupation or the gender of children), but the details of the stories themselves were left intact.

I was always humbled by people's willingness to share such personal details about their lives and experiences. Whereas friends and family are often reluctant to talk to each other about financial matters, people seemed to be comfortable speaking with me. Because financial issues are often embedded in family dynamics and are so emotionally laden because of their association with such strong emotions as love, envy, jealousy, power, and self-worth,[6] people interviewed may have welcomed the opportunity to speak to someone who is a neutral party.

Others simply thought it would be fun to participate or were curious about the topic, perhaps because it is often not discussed regularly with others. I will always be grateful to those who shared their experiences and thoughts. Without them, this book would not be possible.

Description of Variables for Multivariate Analyses

At various points throughout the book, I have employed multivariate analyses (OLS regression, quantile regression, logistic regression) to examine the effects of variables while holding others constant. The issue of whether one should use weighted or unweighted data in regression analysis is open to debate.[7] For the multivariate analyses, I present results of analyses using unweighted data, but the substantive conclusions are similar when weights are used. The main difference is that most variables in the models are statistically significant when weights are employed, as would be expected given the shift in sample size when weights are used. Descriptive information on the variables employed in the multivariate analyses is provided in table A1.

The Survey of Consumer Finances data include multiple imputation of missing values in which each respondent has five records ("implicates") rather than one. The codebook contains information about the use of multiple imputation (and references) and also Stata and SAS programs that can be used to conduct multivariate analyses that take into account the effects of imputation on the estimates. I conducted all multivariate analyses using these programs. However, these programs do not calculate an R^2 value. To give the reader a rough idea of model fit, I have run regressions separately for each implicate and averaged the R^2 value across the five implicates. Further discussion of the imputation and the software programs designed to handle the effects of imputation can be found in the Survey of Consumer Finances codebook.

TABLE A1. Description of variables in multivariate analyses (nonmarried men and women under age 65)

Variable	Description	Mean	Standard deviation
Dependent variables			
Wealth (log)	Logged dollar value of wealth (net worth)	5.47	8.34
Net worth (nonlogged)	Wealth (net worth)	155,789	1,158,339
Owns cash account(s)	Owns a cash account (checking, savings, money market, or certificates of deposit)	0.87	0.34
Owns home	Owns own home	0.48	0.50
Owns stock	Owns stock (directly or indirectly via mutual funds, including retirement accounts)	0.39	0.49
Owns other real estate	Owns real estate other than own home	0.11	0.32
Owns privately held business	Owns privately held business assets	0.07	0.25
Independent variables			
Female	1 = female; 0 = male	0.62	0.49
Age	Age at time of survey	41.80	12.59
Inheritance (log)	Logged dollar value of any inheritances received	1.60	3.75
White	1 = white; 0 = nonwhite	0.65	0.48
Income (log)	Logged annual income from all sources in 2003	10.04	1.34
Unemployment	1 = respondent was unemployed during the past 12 months; 0 = otherwise	0.19	0.39
Bankruptcy	1 = ever declared bankruptcy; 0 = otherwise	0.14	0.35
Self-employed	1 = respondent is self-employed; 0 = otherwise	0.09	0.28
Years full-time	Total number of years that respondent has worked full-time	17.38	12.24
Education	1 = less than high school; 2 = high school diploma/GED; 3 = some college; 4 = 4-year college degree; 5 = graduate school or advanced degree	2.89	1.19

Retired	1 = retired; 0 = otherwise	0.05	0.21
Financial risk tolerance	1 = "not willing to take any financial risks"; 2 = "take average financial risks, expecting to earn average returns"; 3 = "take above-average financial risks, expecting to earn above-average returns"; 4 = "take substantial financial risks, expecting to earn substantial returns"[a]	1.78	0.86
Never married	1 = never married; 0 = otherwise	0.46	0.49
Number of children	Number of children of any age, whether or not they live with respondent	1.46	1.61
Parent	1 = parent; 0 = otherwise	0.61	0.49
Number of children in household	Number of children under age 18 who live in the household	0.41	0.83

The only variables with correlations higher than .5 were the following pairs: years worked full-time and age ($r = .778$), never married and age ($r = -.526$), never married and parent ($r = -.547$), and owns business assets and self-employed ($r = .557$).

[a] The values were recoded from the original data set so that higher numbers would indicate higher financial risk tolerance.

Quantile and OLS regression results predicting (log) wealth for nonmarried men and women, ages 18–64

	Quantile regression	OLS regression
Female	–0.473*	–0.975*
	(0.228)	(0.468)
Age	0.076***	0.128***
	(0.015)	(0.031)
Inheritance (log)	0.127***	0.201***
	(0.028)	(0.058)
White	1.167***	1.239*
	(0.230)	(0.487)
Income (log)	1.271***	1.061***
	(0.082)	(0.159)
Unemployment	–0.339	–0.174
	(0.282)	(0.574)
Bankruptcy	–1.008***	–2.621***
	(0.295)	(0.625)
Self-employed	1.305**	3.233***
	(0.311)	(0.670)
Years full-time	0.029*	0.073*
	(0.014)	(0.029)
Education	0.346***	0.257
	(0.096)	(0.204)
Retired	0.606	1.091
	(0.526)	(1.115)
Financial risk tolerance	0.346*	0.796**
	(0.139)	(0.272)
Never married	–0.739**	–0.436
	(0.252)	(0.536)
Number of children	–0.196**	0.031
	(0.076)	(0.160)
Constant	–9.753	–14.819
	(0.990)***	(1.861)***
Sample size	1,179	1,179
R^2	0.198	0.305

Note: Because one cannot take the log of zero, those with zero net worth were assigned a value of zero for the logged value of net worth.
* $p \leq .05$ ** $p \leq .01$ *** $p \leq .001$ (two-tailed)
Standard errors in parentheses.

TABLE A3. OLS regression results predicting (nonlogged) wealth for nonmarried men and women, ages 18–64

	Men	Women
Income (nonlogged)	5.73***	3.84***
	(0.699)	(1.25)
Age	18,879	22,293
	(73,658)	(52,493)
Inheritance (log)	245,994	–9,553
	(153,.81)	(108,281)
White	28,833	171,378
	(883,912)	(828,216)
Unemployment	–337,615	–648,230
	(1,003,797)	(996,469)
Bankruptcy	–1,145,874	–736,751
	(1,132,159)	(1,077,744)
Self-employed	2,913,569**	6,683,990***
	(1,053,739)	(1,691,214)
Years full-time	27,354	–30,544
	(70,217)	(51,970)
Education	91,299	703,420+
	(358,942)	(366,693)
Retired	–577,917	776,891
	(1,920,649)	(1,989,442)
Financial risk tolerance	594,990	515,335
	(450,760)	(491,543)
Never married	–105,842	–1,094,733
	(1,000,772)	(909,913)
Number of children	57,610	310,555
	(300,523)	(277,883)
Constant	–2,854,897	–3,251,830
	(2,507,694)	(2,382,193)
Sample size	1,179	1,179
R^2	0.439	0.658

Note: In these regression analyses, I used nonlogged income and wealth to allow me to present the dollar contribution of income to wealth in a straightforward manner. See Shapiro, Thomas M. 2004. *The Hidden Cost of Being African American: How Wealth Perpetuates Inequality.* NY: Oxford University Press.

+ $p \le .10$ * $p \le .05$ ** $p \le .01$ *** $p \le .001$ (two-tailed)
Standard errors in parentheses.

Quantile regression results predicting (log) wealth for
nonmarried men and women, ages 18–64

	Model 1 (from table A2)	Model 2
Female	−0.473*	−0.251
	(0.228)	(0.278)
Age	0.076***	0.065**
	(0.015)	(0.022)
Inheritance (log)	0.127***	0.123***
	(0.028)	(0.031)
White	1.167***	1.169***
	(0.230)	(0.277)
Income (log)	1.271***	1.260***
	(0.082)	(0.090)
Unemployment	−0.339	−0.336
	(0.282)	(0.314)
Bankruptcy	−1.008***	−1.119**
	(0.295)	(0.350)
Self-employed	1.305**	1.388***
	(0.311)	(0.363)
Years full-time	0.029*	0.031
	(0.014)	(0.020)
Education	0.346***	0.349**
	(0.096)	(0.112)
Retired	0.606	0.589
	(0.526)	(0.617)
Financial risk tolerance	0.346*	0.326*
	(0.139)	(0.148)
Never married	−0.739**	−0.952**
	(0.252)	(0.311)
Number of children	−0.196**	
	(0.076)	
Parent		−0.752*
		(0.354)
Number of children in household		−0.310+
		(0.175)
Constant	−9.753***	−8.896***
	(0.990)	(1.174)
Sample size	1,179	1,179
R^2	0.198	0.200

Note: Because one cannot take the log of zero, those with zero net worth were assigned a value
of zero for the logged value of net worth.
+ $p \leq .10$ * $p \leq .05$ ** $p \leq .01$ *** $p \leq .001$ (two-tailed)
Standard errors in parentheses.

TABLE A5. Logistic regression analyses predicting ownership of cash accounts, homes, stock, other real estate, and privately held business assets for nonmarried men and women (ages 18–64)

	Cash	Home	Stock	Other real estate	Privately held business
Female	0.697**	−0.030	0.247	−0.049	−0.816**
	(0.256)	(0.156)	(0.198)	(0.220)	(0.313)
Age	−0.026⁺	0.028**	0.011	0.029⁺	0.054*
	(0.014)	(0.010)	(0.012)	(0.016)	(0.023)
Inheritance (log)	0.048	0.049**	0.060**	0.152***	0.042
	(0.039)	(0.019)	(0.021)	(0.021)	(0.032)
White	0.913***	0.493**	0.774***	−0.343	0.026
	(0214)	(0.158)	(0.219)	(0.248)	(0.357)
Income (log)	0.305***	0.195***	0.701***	0.500***	0.367**
	(0.068)	(0.092)	(0.112)	(0.101)	(0.114)
Unemployment	−0.630**	−0.405*	−0.512*	−0.073	−01.198*
	(0.233)	(0.197)	(0.226)	(0.323)	(0.509)
Bankruptcy	−0.283	−0.753***	−0.249	−0.258	−0.190
	(0.292)	(0.196)	(0.220)	(0.308)	(0.438)
Self-employed	0.371	0.629**	0.035	1.335***	3.738***
	(0.393)	(0.229)	(0.253)	(0.246)	(0.290)
Years full-time	0.035**	0.022*	0.026*	−0.001	−0.013
	(0.013)	(0.009)	(0.017)	(0.014)	(0.019)
Education	0.869***	0.166*	0.329***	0.092	0.087
	(0.116)	(0.069)	(0.076)	(0.097)	(0.137)
Retired	0.680	0.100	−0.710⁺	0.204	−1.288
	(0.586)	(0.355)	(0.409)	(0.446)	(1.064)

(continued)

153

TABLE A5. (continued)

	Cash	Home	Stock	Other real estate	Privately held business
Financial risk tolerance	0.156	0.056	0.724***	0.400**	0.456*
	(0.138)	(0.087)	(0.095)	(0.123)	(0.181)
Never married	-0.357	-0.591**	0.385+	-0.446	-0.187
	(0.260)	(0.181)	(0.219)	(0.276)	(0.377)
Parent	-0.787*	0.203	-0.197	-0.014	-0.212
	(0.362)	(0.205)	(0.254)	(0.284)	(0.385)
Number of children in household	-0.133	0.123	-0.158	-0.174	0.245
	(0.124)	(0.104)	(0.141)	(0.193)	(0.236)
Constant	-3.005***	-7.741***	-11.536***	-9.642***	-10.021***
	(0.895)	(0.994)	(1.299)	(1.139)	(1.400)
Sample size	1,179	1,179	1,179	1,179	1,179
Log likelihood	-659.2	-1248.8	-1088.6	-685.3	-388.7
Chi squared	285.5***	371.5***	508.7***	280.5***	451.4***

+$p \leq .10$ *$p \leq .05$ **$p \leq .01$ ***$p \leq .001$ (two-tailed)
Standard errors in parentheses.

Notes

Chapter 1

1. The American Prospect: www.prospect.org/cs/articles?article=tap_talks_with_lilly_ledbetter; www.gibbonslaw.com/news_publications/articles.php?action=display_publication&publication_id=2173

2. The full text of the Supreme Court opinion (Alito) and dissent (Ginsburg) can be found at www.law.cornell.edu/supct/html/05-1074.ZS.html. The National Women's Law Center provides commentary on the Ledbetter Act at http://www.nwlc.org/pdf/Ledbetter%20Fair%20Pay%20Act%200f%202009%20%20-%20Summary%200f%20case%20and%20Bill.pdf.

3. The act states that the 180-day statute of limitations for filing a Title VII pay discrimination claim resets with each discriminatory paycheck if based on a prior discriminatory pay decision.

4. Stolberg, Sheryl Gay. 2009. "Obama Signs Equal-Pay Legislation." *New York Times* January 30.

5. Figures for the gender wage ratio come from the Institute for Women's Policy Research. 2009. "Fact Sheet: The Gender Wage Gap 2008." IWPR No. C350. April. The ratio includes full-time full-year workers only. Data on younger Americans' full-time earnings come from the U.S. Census Bureau, Current Population Survey, 2008 Annual Social and Economic Supplement, which refers to total money earnings in 2007 for people ages 15–24 working full-time for 50 weeks or more. Women's median earnings were $22,075, and men's were $23,174.

6. In families in which both husbands and wives have earnings, 25.7% of wives earned more than their husbands in 2006. In families in which wives have earnings but husbands may not, 33.4% of wives earned more than their husbands.

U.S. Department of Labor. 2008. "Women in the Labor Force: A Databook" (2008 ed.). www.bls.gov/cps/wlf-databook2008.htm. For more information on metropolitan areas where women outearn men, see Roberts, Sam. 2007. "For Young Earners in Big City, a Gap in Women's Favor." *New York Times* August 3.

7. Horn, Laura. 2006. *Placing College Graduation Rates in Context: How 4-Year College Graduation Rates Vary with Selectivity and the Size of Low-Income Enrollment.* NCES 2007–161. U.S. Department of Education. Washington, D.C.: National Center for Educational Statistics. www.nces.ed.gov/pubs2007/2007161.pdf

8. For further information on the likelihood that gender equality is in reach, see Blau, Francine D., Mary C. Brinton, and David B. Grusky (eds.). 2006. *The Declining Significance of Gender?* NY: Russell Sage Foundation.

9. Wealth was calculated using the SAS program provided in the codebook of the 2004 Survey of Consumer Finances, except that I did not include the value of vehicles owned because for most people vehicles are not investments (they do not hold their value and do not provide monetary returns such as interest or capital gains). Wealth, or net worth, was defined as the total value of assets minus the total value of debts. If assets are owned with others, the value is prorated to reflect the percentage owned by the respondent. For years prior to 2004, I also used the calculation of wealth provided in the corresponding year's codebook, without including the value of vehicles. Further information pertaining to the details of the calculation of net worth is available at www.federalreserve.gov/pubs/OSS/oss2/bulleting.macro.txt

10. Domhoff, G. William. 2002. *Who Rules America?* (4th ed.). NY: McGraw-Hill; Jacobs, Lawrence R., and Theda Skocpol (eds.). 2005. *Inequality and American Democracy: What We Know and What We Need to Learn.* NY: Russell Sage Foundation.

11. Andreoni, James, Eleanor Brown, and Isaac Rischall. 2003. "Charitable Giving by Married Couples: Who Decides and Why Does It Matter?" *The Journal of Human Resources* 38:111–133; Ostrower, Francie. 1995. *Why the Wealthy Give: The Culture of Elite Philanthropy.* NJ: Princeton University Press.

12. Eller, Martha Britton. 1997. "Federal Taxation of Wealth Transfers, 1992–1995." *Statistics of Income Bulletin* 16:8–63. www.irs.gov/pub/irs-soi/92–95fedtaxwt.pdf

13. Sullivan, Teresa A., Elizabeth Warren, and Jay Lawrence Westbrook. 2002. *The Fragile Middle Class: Americans in Debt.* CT: Yale University Press.

14. Income data refer to 2003. Source: Wolff, Edward N. 2007. "Recent Trends in Household Wealth in the United States: Rising Debt and the Middle-Class Squeeze." Levy Economics Institute Working Paper No. 502. www.levy.org/pubs/wp_502.pdf

15. Sierminska, Eva, Andera Brandolini, and Timothy M. Smeeding. 2006. "Comparing Wealth Distribution Across Rich Countries: First Results from the Luxembourg Wealth Study." Luxembourg Wealth Study Working Paper No. 1; Wolff, Edward N. (ed.). 2006. *International Perspectives on Household Wealth.* MA: Edward Elgar; Wolff, Edward N. 2002. *Top Heavy: The Increasing Inequality of Wealth in America and What Can Be Done About It.* NY: The New Press.

16. Wolff, Edward N. 2007. "Recent Trends in Household Wealth in the United States: Rising Debt and the Middle-Class Squeeze." Levy Economics Institute Working Paper No. 502. www.levy.org/pubs/wp_502.pdf

17. Mishel, Lawrence, Jared Bernstein, and Sylvia Allegretto. 2007. *The State of Working America 2006/2007*. NY: ILR Press.

18. U.S. Census Bureau. 2008 *Statistical Abstract*. Table 58. http://www.census.g08s0058.pdfov/compendia/statab/tables/

19. Kreider, Rose M., and Jason M. Fields. 2002. *Number, Timing, and Duration of Marriages and Divorces: 1996*. Current Population Report P70–80. Washington, D.C.: U.S. Census Bureau.

20. Kreider, Rose M., and Jason M. Fields. 2002. *Number, Timing, and Duration of Marriages and Divorces: 1996*. Current Population Report P70–80. Washington, D.C.: U.S. Census Bureau.

21. DePaulo, Bella. 2006. *Singled Out: How Singles Are Stereotyped, Stigmatized, and Ignored and Still Live Happily Ever After*. NY: St. Martin's Press.

22. Cherlin, Andrew J. 1992. *Marriage, Divorce, Remarriage*. MA: Harvard University Press.

23. Conley, Dalton. 1999. *Being Black, Living in the Red: Race, Wealth, and Social Policy in America*. CA: University of California Press; Elmelech, Yuval. 2006. "Determinants of Intragroup Wealth Inequality Among Whites, Blacks, and Latinos." Chapter 3 in Gordon Nembhard, Jessica and Ngina Chiteji (eds.). *Wealth Accumulation and Communities of Color in the United States: Current Issues*. MI: University of Michigan Press; Keister, Lisa A. 2000. *Wealth in America: Trends in Wealth Inequality*. NY: Cambridge University Press; Shapiro, Thomas M., and Edward N. Wolff (eds.). 2001. *Assets for the Poor: The Benefits of Spreading Asset Ownership*. NY: Russell Sage Foundation; Sherraden, Michael (ed.). 2005. *Inclusion in the American Dream: Assets, Poverty, and Public Policy*. NY: Oxford University Press; Sherraden, Michael. 1991. *Assets and the Poor: A New American Welfare Policy*. NY: Sharpe.

24. I did find some notable exceptions to the lack of research on the U.S. gender wealth gap. The first is the January/April 2006 special issue of *Feminist Economics* on Women and Wealth (which was later published as *Women and the Distribution of Wealth: Feminist Economics* in 2007). However, of those articles in the special edition that address gender and wealth in the United States (Deere and Doss; Schmidt and Sevak; Yamokoski and Keister), none incorporated qualitative data or were able to present the level of detail on the wealth gap that I provide in this book. The second notable exception is *Women, Marriage and Wealth* by Joyce (2007), which uses the Health and Retirement Study to examine how marital status impacts wealth for women age 50 and older. Other exceptions include work by Janet Gornick et al. (2006), Dalton Conley and Miriam Ryvicker (2004), Tracy Warren et al. (2001), and Lena Edlund and Wojciech Kopczuk (2009). I encourage the reader to seek out these important resources for additional research.

25. Because wealth has been conceptualized as a household asset, gender differences in wealth have historically been examined by comparing households headed by women with households headed by men. But gender of the household head does

not really capture the relation between gender and personal wealth. Even within married couples (which are usually defined as "male-headed"), gender differences most likely exist in the ownership of wealth.

26. Scholars still actively debate whether the individual or the household is the correct unit in social stratification research (i.e., the study of how social goods like income and education are distributed in society). For reviews of this debate, see Baxter and Western (2001) and Sorensen (1994).

27. Blumstein, Phillip, and Pepper Schwartz. 1985. *American Couples*. NY: Pocket Books; Burgoyne, Carole B. 1990. "Money in Marriage: How Patterns of Allocation Both Reflect and Conceal Power." *Sociological Review* 634–665; Hertz, Rosanna.1986. *More Equal than Others: Men and Women in Dual Career Marriages*. CA: University of California Press; Pahl, Jan. 1983. "The Allocation of Money and the Structuring of Inequality Within Marriage." *The Sociological Review* 31:237–262; Pahl, Jan. 1980. "Patterns of Money Management Within Marriage." *Journal of Social Policy* 9:313–335; Tichenor, Veronica Jaris. 2005. *Earning More and Getting Less: Why Successful Wives Can't Buy Equality*. NJ: Rutgers University Press; Zelizer, Viviana. 1997. *The Social Meaning of Money*. NJ: Princeton University Press.

28. Bittman, Michael, Paula England, Liana Sayer, Nancy Folbre, and George Matheson. 2003. "When Does Gender Trump Money? Bargaining and Time in Household Work." *American Journal of Sociology* 109:186–214; Brines, Julie. 1994. "Economic Dependency, Gender, and the Division of Labor at Home." *American Journal of Sociology* 100:652–688; England, Paula, and Barbara Stanek Kilbourne. 1990. "Markets, Marriage and Other Mates: The Problem of Power." Chapter 6 in Roger Friedland and A. Robertson (eds.). *Beyond the Marketplace: Rethinking Economy and Society*. NY: Aldine de Gruyter.

29. For a review, see Sorensen, Annemette, and Sara McLanahan. 1987. "Married Women's Economic Dependency, 1940–1980." *American Journal of Sociology* 93:659–687.

30. Husband's income and the presence of children are less predictive of women's labor force participation than they once were (see Blau, Francine D., and Lawrence M. Kahn. 2005. "Changes in the Labor Supply Behavior of Married Women: 1980–2000." NBER Working Paper 11230). I provide further discussion of the economic and sociological factors that shape women's labor force participation and household decision making in later chapters.

31. For example, Norway, the United Kingdom, and France provide public pension credits for caregivers. AARP. 2006. "AARP European Leadership Study: European Experiences with Long-Term Care." http://assets.aarp.org/www.aarp.org_/cs/gap/ldrstudy_longterm.pdf

32. Morris, Betsy. 1998. "It's Her Job Too: Lorna Wendt's $20 Million Divorce Case Is the Shot Heard 'Round the Water Cooler." *Fortune* February 2.

33. Cohn, Bob. 1998. "What a Wife's Worth." *Stanford Magazine* March/April.

34. Duncan, Greg J., and Saul D. Hoffman. 1985. "A Reconsideration of the Economic Consequences of Marital Dissolution." *Demography* 22:485–497;

Holden, Karen C., and Pamela J. Smock. 1991. "The Economic Costs of Marital Dissolution: Why Do Women Bear a Disproportionate Cost?" *Annual Review of Sociology* 17:51–78; Peterson, Richard R. 1996. "A Re-Evaluation of the Economic Consequences of Divorce." *American Sociological Review* 61:528–536; Weitzman, Lenore. 1996. "The Economic Consequences of Divorce Are Still Unequal: Comment on Peterson." *American Sociological Review* 61:537–538.

35. McGarry, Kathleen, and Robert F. Schoeni. 2005. "Widow(er) Poverty and Out-of-Pocket Medical Expenditures near the End of Life." *The Journals of Gerontology Series B: Psychological Sciences and Social Sciences* 60:S160–S168.

36. Holden, Karen C., and Pamela J. Smock. 1991. "The Economic Costs of Marital Dissolution: Why Do Women Bear a Disproportionate Cost?" *Annual Review of Sociology* 17:51–78.

37. For facts about widows and poverty, see Smeeding, Timothy M. 1999. *Social Security Reform: Improving Benefit Adequacy and Economic Security for Women.* Center for Retirement Research Working Paper No. 16/1999. http://escholarship. bc.edu/retirement_papers/25 (accessed January 7, 2008); Weir, David R., Robert J. Willis, and Purvi Sevak. 2002. *The Economic Consequences of Widowhood.* University of Michigan Retirement Research Center Working Paper 2002–023. For more on the poverty of elderly couples, see McGarry, Kathleen, and Robert F. Schoeni. 2005. "Widow(er) Poverty and Out-of-Pocket Medical Expenditures near the End of Life." *The Journals of Gerontology Series B: Psychological Sciences and Social Sciences* 60:S160–S168.

38. The age given for widowhood refers to first marriage. U.S. Census Bureau. 2007. Detailed Tables: Number, Timing, and Duration of Marriages and Divorces 2004, Table 5. www.census.gov/population/www/socdemo/marr-div/2004detailed_tables.html. In 2004, female life expectancy was 80.4 years. Center for Disease Control. *National Vital Statistics Reports*, Vol. 56, No. 9. www.cdc.gov/nchs/data/nvsr56/nvsr56_09.pdf

39. If we divide households according to their wealth into a continuum from least wealth to most wealth, the bottom quintile consists of the poorest 20% of households. In contrast, the top quintile consists of the wealthiest 20% of households. The middle three quintiles are composed of households in the second, third, and fourth quintiles (the middle 60% of households), which can be thought of as the middle class. In 2004, these households had a net worth between $500 and $406,450. Source: Wolff, Edward N. 2007. "Recent Trends in Household Wealth in the United States: Rising Debt and the Middle-Class Squeeze." Levy Economics Institute Working Paper No. 502. www.levy.org/pubs/wp_502.pdf

40. These statistics refer to defined contribution plans which are funded by employee contributions. Bajtelsmit, Vickie L., and Jack L. VanDerhei. 1997. "Risk Aversion and Pension Investment Choices." Chapter 4 in Michael S. Gordon, Olivia S. Mitchell, and Mac M. Twinney (eds.). *Positioning Pensions for the Twenty-First Century.* PA: Pension Research Council and the University of Pennsylvania Press.

41. Bajtelsmit, Vickie L., and Jack L. VanDerhei. 1997. "Risk Aversion and Pension Investment Choices." Chapter 4 in Michael S. Gordon, Olivia S. Mitchell, and

Mac M. Twinney (eds.). *Positioning Pensions for the Twenty-First Century*. PA: Pension Research Council and the University of Pennsylvania Press.

42. Bajtelsmit, Vickie L., and Nancy A. Jianakoplos. 2000. "Women and Pensions: A Decade of Progress?" Employee Benefit Research Institute Issue Brief Number 227, November, p. 5.

43. In 1998, the male life expectancy was 73.8 years and the female life expectancy was 79.5 years. Center for Disease Control. *National Vital Statistics Reports*, Vol. 48, No. 18. www.cdc.gov/nchs/fastats

44. Sam's daughter, Alice, and his three sons *did* appear on the list along with Sam in the year prior to his death. In explaining the shift in ownership of the Walton fortune from Sam exclusively to Sam and his children, *Forbes* (1989) said: "At what point does actual control of the family fortune pass from parent to child, and therefore at what point should the family's wealth be realigned? In Sam's case, he has made it relatively easy for us. Age 71 this year, he clearly is becoming less active. He has given up the job of chief executive officer at the company he founded and built, retaining only the chairmanship. The children—who are all active adults in their 40s with professional interests and families of their own—are taking an increasing role in investment decisions for the family holding company. Even the holding company itself is being reorganized this year from the family corporation Sam initially set up into a straightforward partnership, with Sam and each of his four children full and equal partners" (p. 146).

45. The Census Bureau measures poverty according to income thresholds that vary according to family size and composition. See www.census.gov/hhes/www/poverty/povdef.html. Statistics on the duration of poverty are found in Stern, Sharon M. 2008. "Poverty Dynamics: 2001–2003." May 15. http://www.census.gov/hhes/www/poverty/dynamics01/pdf/PovertyDynamics.pdf (accessed June 3, 2008).

46. http://www.census.gov/hhes/www/poverty/histpov/hstpov4.html

47. Pearce, Diana. 1978. "The Feminization of Poverty: Women, Work and Welfare." *Urban and Social Change Review* 11:28–36.

48. These statistics are based on my calculations from the 2004 Survey of Consumer Finances and will be explored further in chapter 2.

49. The survey collects detailed financial information for the "primary economic unit" of the household: an economically dominant individual or couple (married or cohabitating as partners) and any persons in the household who are financially interdependent with the economically dominant person or couple. For purposes of simplicity, however, I use the term "household" throughout the book rather than the term "primary economic unit." For further information on the distinction between the primary economic unit and the household with respect to the collection of data, see Bucks, Brian K., Arthur B. Kennickell, and Kevin B. Moore. 2006. "Recent Changes in U.S. Family Finances: Evidence from the 2001 and 2004 Survey of Consumer Finances." *Federal Reserve Bulletin*.

50. For discussions of how the Survey of Consumer Finances compares with other household surveys of wealth, see Curtin, Richard F., Thomas Juster, and James Morgan. 1989. "Survey Estimates of Wealth: An Assessment of Quality." Pages

473–551 in Robert E. Lipsey and Helen Stone Tice (eds.). *The Measurement of Savings, Investment, and Wealth*. IL: University of Chicago Press; Oliver, Melvin L., and Thomas M. Shapiro. 2006. *Black Wealth/White Wealth: A New Perspective on Racial Inequality* (10th anniversary ed.). NY: Routledge; Wolff, Edward N. 2002. *Top Heavy: The Increasing Inequality of Wealth in America and What Can Be Done About It*. NY: The New Press, appendix.

51. Elmelech, Yuval. 2008. *Transmitting Inequality: Wealth and the American Family*. Maryland: Rowman Littlefield.

52. For additional discussion of the data challenges involved in studying the gender wealth gap and the challenges of attributing ownership of household wealth, see Deere, Carmen Diana, and Cheryl R. Doss. 2006. "The Gender Asset Gap: What Do We Know and Why Does It Matter?" *Feminist Economics* 12:1–50.

53. Raymond, Joan. 2001. "The Ex-Files—Corporate Marketing Campaigns Focusing on Divorced Women." *American Demographics* February.

Chapter 2

1. The mean is the mathematical average, and median wealth is the amount of wealth at which half have more wealth and half have less wealth.

2. The design of the Survey of Consumer Finances makes it difficult to separate the assets of cohabiting couples. Generally speaking, married couples are much wealthier than cohabiting couples, but because the focus of the book is on noncoupled households, it is less important to distinguish between married and cohabiting couples in the context of this book.

3. Nonmarried (never-married, divorced, or widowed) households consist of noncoupled men and women, regardless of whether they are supporting children or other dependents.

4. Of the couple households, 85% are married. As mentioned in note 2, the design of the Survey of Consumer Finances makes it difficult to separate the assets of cohabiting couples, recognizing that their finances are likely to be entwined in ways more similar to those of married couples than those of single heads of households. Because the focus of the book is on single-headed households, combining married and cohabiting households is simpler and does not detract from the arguments presented.

5. Hao, Lingxin. 1996. "Family Structure, Private Transfers, and the Economic Well-Being of Families with Children." *Social Forces* 75:269–292; Hirschl, Tomas A., Joyce Altobelli, and Mark R. Rank. 2003. "Does Marriage Increase the Odds of Affluence? Exploring the Life Course Probabilities." *Journal of Marriage and Family* 65:927–938; Schmidt, Lucie, and Purvi Sevak. 2006. "Gender, Marriage, and Asset Accumulation in the United States." *Feminist Economics* 12:139–166; Waite, Linda J., and Maggie Gallagher. 2000. *The Case for Marriage: Why Married People Are Happier, Healthier, and Better Off Financially*. NY: Broadway Books; Wilmoth, Janet, and Gregor Koso. 2002. "Does Marital History Matter? Marital Status and Wealth Outcomes Among Preretirement Adults." *Journal of Marriage and Family* 64:254–268.

6. The bottom quintile (quintile 1) consists of the 20% of the population with the least wealth, and the top quintile (quintile 5) consists of the 20% of the population with the most wealth. Quintiles are defined for households under age 65. For married or cohabitating households, the age of the older spouse or partner is used. Because slightly more than 20% of households under age 65 have zero or negative wealth, quintile 1 consists of the bottom 20.2% of the wealth distribution and quintile 2 consists of the next 19.8% of the distribution. The substantive conclusions using households under age 65 are similar to those when there is no age restriction (women are more likely to be in the bottom quintile and less likely to be in the top quintile than men).

7. The "divorced" category also includes people who are legally separated and reported assets that were owned (solely or primarily) by them in the survey.

8. Surviving spouses do not always inherit all household assets, but in most cases they do inherit the majority of household assets.

9. Goldin, Claudia. 1990. *Understanding the Gender Gap: An Economic History of American Women*. NY: Oxford University Press.

10. www.bls.gov/cps/wlf-table1–2005.pdf

11. Horn, Laura. 2006. *Placing College Graduation Rates in Context: How 4-Year College Graduation Rates Vary with Selectivity and the Size of Low-Income Enrollment*. NCES 2007–161. U.S. Department of Education. Washington, D.C.: National Center for Educational Statistics. www.nces.ed.gov/pubs2007/2007161.pdf (accessed January 26, 2008).

12. These statistics refer to the median annual earnings ratio of full-time, year-round workers. Institute for Women's Policy Research. 2009. "Fact Sheet: The Gender Wage Gap 2008." IWPR No. C350. April. www.iwpr.org/pdf/C350.pdf (accessed June 15, 2009).

13. Income refers to their reported income from 2003 or their normal income if they reported that their 2003 income was unusually high or unusually low. To determine their typical monthly income, I divided their annual income by 12. Total amount of savings is their financial assets that can be easily liquidated (savings accounts, checking accounts, money market accounts, call accounts).

14. The average number of months of income available in savings for married couples (excluding cohabitating couples) is 2.5 months.

15. Married households are likely to have higher expenses associated with raising children and are also more likely to be homeowners, both of which may reduce their cash savings.

16. Conley, Dalton. 1999. *Being Black, Living in the Red: Race, Wealth, and Social Policy in America*. CA: University of California Press; Gordon Nembhard, Jessica, and Ngina Chiteji (eds.). 2006. *Wealth Accumulation and Communities of Color in the United States*. MI: The University of Michigan Press; Kijakazi, Kilolo. 2003. "Impact of Unreported Social Security Earnings on Women and People of Color." Chapter 11 in Kathleen Buto, Martha Priddy Patterson, William E. Spriggs, and Maya Rockeymoore (eds.). *Strengthening Community: Social Insurance in a Diverse America*. National Academy of Social Insurance; Lui, Meizhu. 2009.

"Laying the Foundation for National Prosperity: The Imperative of Closing the Racial Wealth Gap." Insight Center for Community Economic Development. March; Lui, Meizhu, Barbara Robles, Betsy Leondar-Wright, Rose Brewer, and Rebecca Adamson, with United for a Fair Economy. 2006. *The Color of Wealth: The Story Behind the U.S. Racial Wealth Divide.* NY: The New Press; Oliver, Melvin L., and Thomas M. Shapiro. 2006. *Black Wealth/White Wealth: A New Perspective on Racial Inequality* (10th anniversary ed.). NY: Routledge; Shapiro, Thomas M. 2004. *The Hidden Cost of Being African American: How Wealth Perpetuates Inequality.* NY: Oxford University Press.

17. Asian, American Indian/Alaska Native, Native Hawaiian/Pacific Islander, and Other are combined into a single category in the Survey of Consumer Finances data, and therefore I am unable to provide information for these groups individually.

18. Asian-Americans of Chinese, Japanese, and Indian ancestry may have particularly high levels of wealth in part because they have lived in the United States longer and in part because they are more likely to have come to the United States with EB-5 visas, which stipulate that they must bring at least $500,000 with them to invest in a business. In contrast, other Asian groups, such as the Vietnamese and Hmong, are more likely to have come to the United States as refugees with very little wealth (Leigh 2006). However, using data from the Survey of Income and Program Participation (SIPP), Ong and Patraporn (2006) find that white households have greater wealth than Asian households. The different position of Asians vis-à-vis whites may be a result of the different data sets. The proportion of Asians among the wealthiest 1% doubled between 1983 and 1995 (Wolff 1998), and the Survey of Consumer Finances oversamples wealthy households, which are less likely to show up in other surveys such as the SIPP.

19. Cobb-Clark, Deborah A., and Vincent A. Hildebrand. 2006. "The Portfolio Choices of Hispanic Couples." *Social Science Quarterly* 87:1344–1363; Cobb-Clark, Deborah A., and Vincent A. Hildebrand. 2006. "The Wealth of Mexican Americans." *The Journal of Human Resources* 41:841–868; Kochhar, Rakesh. 2004. "The Wealth of Hispanic Households: 1996 to 2002." Washington, D.C.: Pew Hispanic Center Report.

20. Elmelech, Yuval. 2008. *Transmitting Inequality: Wealth and the American Family.* Maryland: Rowman Littlefield; Hao, Lingxin. 2007. *Color Lines, Country Lines: Race, Immigration, and Wealth Stratification in America.* NY: Russell Sage Foundation; Krivo, Lauren J. 1995. "Immigrant Characteristics and Hispanic-Anglo Housing Inequality." *Demography* 32:599–615; Robles, Barbara J. 2006. "Wealth Creation in Latino Communities." Chapter 10 in Gordon Nembhard, Jessica, and Chiteji (eds.). *Wealth Accumulation and Communities of Color in the United States: Current Issues.* MI: University of Michigan Press.

21. Horn, Laura. 2006. *Placing College Graduation Rates in Context: How 4-Year College Graduation Rates Vary with Selectivity and the Size of Low-Income Enrollment.* NCES 2007–161. U.S. Department of Education. Washington, D.C.: National Center for Educational Statistics. www.nces.ed.gov/pubs2007/2007161.pdf (accessed January 26, 2008).

22. Jackson, Robert Max. 1998. *Destined for Equality: The Inevitable Rise of Women's Status*. MA: Harvard University Press, p. 242.

23. Institute for Women's Policy Research. 2009. "Fact Sheet: The Gender Wage Gap 2008." IWPR No. C350. April. www.iwpr.org/pdf/C350.pdf (accessed June 15, 2009).

24. The Survey of Consumer Finances is not used here for years prior to 1989 because the sample and weighting procedures for these prior years are not consistent with those for the surveys from 1989 onward. Following a major redesign, the Federal Reserve Board has made great efforts to assure the over-time comparability of the surveys beginning in 1989. For further information, see Kennickell, Arthur B. 2006. "A Rolling Tide: Changes in the Distribution of Wealth in the US, 1989–2001." Chapter 2 in Edward N. Wolff (ed.). *International Perspectives on Household Wealth*. MA: Edward Elgar; Kennickell, Arthur B., and R. Louise Woodburn. 1999. "Consistent Weight Design for the 1989, 1992, and 1995 SCFs, and the Distribution of Wealth." *Review of Income and Wealth* 45:193–214.

25. As new Survey of Consumer Finances data are released, this figure will be updated at the following Web site: www.mariko-chang.com/shortchanged.

26. In contrast to the wealth gap, which increased, the gender wage ratio for full-time year-round workers improved from 73.2 in 1998 to 76.6 in 2004. Institute for Women's Policy Research. 2009. "Fact Sheet: The Gender Wage Gap 2008." IWPR No. C350. April. www.iwpr.org/pdf/C350.pdf (accessed June 15, 2009).

27. Increasing levels of wealth inequality are mirrored in other groups as well. For example, wealth inequality between college graduates and high school graduates narrowed between 1989 and 1995 and then increased until 2001 (Yamashita 2009), which is attributed primarily to differences in portfolio composition (the stock market and housing booms increased the values of assets that are more likely to be owned by college graduates than by high school graduates). The racial wealth gap was stable during most of the 1990s, but grew between 1998 and 2001, which has been attributed to lower stock ownership of nonwhite households (Wolff 2006).

28. The economic expansion that characterized much of the 1990s began losing momentum with the stock market decline in the second half of 2000. Because differences in stock holdings and home ownership have been cited as affecting inter-group wealth inequality during this time period (see note 27), I examined trends in stock and home ownership between single men and women between 1998 and 2004, but found that ownership rates remained remarkably stable during this time period. In contrast, gender differences in characteristics of debt changed dramatically between 1998 and 2004. I also examined whether key demographic characteristics of single male and single female households changed during the 1998–2004 time period, but found no major changes.

29. Data on debt from 1998 to 2004 are from Weller, Christian. 2006. "Drowning in Debt: America's Middle Class Falls Deeper in Debt as Income Growth Slows and Costs Climb." Center for American Progress. www.americanprogress.org/issues/2006/05/b1655517.html (accessed May 6, 2009).

30. Rising indebtedness was not limited to single women. Wolff (2007) documents that indebtedness declined during the late 1990s but then "skyrocketed in the early 2000s. Among the middle class, the debt-to-income ratio reached its highest level in 20 years" (p. 1).

31. Hartmann, Heidi. 2000. "Closing the Gap: Women's Economic Progress and Future Prospects." Chapter 9 in Ray F. Marshall (ed.). *Back to Shared Prosperity: The Growing Inequality of Wealth and Income in America*. NY: M.E. Sharpe; U.S. Bureau of Labor Statistics. 2005. "Highlights of Women's Earnings in 2004." Report 987. Washington, D.C. www.bls.gov/cps/cpswom2004.pdf

32. These calculations do not adjust for inflation.

Chapter 3

1. Edin, Kathryn, and Laura Lein. 1997. *Making Ends Meet: How Single Mothers Survive Welfare and Low-Wage Work*. NY: Russell Sage Foundation; Ehrenreich, Barbara. 2001. *Nickel and Dimed: On (Not) Getting By in America*. NY: Metropolitan Books; Newman, Katherine S., and Victor Tan Chen. 2007. *The Missing Class: Portraits of the Near Poor in America*. MA: Beacon Press.

2. I conducted two analyses that predict the log of wealth: ordinary least squares (OLS) regression and quantile regression. OLS regression examines the effects of the variables in the model on the conditional mean of the dependent variable, and quantile regression examines the effects of the variables on the median of the dependent variable. In cases such as that of wealth, in which the dependent variable is highly skewed and there are many households at zero net worth, some have argued that quantile regression is a more appropriate choice. Results of both analyses are presented in the appendix, table A2.

3. Rubenstein, Carin. 1981. "Money and Self Esteem, Relationships, Secrecy, Envy, and Satisfaction." *Psychology Today* (May):29–44.

4. O'Rand, Angela M. 1986. "The Hidden Payroll: Employee Benefits and the Structure of Workplace Inequality." *Sociological Forum* 1:657–683, p. 659.

5. U.S. Department of Labor. 2009. "Employer Costs for Employee Compensation— March 2009." www.bls.gov/news.release/pdf/ecec.pdf (accessed June 10, 2009).

6. Weller, Christian, and Edward N. Wolff. 2005. *Retirement Income: The Crucial Role of Social Security*. Washington, D.C.: Economic Policy Institute.

7. For an overview of pension types, see Gordon, Michael S., Olivia S. Mitchell, and Marc M. Twinney. 1997. *Positioning Pensions for the Twenty-First Century*. PA: University of Pennsylvania Press; Harrington Meyer, Madonna, and Pamela Herd. 2007. *Market Friendly or Family Friendly? The State and Gender Inequality in Old Age*. NY: Russell Sage Foundation.

8. Even, William E., and David A. Macpherson. 1994. "Gender Differences in Pensions." *Journal of Human Resources* 29:555–587; He, Wan, Manisha Sengupta, Victoria A. Velkoff, and Kimberly A. DeBarros. 2005. *65+ in the United States: 2005*. Current Population Report P23–209. Washington, D.C.: U.S. Census Bureau; Knoke, David. 1994. "Cui Bono? Employee Benefit Packages." *American Behavioral Scientist* 37:963–978; Mitchell, Olivia S.,

Phillip B. Levine, and John W. Phillips. 1999. "The Impact of Pay Inequality, Occupational Segregation, and Lifetime Work Experience on the Retirement Income of Women and Minorities." Washington, D.C.: AARP Public Policy Institute; O'Rand, Angela M., and Kim M. Shuey. 2007. "Gender and the Devolution of Pension Risks in the US." *Current Sociology* 55:287–304; Quadagno, Jill. 1988. "Women's Access to Pensions and the Structure of Eligibility Rules: Systems of Production and Reproduction." *The Sociological Quarterly* 29:541–558; Seccombe, Karen. 1993. "Employer Sponsored Medical Benefits: The Influence of Occupational Characteristics and Gender." *The Sociological Quarterly* 34:557–580; Shuey, Kim M., and Angela M. O'Rand. 2004. "New Risks for Workers: Pensions, Labor Markets, and Gender." *Annual Review of Sociology* 30:453–477.

9. Mitchell, Olivia S., Phillip B. Levine, and John W. Phillips. 1999. "The Impact of Pay Inequality, Occupational Segregation, and Lifetime Work Experience on the Retirement Income of Women and Minorities." Washington, D.C.: AARP Public Policy Institute; Purcell, Patrick J. 2003. "Pension Issues: Lump Sum Distributions and Income Security." Washington, D.C.: Congressional Research Service, The Library of Congress; Shaw, Lois, and Catherine Hill. 2001. "The Gender Gap in Pension Coverage: What Does the Future Hold?" Institute for Women's Policy Research Publication E507. www.iwpr.org/pdf/e507.pdf (accessed September 18, 2008).

10. Shaw, Lois, and Catherine Hill. 2001. "The Gender Gap in Pension Coverage: What Does the Future Hold?" Institute for Women's Policy Research Publication E507. www.iwpr.org/pdf/e507.pdf (accessed September 18, 2008). On average, women are lower earners and have less money accumulated in their retirement accounts, both of which decrease the likelihood that lump sum payments will be rolled over into another retirement account.

11. Harrington Meyer, Madonna, and Pamela Herd. 2007. *Market Friendly or Family Friendly? The State and Gender Inequality in Old Age.* NY: Russell Sage Foundation.

12. Purcell (2003) found that the strongest predictor of whether a lump sum was rolled over was the size of the distribution (with rollover more likely the larger the amount in the retirement plan). When controlling for other factors that affect distribution decisions (income, age, education, marital status, children in the family, etc.), women were less likely than men to cash out. Purcell, Patrick J. 2003. "Pension Issues: Lump Sum Distributions and Income Security." Washington, D.C.: Congressional Research Service, The Library of Congress.

13. The Economic Growth and Tax Relief Reconciliation Act of 2001 reduced the vested amount that could be involuntarily cashed out from $5,000 to $1,000 (this change became effective in 2005). www.investopedia.com/articles/retirement/05/042505.asp (accessed June 8, 2009).

14. Iqbal, Zahid, O. Sewon, and H. Young Baek. 2006. "Are Female Executives More Risk-Averse than Male Executives?" *Atlantic Economic Journal.* http://goliath.ecnext.com/coms2/summary_0199-689286_ITM

15. Seccombe, Karen. 1993. "Employer Sponsored Medical Benefits: The Influence of Occupational Characteristics and Gender." *The Sociological Quarterly* 34:557–580.

16. Data from the Bureau of Labor Statistics Current Population Survey for the year 2008. www.bls.gov/cps/tables.htm#annual

17. www.paidsickdays.nationalpartnership.org/site/PageServer?pagename=psd_index. The Healthy Families Act, currently before Congress, would provide employees working at firms with 15 or more employees with seven paid sick days per year to recover from their own illness or to care for a sick family member.

18. McCaffery, Edward J. 1997. *Taxing Women*. IL: University of Chicago Press, pp. 126–127.

19. www.smartmoney.com/Spending/Deals/The-Best-Way-to-Save-on-Health-Care-Costs-13065/ (accessed June 9, 2009).

20. McCaffery, Edward J. 1997. *Taxing Women*. IL: University of Chicago Press.

21. The Small Business Job Protection Act of 1996, effective starting 1997, allowed nonworking spouses to contribute the same amount (at that time, $2,000) as their working spouses to a tax-deductible IRA.

22. On top of the maximum contributions, as of 2008 the IRS allowed people age 50 and over to make "catch up" contributions of an additional $1,000 for IRAs and an additional $5,000 for 401(k) and 403(b) plans.

23. Long-term capital gains refer to those gains (or losses) on capital held more than one year.

24. Abramovitz, Mimi, and Sandra Morgen. 2006. *Taxes Are a Woman's Issue*. NY: Feminist Press at the City University of New York.

25. www.bankrate.com/brm/itax/news/taxguide/review-rates1.asp?caret=7a (accessed June 9, 2009).

26. In 2011, the long-term capital gains tax rates will increase to 10% for those in the 10%–15% tax bracket and to 20% for those in the 25%–35% tax bracket (reverting to their pre-2003 levels) unless the lower rates are extended by Congress. www.usatoday.com/money/perfi/taxes/2007–06–15-mym-capital-gains_N.htm (accessed June 9, 2009).

27. Some might argue that those in higher tax brackets (35%) are paying much higher taxes and therefore should have higher deductions. The IRS reported that after deductions and other adjustments, the average tax rate for the 400 individuals with the highest adjusted gross incomes in 2006 was 17%. www.irs.gov/pub/irs-soi/06intop400.pdf (accessed May 11, 2009).

28. Citizens for Tax Justice. 1996. "The Hidden Entitlements." www.ctj.org/pdf/hident.pdf (accessed May 11, 2009).

29. Insight Center for Community Economic Development. 2009. "Fact Sheet: Social Insurance and Communities of Color." Spring: Simms, Margaret C. 2008. "Weathering Job Loss: Unemployment Insurance." New Safety Net Paper 6. The Urban Institute. July.

30. Institute for Women's Policy Research. 2008. "Fact Sheet: Women and Unemployment Insurance: Outdated Rules Deny Benefits That Workers Need and Have Earned." Washington, D.C.: Institute for Women's Policy Research, January.

31. Nam, Yunju. 2008. "Welfare Reform and Asset Accumulation: Asset Limit Changes, Financial Assets, and Vehicle Ownership." *Social Science Quarterly* 89:133–154; Sherraden, Michael. 1991. *Assets and the Poor: A New American Welfare Policy*. NY: Sharpe.

32. Before the Family Support Act of 1988 was enacted, the vehicle asset limit was $1,500 in all states. Vehicle limits vary by state, and about half of states currently have no asset limit on the value of vehicles. Nam, Yunju. 2008. "Welfare Reform and Asset Accumulation: Asset Limit Changes, Financial Assets, and Vehicle Ownership." *Social Science Quarterly* 89:133–154.

33. Ong, Paul. 2002. "Car Ownership and Welfare-to-Work." *Journal of Policy Analysis and Management* 21:239–252; Raphael, Steven, and Lorien Rice. 2002. "Car Ownership, Employment, and Earnings," *Journal of Urban Economics* 52:109–130.

34. Nam, Yunju. 2008. "Welfare Reform and Asset Accumulation: Asset Limit Changes, Financial Assets, and Vehicle Ownership." *Social Science Quarterly* 89:133–154.

35. Unlike other retirement wealth, Social Security (and some pension wealth) cannot be transferred across generations. However, Social Security and pension wealth are often treated as a form of "augmented wealth" because they can affect, or even offset, the need to save for retirement in other ways and because they contribute to economic well-being. See Weller, Christian, and Edward N. Wolff. 2005. *Retirement Income: The Crucial Role of Social Security*. Washington, D.C.: Economic Policy Institute.

36. Government Accounting Office. 1997. "Social Security Reform: Implications for Women's Retirement Income." December.

37. Weller, Christian, and Edward N. Wolff. 2005. *Retirement Income: The Crucial Role of Social Security*. Washington, D.C.: Economic Policy Institute.

38. Weller (2006) reports that the tremendous increase in indebtedness is primarily a result of increased housing and educational debt. Weller, Christian. 2006. "Drowning in Debt: America's Middle Class Falls Deeper in Debt as Income Growth Slows and Costs Climb." Center for American Progress. www.americanprogress.org/issues/2006/05/b1655517.html (accessed May 6, 2009).

39. The Survey of Consumer Finances includes education loans in this category, but I have separated them into their own category.

40. Fishbein, Allen J., and Patrick Woodall. 2006. "Women Are Prime Targets for Subprime Lending: Women Are Disproportionately Represented in High-Cost Mortgage Market." Washington, D.C.: Consumer Federation of America, December. www.consumerfed.org/pdfs/womenprimetargetsstudy120606.pdf (accessed September 11, 2008).

41. Women are more likely to receive subprime loans across mortgage product lines (loans for purchase, home improvement loans, and refinances), but the problem is particularly salient for home improvement loans and refinances, which are more likely to be subprime overall.

42. These statistics refer to purchase mortgages.

43. Draut, Tamara. 2007. *Strapped: Why America's 20- and 30-Somethings Can't Get Ahead*. NY: Anchor Books; Kamenetz, Anya. 2006. *Generation Debt: Why Now Is a Terrible Time to Be Young*. NY: Riverhead Books.

44. U.S. Department of Education, National Center for Educational Statistics. 2004. "The Condition of Education 2004." NCES 2004–077. Washington, D.C.: U.S. Government Printing Office. www.nces.ed.gov/pubs2004/2004077.pdf (accessed July 24, 2008).

45. Among 1999–2000 bachelor's degree recipients, 65.9% of women and 64.7% of men borrowed for their undergraduate education. Among those who borrowed, women borrowed an average of $19,500 and men an average of $19,100. A year after graduation, men's average monthly salary was $3,100 and women's average monthly salary was $2,600. The median debt burden (defined as the monthly loan payment as a percentage of monthly income) was 6.4% for men and 7.3% for women. See U.S. Department of Education, National Center for Educational Statistics. 2004. "The Condition of Education 2004." NCES 2004–077. Washington, D.C.: U.S. Government Printing Office. www.nces.ed.gov/pubs2004/2004077.pdf (accessed July 24, 2008).

46. Horn, Laura. 2006. *Placing College Graduation Rates in Context: How 4-Year College Graduation Rates Vary with Selectivity and the Size of Low-Income Enrollment*. NCES 2007–161. U.S. Department of Education. Washington, D.C.: National Center for Educational Statistics. www.nces.ed.gov/pubs2007/2007161.pdf (accessed January 26, 2008).

47. Garcia, Jose, James Lardner, and Cindy Zeldin. 2008. *Up To Our Eyeballs: How Shady Lenders and Failed Economic Policies Are Drowning Americans in Debt*. NY: The New Press, p. 16.

48. Brown, Ralph J. 1998. "Saving Rate Estimates for Single Persons by Income, Age, and Gender." *Journal of Legal Economics* 8:49–62; Paulin, Geoffrey D., and Yoon G. Lee. 2002. "Expenditures of Single Parents: How Does Gender Figure In?" *Monthly Labor Review* 125:16–37.

49. Draut, Tamara, and Javier Silva. 2003. *Borrowing to Make Ends Meet: The Growth of Credit Card Debt in the 90s*. NY: Demos. http://www.demos-usa.org/pubs/borrowing_to_make_ends_meet.pdf#search='Borrowing%20to%20Make%20Ends%20Meet'; McGhee, Heather, and Tamara Draut. 2004. *Retiring in the Red: The Growth of Debt Among Older Americans*. NY: Demos. http://www.demos-usa.org/pubs/Retiring_2ed.pdf#search='do%20women%20have%20higher%20credit%20card%20debt%20than%20men%3F'

50. Sullivan, Teresa A., Elizabeth Warren, and Jay Lawrence Westbrook. 2002. *The Fragile Middle Class: Americans in Debt*. CT: Yale University Press.

51. Wheary, Jennifer, and Tamara Draut. 2007. "Who Pays? The Winners and Losers of Credit Card Deregulation." Washington, D.C.: Demos, August 1. www.demos.org/pub1463.cfm (accessed July 22, 2008).

52. Author's calculations from the Survey of Consumer Finances, 2004, for single (nonmarried and noncohabitating) women and men under age 65. Gender differences are statistically significant (p < .001).

Chapter 4

1. Refers to a child born in 2004. See the USDA's "Expenditures on Children by Families, 2004." www.usda.gov/cnpp/Crc/crc2004.pdf

2. For further information on the cost of children, see Folbre, Nancy. 2008. *Valuing Children: Rethinking the Economics of the Family*. MA: Harvard University Press.

3. The terms *custodial parent* and *single parent* will be used interchangeably to refer to the unmarried parent who has custody of his or her child(ren).

4. Grall, Timothy S. 2006. "Custodial Mothers and Fathers and Their Child Support: 2003." Current Population Report P60–230. Washington, D.C.: U.S. Census Bureau. http://www.census.gov/prod/2006pubs/p60–230.pdf (accessed September 10, 2008).

5. In addition to the expenses associated with raising children, Folbre (2008) has estimated the replacement cost of parental time spent on children to underscore the economic effects of having children. See Folbre, Nancy. 2008. *Valuing Children: Rethinking the Economics of the Family*. MA: Harvard University Press.

6. U.S. Census Bureau. 2004. http://pubdb3.census.gov/macro/032004/pov/new31_100_005_01.htm and…new31_100_006_01.htm

7. Grall, Timothy S. 2006. "Custodial Mothers and Fathers and Their Child Support: 2003." Current Population Report P60–230. Washington, D.C.: U.S. Census Bureau. http://www.census.gov/prod/2006pubs/p60–230.pdf (accessed September 10, 2008).

8. Matthews, Linda. 1995. "Divorced Father's Case Raises Difficult Issues of Who Pays Tuition." *New York Times*, November 15.

9. Beller, Andrea H., and John W. Graham. 1993. *Small Change: The Economics of Child Support*. CT: Yale University Press.

10. Data for the "Asian and other" category are not provided because the nonweighted sample sizes for some of the parental status categories when broken down by gender contain fewer than 10 households.

11. Elmelech, Yuval. 2006. "Determinants of Intragroup Wealth Inequality Among Whites, Blacks, and Latinos." Chapter 3 in Gordon Nembhard, Jessica and Ngina Chiteji (eds.). *Wealth Accumulation and Communities of Color in the United States: Current Issues*. MI: University of Michigan Press; Hao, Lingxin. 2007. *Color Lines, Country Lines: Race, Immigration, and Wealth Stratification in America*. NY: Russell Sage Foundation; Robles, Barbara J. 2006. "Wealth Creation in Latino Communities." Chapter 10 in Gordon Nembhard, Jessica and Ngina Chiteji (eds.). *Wealth Accumulation and Communities of Color in the United States: Current Issues*. MI: University of Michigan Press.

12. Martin, Joyce A., Brady E. Hamilton, Paul D. Sutton, Stephanie J. Ventura, Fay Menacker, and Martha L. Munson. 2003. "Births: Final Data for 2002." National Vital Statistics Reports, Vol. 52, No. 10. U.S. Department of Health and Human Services, tables 14 and 17.

13. Matthews, T. J., and Brady E. Hamilton. 2002. "Mean Age of Mother, 1970–2000." National Vital Statistics Reports, Vol. 51, No. 1. U.S. Department of

Health and Human Services. In addition, birth rates are higher for Hispanic teenagers than for blacks, whites, or other minority groups. In 2002, the birth rate for unmarried teenagers (rate per 1,000 unmarried women ages 15–19) was 66.1 for Hispanics, 64.8 for non-Hispanic blacks, 22.1 for non-Hispanic whites, and 13.4 for Asian or Pacific Islanders. (See Martin, Joyce A., Brady E. Hamilton, Paul D. Sutton, Stephanie J. Ventura, Fay Menacker, and Martha L. Munson. 2003. "Births: Final Data for 2002." National Vital Statistics Reports, Vol. 52, No. 10. U.S. Department of Health and Human Services.) Delaying first birth by even a year results in higher wages for women, even those earning low wages. (See Buckles, Kasey. 2008. "Women, Finances, and Children: Understanding the Returns to Delayed Childbearing for Working Women." *American Economic Review: Papers and Proceedings* 98:403–407.)

14. Ventura, Stephanie J., and Christine A. Bachrach. 2000. "Nonmarital Childbearing in the United States, 1940–1999." National Vital Statistics Reports, Vol. 48, No. 16. National Center for Health Statistics.

15. Stone, Pamela. 2007. *Opting Out? Why Women Really Quit Careers and Head Home.* CA: University of California Press.

16. Rose, Stephen J., and Heidi I. Hartmann. 2004. "Still a Man's Labor Market: The Long-Term Earnings Gap." Washington, D.C.: Institute for Women's Policy Research.

17. Anderson, Deborah, Melissa Binder, and Kate Krause. 2003. "The Motherhood Wage Penalty Revisited: Experience, Heterogeneity, Work Effort, and Work-Schedule Flexibility." *Industrial and Labor Relations Review* 56:10–31; Budig, Michelle J., and Paula England. 2001. "The Wage Penalty for Motherhood." *American Sociological Review* 66:204–225; Waldfogel, Jane. 1997. "The Effects of Children on Women's Wages." *American Sociological Review* 62:209–217.

18. Waldfogel, Jane. 1997. "The Effects of Children on Women's Wages." *American Sociological Review* 62:209–217.

19. Correll, Shelley J., Stephen Benard, and Im Paik. 2007. "Getting a Job: Is There a Motherhood Penalty?" *American Journal of Sociology* 112:1297–1338; Cuddy, Amy J. C., Susan T. Fiske, and Peter Glick. 2004. "When Professionals Become Mothers, Warmth Doesn't Cut the Ice." *Journal of Social Issues* 60:701–718; Fuegen, Kathleen, Monica Biernat, Elizabeth Haines, and Kay Deaux. 2004. "Mothers and Fathers in the Workplace: How Gender and Parental Status Influence Judgments of Job-Related Competence." *Journal of Social Issues* 60:737–754; Ridgeway, Cecilia L., and Shelley J. Correll. 2004. "Motherhood as a Status Characteristic." *Journal of Social Issues* 60:683–700.

20. Bielby Denise, and William T. Bielby. 1984. "Work Commitment, Sex-Role Attitudes, and Women's Employment." *American Sociological Review* 49:234–247; Marsden, Peter V., Arne L. Kalleberg, and Cynthia R. Cook. 1993. "Gender Differences in Organization Commitment." *Work and Occupations* 20:368–390.

21. Stone, Pamela. 2007. *Opting Out? Why Women Really Quit Careers and Head Home.* CA: University of California Press.

22. Fuegen, Kathleen, Monica Biernat, Elizabeth Haines, and Kay Deaux. 2004. "Mothers and Fathers in the Workplace: How Gender and Parental Status Influence Judgments of Job-Related Competence." *Journal of Social Issues* 60:737–754; Townsend, Nicholas W. 2002. *The Package Deal: Marriage, Work, and Fatherhood in Men's Lives*. PA: Temple University Press.

23. Lundberg, Shelly, and Elaina Rose. 2000. "Parenthood and the Earnings of Married Men and Women." *Labour Economics* 7:689–710.

24. Correll, Shelley J., Stephen Benard, and Im Paik. 2007. "Getting a Job: Is There a Motherhood Penalty?" *American Journal of Sociology* 112:1297–1338.

25. Shuey, Kim M., and Angela M. O'Rand. 2004. "New Risks for Workers: Pensions, Labor Markets, and Gender." *Annual Review of Sociology* 30:453–477.

26. Farkas, Janice I., and Angela M. O'Rand. 1998. "The Pension Mix for Women in Middle and Late Life: The Changing Employment Relationship." *Social Forces* 76:1007–1032.

27. U.S. General Accounting Office. 2000. "Contingent Workers: Incomes and Benefits Lag Behind Those of the Rest of the Workforce." www.gao.gov/archive/2000/he00076.pdf (accessed March 14, 2008).

28. Williams, Joan C., and Holly Cohen Cooper. 2004. "The Public Policy of Motherhood." *Journal of Social Issues* 60:849–865.

29. Fernandez, Raquel, and Richard Rogerson. 2001. "Sorting and Long-Run Inequality." *Quarterly Journal of Economics* 116:1305–1341; Mare, Robert D. 1991. "Five Decades of Educational Assortative Mating." *American Sociological Review* 56:15–32.

30. For an economic interpretation of this pattern (compensating differentials in marriage), see Grossbard-Shechtman, Shoshana. 1993. *On the Economics of Marriage: A Theory of Marriage, Labor, and Divorce*. CO: Westview Press.

31. Glass, Jennifer. 2000. "Envisioning the Integration of Family and Work: Toward a Kinder, Gentler Workplace." *Contemporary Sociology* 29:129–143.

32. The ideal worker norm derived from traditional gender roles in which male workers were perceived as being unencumbered by family responsibilities because they had wives who not only took care of family matters but also managed all other aspects of their lives to ensure they had adequate time and energy to devote to work. However, as women have continued to move into the labor force full-time, they are also expected to adhere to the ideal worker norm if they are to succeed and climb the corporate ladder.

33. Chun, Hyuanbae, and Injae Lee. 2001. "Why Do Married Men Earn More: Productivity or Marriage Selection?" *Economic Inquiry* 39:307–319; Lewin, Tamar. 1994. "Men Whose Wives Work Earn Less, Studies Show." *New York Times* October 12; Thomas, Adam, and Isabel Sawhill. 2005. "For Love and Money? The Impact of Family Structure on Family Income." *The Future of Children* 15:57–74. But see Jacobsen, Joyce P., and Rayack, Wendy L. 1996. "Do Men Whose Wives Work Really Earn Less?" *The American Economic Review* 86:268–273.

34. Becker, Gary. 1991. *A Treatise on the Family*. MA: Harvard University Press; Waite, Linda J., and Maggie Gallagher. 2000. *The Case for Marriage: Why Married People Are Happier, Healthier, and Better Off Financially*. NY: Broadway Books.

35. Williams, Joan. 2000. *Unbending Gender: Why Family and Work Conflict and What to Do About It*. NY: Oxford University Press, p. 139.

36. Blair-Loy, Mary. 2003. *Competing Devotions: Career and Family among Women Executives*. MA: Harvard University Press, p. 18.

37. Warren, Elizabeth, and Amelia Warren Tyagi. 2003. *The Two-Income Trap: Why Middle-Class Mothers and Fathers Are Going Broke*. NY: Basic Books, p.104.

Chapter 5

1. From www.dikenh.k12.ia.us/NHSERVER/Resources/Web%20Quest/Diane/index.html

2. Brown, Ralph J. 1998. "Saving Rate Estimates for Single Persons by Income, Age, and Gender." *Journal of Legal Economics* 8:49–62; Paulin, Geoffrey D., and Yoon G. Lee. 2002. "Expenditures of Single Parents: How Does Gender Figure In?" *Monthly Labor Review* 125:16–37.

3. For this discussion, it is useful to think of U.S. households, divided according to their wealth, as on a continuum from least wealthy to most wealthy. The bottom quintile would consist of the poorest 20% of households; in contrast, the top quintile would contain the wealthiest 20% of households. The middle three quintiles, composed of households in the second, third, and fourth quintiles (the middle 60% of households), can be thought of as the middle class.

4. Keister, Lisa A. 2005. *Getting Rich: America's New Rich and How They Got That Way*. NY: Cambridge University Press; Wolff, Edward N. 2002. *Top Heavy: The Increasing Inequality of Wealth in America and What Can Be Done About It*. NY: The New Press.

5. Reuters. 2000. "Overly Cautious Savers Risk Losing a Fortune." *New York Times*. November 19.

6. Calculated at www.moneychimp.com/calculator/compound_interest_calculator.htm. Calculations assume $260 principal ($5 per week for $52 weeks), $260 annual addition, compound interested calculated annually, with 40 years to grow.

7. Caskey, John P. 1994. *Fringe Banking: Check-Cashing Outlets, Pawnshops, and the Poor*. NY: Russell Sage Foundation.

8. Cash accounts include saving accounts, checking accounts, money market accounts, and CDs.

9. Wolff, Edward N. 2001. "Recent Trends in Wealth Ownership, from 1983 to 1998." Chapter 2 in Thomas M. Shapiro and Edward N. Wolff (eds.). *Assets for the Poor: The Benefits of Spreading Asset Ownership*. NY: Russell Sage Foundation, table 2.13.

10. Fannie Mae. 1996. National Housing Survey. www.fanniemae.com/news/housingsurvey/1996_nhs.html

11. As of 2008, the first $250,000 in capital gains were not taxed for single filers and the first $500,000 in capital gains were not taxed for married couples.

12. Bucks, Brian K., Arthur B. Kennickell, and Kevin B. Moore. 2006. "Recent Changes in U.S. Family Finances: Evidence from the 2001 and 2004 Survey of Consumer Finances." *Federal Reserve Bulletin*. Vol. 92, pp. A1–A38.

13. Wolff, Edward N. 2007. "Recent Trends in Household Wealth in the United States: Rising Debt and the Middle-Class Squeeze." Levy Economics Institute Working Paper No. 502. www.levy.org/pubs/wp_502.pdf

14. Gross, Daniel. 2000. *Bull Run: Wall Street, the Democrats, and the New Politics of Personal Finance.* NY: Public Affairs (member of the Perseus Books Group).

15. Projector, Dorothy S. 1964. "Survey of Financial Characteristics of Consumers." *Federal Reserve Bulletin* 51:285–293.

16. Bucks, Brian K., Arthur B. Kennickell, and Kevin B. Moore. 2006. "Recent Changes in U.S. Family Finances: Evidence from the 2001 and 2004 Survey of Consumer Finances." *Federal Reserve Bulletin.* Vol. 92, pp. A1-A38.

17. Stock ownership is broadly defined and includes direct ownership of stocks, indirect ownership through mutual funds, and ownership within retirement funds such as IRAs and defined contribution pension plans; 401(k) and 403(b) accounts are common forms of defined contribution plans.

18. Explanations for lower stock ownership among minority groups include differences in exposure to stock investment from parents or others in one's social network. (See Brimmer, Andrew. 1988. "Income, Wealth, and Investment Behavior in the Black Community." *American Economic Review* 78:151–155; Chang, Mariko Lin. 2005. "With a Little Help from My Friends (and My Financial Planner)." *Social Forces* 83:1469–1498; Charles, Kerwin K., and Erik Hurst. 2003. "The Correlation of Wealth Across Generations." *Journal of Political Economy* 111:1155–1182; Chiteji, Ngina S., and Frank P. Stafford. 1999. "Portfolio Choices of Parents and Their Children as Young Adults: Asset Accumulation by African-American Families." *American Economic Review* 89:377–380.) They also include cultural or language barriers that limit access to or trust in financial institutions. (See Atlas, Riva D. 2001. "Why Juan Won't Save." *New York Times* June 20; Mabry, Tristan. 1999. "Black Investors Shy Away from Stocks." *Wall Street Journal* May 14; Osilli, Una Okonkwo, and Anna Paulson. 2004. "Prospects for Immigrant-Native Wealth Assimilation: Evidence from Financial Market Participation." Working Paper 04-18. Federal Reserve Bank of Chicago.)

19. Clemence, Sara. 2005. "Real Estate vs. Stocks " *Forbes.com*. www.forbes.com/lifestyle/2005/05/27/cx_sc_0527home.html?partner=sify; Cobb-Clark, Deborah A., and Vincent A. Hildebrand. 2006. "The Wealth of Mexican Americans." *The Journal of Human Resources*, 41:841–868; Updegrave, Walter. 2005. "Is Real Estate Right for Your IRA?" August 11. www.money.cnn.com/2005/08/11/pf/updegrave_0509/index.htm

20. Jackson, Jesse L., Sr., and Jesse L. Jackson, Jr. 1999. *It's About the Money!* NY: Random House.

21. Edlund, Lena, and Wojciech Kopczuk. 2009. "Women, Wealth, and Mobility." *American Economic Review* 99:146–178.

22. Conley, Dalton, and Miriam Ryvicker. 2004. "The Price of Female Hardship: Gender, Inheritance, and Wealth Accumulation in the United States." *Journal of Income Distribution* 13:41–56; Deere, Carmen Diana, and Cheryl R. Doss. 2006. "The Gender Asset Gap: What Do We Know and Why Does It Matter?" *Feminist*

Economics 12:1–50; Edlund, Lena, and Wojciech Kopczuk. 2009. "Women, Wealth, and Mobility." *American Economic Review* 99:146–178; Menchik, Paul L. 1980. "Primogeniture, Equal Sharing, and the U.S. Distribution of Wealth." *The Quarterly Journal of Economics* 94:299–316. However, there is some evidence that men (but not women) who have ever received an inheritance may be more likely to engage in self-employment (Burke, Andrew E., Felix R. FitzRoy, and Michael A. Nolan. 2008. "What Makes a Die-Hard Entrepreneur? Beyond the 'Employee or Entrepreneur' Dichotomy." *Small Business Economics* 31:93–115; Zissimopoulos, Julie M., and Lynn A. Karoly. 2003. "Transitions to Self-Employment at Older Ages: The Role of Wealth, Health, Health Insurance, and Other Factors." Rand Working Paper 135. *www.rand.org/pubs/working_papers/WR135/WR135.pdf* [accessed September 22, 2008]).

23. Keister, Lisa A. 2005. *Getting Rich: America's New Rich and How They Got That Way*. NY: Cambridge University Press.

24. Analyses of the 2004 Survey of Consumer Finances data reveal that among those under age 65, 4% of divorced women own business assets compared with 12% of divorced men. Likewise, 5% of widowed women own business assets in comparison to 17% of widowed men.

25. U.S. Census Bureau. 2006. *2002 Survey of Business Owners, Company Summary*. Washington, D.C.: U.S. Department of Commerce.

26. The service industry consists of those businesses that produce services rather than goods.

27. Center for Women's Business Research, 2006. "Women-Owned Businesses in the United States, 2006: A Fact Sheet." www.cfwbr.org/assets/344_statesoverview webcolorfac.pdf (accessed September 4, 2008).

28. Buttner, E. Holly, and Dorothy P. Moore. 1997. "Women's Organizational Exodus to Entrepreneurship: Self-Reported Motivations and Correlates with Success." *Journal of Small Business Management* 35:34–46; Cole, R. A., and J. D. Wolken. 1995. "Financial Services Used by Small Businesses: Evidence from the 1993 National Survey of Small Business Finances." *Federal Reserve Bulletin* 629–667; Coleman, Susan. 2002. "Constraints Faced by Women Small Business Owners: Evidence from the Data." *Journal of Developmental Entrepreneurship* 7:151–174; Kalleberg, Arne L., and Kevin T. Leicht. 1991. "Gender and Organizational Performance: Determinants of Small Business Survival and Success." *Academy of Management Journal* 34:136–161; Loscocco, Karyn A., Joyce Robinson, Richard H. Hall, and John K. Allen. 1991. "Gender and Small Business Success: An Inquiry into Women's Relative Disadvantage." *Social Forces* 70:65–85.

29. Thomas, Paulette. 2000. "At 'Camp,' Women Learn to Pitch Deals to Investors." *The Wall Street Journal* July 18.

30. U.S. Census Bureau. 2002. "Survey of Business Owners—Characteristics of Businesses: 2002." www.census.gov/csd/sbo/womensummaryoffindings.htm (accessed September 4, 2008).

31. Hersch, Joni. 1996. "Smoking, Seat Belts, and Other Risky Consumer Decisions: Differences by Gender and Race." *Managerial and Decision Economics* 17: 471–481.

32. Bajtelsmit, Vickie L., and Jack L. VanDerhei. 1997. "Risk Aversion and Pension Investment Choices." Chapter 4 in Michael S. Gordon, Olivia S. Mitchell, and Mac M. Twinney (eds.). *Positioning Pensions for the Twenty-First Century*. PA: Pension Research Council and the University of Pennsylvania Press; Bernasek, Alexandra, and Stephanie Shwiff. 2001. "Gender, Risk, and Retirement." *Journal of Economic Issues* 35:345–356; Hinz, Richard P., David D. McCarthy, and John A. Turner. 1997. "Are Women Conservative Investors? Gender Differences in Participant-Directed Pension Investments." Chapter 6 in Michael S. Gordon, Olivia S. Mitchell, and Mac M. Twinney (eds.). *Positioning Pensions for the Twenty-First Century*. PA: Pension Research Council and the University of Pennsylvania Press. However, see Papke, Leslie E. 1998. "How Are Participants Investing Their Accounts in Participant-Directed Individual Account Pension Plans?" *The American Economic Review* 88:212–216.

33. Apicella, Coren L., Anna Dreber, Benjamin Campbell, Peter B. Gray, Moshe Hoffman, and Anthony C. Little. 2008. "Testosterone and Financial Risk Preferences." *Evolution and Human Behavior* 29:384–390; Barber, Brad M., and Terrance Odean. 2001. "Boys Will Be Boys: Gender, Overconfidence, and Common Stock Investment." *The Quarterly Journal of Economics* 116:261–292; Estes, Ralph, and Jinoos Hosseini. 1998. "The Gender Gap on Wall Street: An Empirical Analysis of Confidence in Investment Decision Making." *The Journal of Psychology* 122:577–590; Newcomb, Michael D., and Jerome Rabow. 1999. "Gender, Socialization, and Money." *Journal of Applied Social Psychology* 29:582–869.

34. Barber, Brad M. and Terrance Odean. 2001. "Boys Will Be Boys: Gender, Overconfidence, and Common Stock Investment." *The Quarterly Journal of Economics* 116:261–292.

35. Barber, Brad M., and Terrance Odean. 2001. "Boys Will Be Boys: Gender, Overconfidence, and Common Stock Investment." *The Quarterly Journal of Economics* 116:261–292; Newcomb, Michael D., and Jerome Rabow. 1999. "Gender, Socialization, and Money." *Journal of Applied Social Psychology* 29:582–869.

36. Kaba, Amadu Jacky. 2008. "Race, Gender and Progress: Are Black American Women the New Model Minority?" *Journal of African American Studies* 12:309–335; Kaba, Amadu Jacky. 2005. "The Gradual Shift of Wealth and Power from African American Males to African American Females." *Journal of African American Studies* 9:33–44; Mincy, Ronald B. 2006. *Black Males Left Behind*. Washington, D.C.: Urban Institute Press; Wilson, William Julius. 2009. *More than Just Race: Being Black and Poor in the Inner City*. NY: W.W. Norton and Company.

37. U.S. Department of Labor. 2007. "Labor Force Characteristics by Race and Ethnicity, 2007." http://www.bls.gov/cps/cpsrace2007.pdf (accessed June 15, 2009).

Chapter 6

1. Bittman, Michael, Paula England, Liana Sayer, Nancy Folbre, and George Matheson. 2003. "When Does Gender Trump Money? Bargaining and Time in Household Work." *American Journal of Sociology* 109:186–214; Brines, Julie. 1994. "Economic Dependency, Gender, and the Division of Labor at Home." *American Journal of*

Sociology 100:652–688. The wife's income also affects household expenditures on female tasks and on child care. See Brandon, Peter D. 1999. "Income-Pooling Arrangements, Economic Constraints, and Married Mothers' Child Care Choices." *Journal of Family Issues* 20:350–370; Phipps, Shelley, and Peter Burton. 1998. "What's Mine Is Yours? The Influence of Male and Female Incomes on Patterns of Household Expenditure." *Economica* 65:599–613; Treas, Judith, and Esther De Ruuter. 2008. "Earnings and Expenditures on Household Services in Married and Cohabiting Unions." *Journal of Marriage and the Family* 70:796–805.

2. For a discussion of the application of exchange theory and game theory to marital power, see England, Paula, and Barbara Stanek Kilbourne. 1990. "Markets, Marriage and Other Mates: The Problem of Power." Chapter 6 in Roger Friedland and A. Robertson (eds.). *Beyond the Marketplace: Rethinking Economy and Society*. NY: Aldine de Gruyter.

3. Women's ability to maintain an autonomous household is cited as a key factor in understanding the status of women across countries (see Orloff, Ann Shola. 1993. "Gender and the Social Rights of Citizenship: The Comparative Analysis of Gender Relations and Welfare States." *American Sociological Review* 58:303–328).

4. Bielby, William T., and Denise D. Bielby. 1992. "I Will Follow Him: Family Ties, Gender Role Beliefs, and Reluctance to Relocate for a Better Job." *American Journal of Sociology* 97:1241–1267; Mahony, Rhona. 1995. *Kidding Ourselves: Breadwinning, Babies, and Bargaining Power*. NY: Basic Books.

5. Andreoni, James, Eleanor Brown, and Isaac Rischall. 2003. "Charitable Giving by Married Couples: Who Decides and Why Does It Matter?" *The Journal of Human Resources* 38:111–133.

6. Although not one of the nine community property states, Alaska in 1998 passed the Alaska Community Property Law, which gives couples the *option* to designate that all assets be held as community property.

7. Exceptions are complicated and do not hold if assets are "commingled."

8. Deere, Carmen Diana, and Cheryl R. Doss. 2006. "The Gender Asset Gap: What Do We Know and Why Does It Matter?" *Feminist Economics* 12:1–50.

9. American Bar Association. 1995. *ABA Guide to Wills and Estates: Everything You Need to Know About Wills, Trusts, Estates, and Taxes*. NY: Three Rivers Press.

10. American Bar Association. 1995. *ABA Guide to Wills and Estates: Everything You Need to Know About Wills, Trusts, Estates, and Taxes*. NY: Three Rivers Press, pp. 21–22.

11. When money is tight and there is barely enough of it to meet basic living expenses, *women* are more likely to have control over the stressful financial juggling act of stretching a dollar the furthest (see Rubin, Lillian B. 1992. *Worlds of Pain: Life in the Working-Class Family*. NY: Basic Books). Interestingly, when there is at least some discretionary income, men often take on the role of managing household investments, planning for retirement, or making the types of decisions that impact wealth.

12. One benefit of this approach is that it lets couples specialize in household tasks, which may contribute to greater combined efficiency overall (see Becker, Gary. 1991. *A Treatise on the Family*. MA: Harvard University Press).

13. On average, women are 2.5 years younger than their husbands. Kreider, Rose M., and Jason M. Fields. 2001. *Number, Timing, and Duration of Marriages and Divorces: Fall 1996*. Current Population Report P70–80. Washington, D.C.: U.S. Census Bureau.

14. Societal expectations about gender are so ingrained that many people who believe in equality between men and women still find themselves re-enacting patterns that reinforce stereotypical male and female tasks.

15. West, Candace, and Donald Zimmerman. 1987. "Doing Gender." *Gender and Society* 1:125–151.

16. Tichenor, Veronica Jaris. 2005. *Earning More and Getting Less: Why Successful Wives Can't Buy Equality*. NJ: Rutgers University Press.

17. Kreider, Rose M., and Jason M. Fields. 2001. *Number, Timing, and Duration of Marriages and Divorces: Fall 1996*. Current Population Report P70–80. Washington, D.C.: U.S. Census Bureau.

18. Hertz (1986) also found that couples kept separate accounts because it was more "fair" and minimized conflicts. Hertz, Rosanna. 1986. *More Equal than Others: Men and Women in Dual Career Marriages*. CA: University of California Press.

19. Tan, Amy. 1989. *The Joy Luck Club*. NY: Ivy Books, pp. 174–177.

20. Zelizer, Viviana. 1997. *The Social Meaning of Money*. NJ: Princeton University Press.

21. Sorensen, Annemette. 2003. "Economic Relations Between Women and Men: New Realities and the Re-Interpretation of Dependence." *Advances in Life Course Research* 8:281–297; Warren, Elizabeth, and Amelia Warren Tyagi. 2003. *The Two-Income Trap: Why Middle-Class Mothers and Fathers Are Going Broke*. NY: Basic Books.

22. Mahony, Rhona. 1995. *Kidding Ourselves: Breadwinning, Babies, and Bargaining Power*. NY: Basic Books, p. 44.

23. Bumpass, Larry, James Sweet, and Teresa Castro Martin. 1990. "Changing Patterns of Remarriage." *Journal of Marriage and the Family* 52:747–756; Sweeney, Megan M. 1997. "Remarriage of Women and Men After Divorce: The Role of Socioeconomic Prospects." *Journal of Family Issues* 18:479–502.

24. For detailed discussions of this issue and its roots in game theory and exchange theory, see England, Paula, and George Farkas. 1986. *Households, Employment, and Gender: A Social, Economic, and Demographic View*. NY: Aldine Publishing Company, chap. 3; England, Paula, and Barbara Stanek Kilbourne. 1990. "Markets, Marriage and Other Mates: The Problem of Power." Chapter 6 in Roger Friedland and A. Robertson (eds.). *Beyond the Marketplace: Rethinking Economy and Society*. NY: Aldine de Gruyter; Mahony, Rhona. 1995. *Kidding Ourselves: Breadwinning, Babies, and Bargaining Power*. NY: Basic Books.

25. Employing statistical models to predict marriage rates for women born between 1960 and 1964, sociologists Goldstein and Kenny (2001) found that in contrast to the case for prior generations, those with a college degree are more likely to marry (although they may do so at later ages) than those without a college degree. Goldstein, Joshua R., and Catherine T. Kenney. 2001. "Marriage Delayed or

Marriage Forgone? New Cohort Forecasts of First Marriage for U.S. Women." *American Sociological Review* 66:506–519.

26. Goldstein, Joshua R., and Catherine T. Kenney. 2001. "Marriage Delayed or Marriage Forgone? New Cohort Forecasts of First Marriage for U.S. Women." *American Sociological Review* 66:506–519.

27. The average age of widowhood is 62 for white non-Hispanic women and 54 for black and Hispanic women. These statistics refer to first marriage. U.S. Census Bureau. 2007. Detailed Tables: Number, Timing, and Duration of Marriages and Divorces 2004, Table 5. www.census.gov/population/www/socdemo/marr-div/2004detailed_tables.html.

28. Angel, Jacqueline L., Cynthia J. Buckley, Ronald J. Angel, and Maren A. Jimenez. 2003. "The Economic Consequences of Marital Disruption for Pre-Retirement Age African-American, Hispanic and Non-Hispanic White Women." Paper presented at the Population Association of America Annual Meeting in Minneapolis, Minnesota, p. 6.

29. Blacks and Hispanics have the lowest levels of wealth overall. For a discussion of causes of the poorer economic situation of minority women upon widowhood, see Angel, Jacqueline L., Maren A. Jimenez, and Ronald J. Angel. 2007. "The Economic Consequences of Widowhood for Older Minority Women." *The Gerontologist* 47:224–234.

30. Harrington Meyer, Madonna, and Pamela Herd. 2007. *Market Friendly or Family Friendly? The State and Gender Inequality in Old Age*. NY: Russell Sage Foundation.

31. For a recent review of the ways that low incomes affect marriage, see McLanahan, Sara, and Christine Percheski. 2008. "Family Structure and the Reproduction of Inequalities." *Annual Review of Sociology* 34:257–276.

32. Fernandez, Raquel, and Richard Rogerson. 2001. "Sorting and Long-Run Inequality." *Quarterly Journal of Economics* 116:1305–1341; Mare, Robert D. 1991. "Five Decades of Educational Assortative Mating." *American Sociological Review* 56:15–32.

33. DePaulo, Bella. 2006. *Singled Out: How Singles Are Stereotyped, Stigmatized, and Ignored and Still Live Happily Ever After*. NY: St. Martin's Press.

34. Carr, Deborah. 2004. "The Desire to Date and Remarry Among Older Widows and Widowers." *Journal of Marriage and Family* 66: 1051–1068; Schoen, Robert, and Robin M. Weinick. 1993. "The Slowing Metabolism of Marriage: Figures from 1988 U.S. Marital Status Life Tables." *Demography* 30:737–746.

35. U.S. Census Bureau. 2006. "Marital Status of the Population 55 Years and Over by Sex and Age: 2006." Table 2. www.census.gov/population/www/socdemo/age/age_2006.html (accessed May 27, 2009).

36. Treas, Judith. 1993. "Money in the Bank: Transaction Costs and the Economic Organization of Marriage." *American Sociological Review* 58:723–734.

37. Research on developing countries indicates that women's bargaining power within marriage increases when they have their own source of wealth. (See Brown, Philip H. 2009. "Dowry and Intrahousehold Bargaining: Evidence from

China." *Journal of Human Resources* 44:25–46; Doss, Cheryl. 2006. "The Effects of Intrahousehold Property Ownership on Expenditure Patterns in Ghana." *Journal of African Economies* 15:149–180; Quisumbing, Agnes R., and John A. Maluccio. 2003. "Resources at Marriage and Intrahousehold Allocation: Evidence from Bangladesh, Ethiopia, Indonesia, and South Africa." *Oxford Bulletin of Economics and Statistics* 65:283–327.) Yet we should not unilaterally assume that women will have equal control over wealth. As Tichenor's (2005) study of high-earning wives revealed, even women who earn more than their husbands often defer control of financial decisions to their husbands as a way of "doing gender." While it is not entirely clear that one can extrapolate directly from income to wealth, I expect that some women with more wealth than their husbands may defer control over resources, but to borrow from the title of Rosanna Hertz's (1986) book, marriages in which women have their own wealth are likely to be "More Equal than Others." And over time, as gender roles continue to evolve toward greater equality, the link between gender and control over financial resources should continue to weaken.

Chapter 7

1. The wage gap refers to the median annual earnings ratio for full-time full-year workers. Institute for Women's Policy Research. 2009. "Fact Sheet: The Gender Wage Gap 2008." IWPR No. C350 April. www.iwpr.org/pdf/C350.pdf (accessed June 15, 2009).
2. Bielby, William T., and James N. Baron. 1986. "Men and Women at Work: Sex Segregation and Statistical Discrimination." *American Journal of Sociology* 91:759–799; Bielby, William T., and James N. Baron. 1984. "A Woman's Place Is with Other Women: Sex Segregation Within Organizations." Pages 25–55 in Barbara F. Reskin (ed.). *Sex Segregation in the Workplace*. Washington, D.C.: National Academy.
3. U.S. Census Bureau. 1995. "Two Different Worlds: Men and Women from 9 to 5." Statistical Brief SB94–24, February, p. 2.
4. Blau, Francine D., and Lawrence M. Kahn. 2006. "The Gender Pay Gap: Going, Going…but Not Gone." Chapter 2 in Blau, Francine D., Mary C. Brinton, and David B. Grusky (eds.). *The Declining Significance of Gender?* NY: Russell Sage Foundation; Peterson, Trond, and Laurie A. Morgan. 1995. "Separate and Unequal. Occupation-Establishment Sex Segregation and the Gender Wage Gap." *American Journal of Sociology* 101:329–361.
5. England, Paula. 1992. *Comparable Worth: Theories and Evidence*. NY: Aldine de Gruyter.
6. www.payequityresearch.com/worth.htm (accessed Jan. 12, 2008).
7. England, Paula. 1992. *Comparable Worth: Theories and Evidence*. NY: Aldine de Gruyter; Nelson, Robert L., and William P. Bridges. 1999. *Legalizing Gender Inequality: Courts, Markets, and Unequal Pay for Women in America*. NY: Cambridge University Press.
8. Hochschild, Arlie. 1989. *The Second Shift*. NY: Avon.

9. California, New Jersey, and Washington now provide paid family leave to employees. Employees are entitled to up to 5 weeks of leave in Washington state and up to 6 weeks of leave in California and New Jersey. www.stateline.org/live/details/story?contentId=309423 (accessed May 13, 2009).

10. Wheary, Jennifer, Thomas M. Shapiro, and Tamara Draut. 2007. "By a Thread: The New Experience of America's Middle Class." Briefing Paper. Washington, D.C.: Demos.

11. Only about 60% of private-sector workers work for employers with 50 or more employees. Folbre, Nancy. 2008. *Valuing Children: Rethinking the Economics of the Family*. MA: Harvard University Press.

12. Glass, Jennifer. 2004. "Blessing or Curse: Work-Family Policies and Mother's Wage Growth over Time." *Work and Occupations* 31:367–394.

13. Nock, Steven L. 1998. *Marriage in Men's Lives*. NY: Oxford University Press.

14. Folbre, Nancy. 2001. *The Invisible Heart: Economics and Family Values*. NY: The New Press, p. 50.

15. Williams, Joan. 2000. *Unbending Gender: Why Family and Work Conflict and What to Do About It*. NY: Oxford University Press, p. 41.

16. Corporation for Enterprise Development. 2004. "Hidden in Plain Sight: A Look at the $335 Billion Federal Asset-Building Budget." Washington, D.C.: Corporation for Enterprise Development. www.cfed.org/publications/Final HIPS Version.pdf

17. For example: Lui, Meizhu. 2009. "Laying the Foundation for National Prosperity: The Imperative of Closing the Racial Wealth Gap." Insight Center for Community Economic Development. March; Lui, Meizhu, Barbara Robles, Betsy Leondar-Wright, Rose Brewer, and Rebecca Adamson, with United for a Fair Economy. 2006. *The Color of Wealth: The Story Behind the U.S. Racial Wealth Divide*. NY: The New Press; Moran, Beverly (ed.). 2008. *Race and Wealth Disparities: A Multidisciplinary Discourse*. MD: Rowman and Littlefield; Oliver, Melvin L., and Thomas M. Shapiro. 2006. *Black Wealth/White Wealth: A New Perspective on Racial Inequality* (10th anniversary ed.). NY: Routledge; Shapiro, Thomas M. 2004. *The Hidden Cost of Being African American: How Wealth Perpetuates Inequality*. NY: Oxford University Press; Shapiro, Thomas M., and Edward N. Wolff (eds.). 2001. *Assets for the Poor: The Benefits of Spreading Asset Ownership*. NY: Russell Sage Foundation; Sherraden, Michael (ed.). 2005. *Inclusion in the American Dream: Assets, Poverty, and Public Policy*. NY: Oxford University Press.

18. Heymann, Jody, Alison Earle, Stephanie Simmons, Stephanie M. Breslow, and April Kuehnhoff. N.d. "The Work, Family, and Equity Index." MA: Harvard School of Public Health, The Project on Global Working Families. www.nationalpartnership.org/site/DocServer/WFE_Index.pdf?docID=361 (accessed February 3, 2008).

19. California, New Jersey, and Washington now provide employees with paid family leave that can be used to care for a newborn. www.stateline.org/live/details/story?contentId=309423 (accessed May 13, 2009).

20. www.lisproject.org/publications/fampol/family%20leave%20policies

21. www.bls.gov/ncs/ebs/sp/ebsm0006.pdf

22. Heymann, Jody, Alison Earle, Stephanie Simmons, Stephanie M. Breslow, and April Kuehnhoff. N.d. "The Work, Family, and Equity Index." MA: Harvard School of Public Health, The Project on Global Working Families. www.nationalpartnership.org/site/DocServer/WFE_Index.pdf?docID=361 (accessed February 3, 2008).

23. Columbia University. 2002. "Mother's Day: More Than Candy and Flowers, Working Parents Need Paid Time-Off." The Clearinghouse on International Developments in Child, Youth, and Family Policies. Issue Brief, Spring.

24. A minimum period of leave should be compulsory, with the option of taking a longer leave. In their book *The War Against Parents*, Sylvia Ann Hewlett and Cornel West recommend paid, job-protected parenting leaves for 24 weeks and also recommend a paid and compulsory 10-day leave for new fathers to help eliminate the stigma of taking paternity leave and help fathers bond with their children. Hewlett, Sylvia Ann, and Cornel West. 1998. *The War Against Parents: What We Can Do for America's Beleaguered Moms and Dads*. NY: Houghton Mifflin Company.

25. Haas, Linda. 1992. *Equal Parenthood and Social Policy: A Study of Parental Leave in Sweden*. NY: SUNY Press.

26. Coltrane, Scott. 1996. *Family Man: Fatherhood, Housework, and Gender Equity*. NY: Oxford University Press; Hewlett, Sylvia Ann, and Cornel West. 1998. *The War Against Parents: What We Can Do for America's Beleaguered Moms and Dads*. NY: Houghton Mifflin Company.

27. For example: Alstott, Anne L. 2004. *No Exit: What Parents Owe Their Children and What Society Owes Parents*. NY: Oxford University Press; Hewlett, Sylvia Ann, and Cornel West. 1998. *The War Against Parents: What We Can Do for America's Beleaguered Moms and Dads*. NY: Houghton Mifflin Company.

28. Alstott, Anne L. 2004. *No Exit: What Parents Owe Their Children and What Society Owes Parents*. NY: Oxford University Press.

29. Misra, Joya, Michelle Budig, and Stephanie Moller. 2006. "Reconciliation Policies and the Effects of Motherhood on Employment, Earnings, and Poverty." Luxembourg Income Study Working Paper No. 429.

30. Hegewisch, Ariane, and Janet C. Gornick. 2008. "Statutory Routes to Workplace Flexibility in Cross-National Perspective." Washington, D.C.: Institute for Women's Policy Research. www.iwpr.org/pdf/B258workplaceflex.pdf (accessed September 22, 2008).

31. www.lisproject.org/publications/fampol/famp0103.htm (accessed December 13, 2006).

32. Burkhauser, Richard V., and Karen C. Holden. 1982. *A Challenge to Social Security: The Changing Roles of Women and Men in American Society*. NY: Academic Press.

33. Misra, Joya, Michelle Budig, and Stephanie Moller. 2006. "Reconciliation Policies and the Effects of Motherhood on Employment, Earnings, and Poverty." Luxembourg Income Study Working Paper No. 429.

34. Hegewisch, Ariane, and Janet C. Gornick. 2008. "Statutory Routes to Workplace Flexibility in Cross-National Perspective." Washington, D.C.: Institute for

Women's Policy Research. www.iwpr.org/pdf/B258workplaceflex.pdf (accessed September 22, 2008).

35. Bardasi, Elena, and Janet C. Gornick. 2008. "Working for Less? Women's Part-Time Wage Penalties Across Countries." *Feminist Economics* 14:37–72.

36. Crittenden, Ann. 2004. *If You've Raised Kids, You Can Manage Anything: Leadership Begins at Home*. NY: Penguin.

37. www.worklifepolicy.org/documents/AthenaPressRelease-April130.pdf

38. Gerson, Kathleen. 2010. *The Unfinished Revolution: How a New Generation Is Reshaping Family, Work, and Gender in America*. NY: Oxford University Press.

39. For example: Land, Michael E. (ed.). 2003. *The Role of the Father in Child Development* (4¹h ed). NY: Wiley; Meers, Sharon, and Joanna Strober. 2009. *Getting to 50/50: How Working Couples Can Have It All by Sharing All*. NY: Bantam Books; Pruett, Kyle D. 2000. *Fatherneed: Why Father Care Is as Essential as Mother Care for Your Child*. NY: Free Press.

40. Hewlett, Sylvia Ann, and Cornel West. 1998. *The War Against Parents: What We Can Do for America's Beleaguered Moms and Dads*. NY: Houghton Mifflin Company; Meers, Sharon, and Joanna Strober. 2009. *Getting to 50/50: How Working Couples Can Have it All by Sharing All*. NY: Bantam Books.

41. Christopher, Karen, Paula England, Timothy M. Smeeding, and Katherin Ross Phillips. 2002. "The Gender Gap in Poverty in Modern Nations: Single Motherhood, the Market, and the State." *Sociological Perspectives* 45:219–242; Misra, Joya, Michelle Budig, and Stephanie Moller. 2006. "Reconciliation Policies and the Effects of Motherhood on Employment, Earnings, and Poverty." Luxembourg Income Study Working Paper No. 429.

42. www.nwlc.org/pdf/AffordabilityFINAL.pdf

43. Burman, Leonard E., Elaine Maag, and Jeffrey Rohaly. 2005. "Tax Credits to Help Low-Income Families Pay for Child Care." Urban-Brookings Tax Policy Center, No. 14, July.

44. Beeferman, Larry W. 2001. "Asset Development Policy: The New Opportunity." Asset Development Institute. The Heller School for Social Policy and Management, Brandeis University. October. www./iasp.brandeis.edu/pdfs/newopportunity.pdf; Oliver, Melvin L., and Thomas M. Shapiro. 2006. *Black Wealth/White Wealth: A New Perspective on Racial Inequality* (10th anniversary ed.). NY: Routledge; Schreiner, Marik, Michael Sherraden, Margaret Clancy, Lissa Johnson, Jami Curley, Min Zhan, Sondra G. Beverly, and Michal Grinstein-Weiss. 2005. "Assets and the Poor: Evidence from Individual Development Accounts." Chapter 10 in Michael Sherraden (ed.). *Inclusion in the American Dream: Assets, Poverty, and Public Policy*. NY: Oxford University Press; Sherraden, Michael. 1991. *Assets and the Poor: A New American Welfare Policy*. NY: Sharpe.

45. Schreiner, Marik, Michael Sherraden, Margaret Clancy, Lissa Johnson, Jami Curley, Min Zhan, Sondra G. Beverly, and Michal Grinstein-Weiss. 2005. "Assets and the Poor: Evidence from Individual Development Accounts." Chapter 10 in Michael Sherraden (ed.). *Inclusion in the American Dream: Assets, Poverty, and Public Policy*. NY: Oxford University Press; Sherraden, Michael. 2001. "Asset-Building

Policy and Programs for the Poor." Chapter 9 in Thomas M. Shapiro and Edward N. Wolff (eds.). *Assets for the Poor: The Benefits of Spreading Asset Ownership*. NY: Russell Sage Foundation; Sherraden, Michael. 1991. *Assets and the Poor: A New American Welfare Policy*. NY: Sharpe.

46. Orszag, Peter, and Robert Greenstein. 2005. "Toward Progressive Pensions: A Summary of the U.S. Pension System and Proposals for Reform." Chapter 13 in Michael Sherraden (ed.). *Inclusion in the American Dream: Assets, Poverty, and Public Policy*. NY: Oxford University Press, p. 269.

47. Orszag, Peter, and Robert Greenstein. 2005. "Toward Progressive Pensions: A Summary of the U.S. Pension System and Proposals for Reform." Chapter 13 in Michael Sherraden (ed.). *Inclusion in the American Dream: Assets, Poverty, and Public Policy*. NY: Oxford University Press, p. 270.

48. Stern, Mark J. 2001. "The Un(credit)worthy Poor: Historical Perspectives on Policies to Expand Assets and Credit." Chapter 8 in Thomas M. Shapiro and Edward N. Wolff (eds.). *Assets for the Poor: The Benefits of Spreading Asset Ownership*. NY: Russell Sage Foundation.

49. Wheary, Jennifer, Thomas M. Shapiro, and Tamara Draut. 2007. *By a Thread: The New Experience of America's Middle Class*. Washington, D.C.: Demos.

50. Keister, Lisa A. 2005. *Getting Rich: America's New Rich and How They Got That Way*. NY: Cambridge University Press.

51. Brush, Candida G., Nancy M. Carter, Patricia G. Greene, Myra M. Hart, and Elizabeth Gatewood. 2002. "The Role of Social Capital and Gender in Linking Financial Suppliers and Entrepreneurial Firms: A Framework for Future Research." *Venture Capital* 4:305–323; Thomas, Paulette. 2000. "At 'Camp,' Women Learn to Pitch Deals to Investors." *The Wall Street Journal* July 18.

52. Manning, Robert D. 2000. *Credit Card Nation: The Consequences of America's Addiction to Credit*. NY: Basic Books.

53. Fairlie, Robert W., Kanika Kapur, and Susan M. Gates. 2008. "Is Employer-Based Health Insurance a Barrier to Entrepreneurship?" RAND Institute for Civil Justice Working Paper; Velamuri, Malathi R. 2008. "Taxes, Health Insurance and Women's Self-Employment." Social Science Research Network: http://ssrn.com/abstract=1141507.

54. Velamuri, Malathi R. 2008. "Taxes, Health Insurance and Women's Self-Employment." Social Science Research Network. http://ssrn.com/abstract=1141507.

55. Williams, Robert J. 2003. "Women on Corporate Boards of Directors and Their Influence on Corporate Philanthropy." *Journal of Business Ethics* 42:1–10.

56. Brush, Candida G., Nancy M. Carter, Patricia G. Greene, Myra M. Hart, and Elizabeth Gatewood. 2002. "The Role of Social Capital and Gender in Linking Financial Suppliers and Entrepreneurial Firms: A Framework for Future Research." *Venture Capital* 4:305–323.

57. Duncan, Greg J., and Saul D. Hoffman. 1985. "A Reconsideration of the Economic Consequences of Marital Dissolution." *Demography* 22:485–497; Holden, Karen C., and Pamela J. Smock. 1991. "The Economic Costs of Marital

Dissolution: Why Do Women Bear a Disproportionate Cost?" *Annual Review of Sociology* 17:51–78; Peterson, Richard R. 1996. "A Re-Evaluation of the Economic Consequences of Divorce." *American Sociological Review* 61:528–536; Weitzman, Lenore. 1996. "The Economic Consequences of Divorce Are Still Unequal: Comment on Peterson." *American Sociological Review* 61:537–538.

58. Not all men experience an improved standard of living after divorce. McManus, Patricia A., and Thomas A. DiPrete. 2001. "Losers and Winners: The Financial Consequences of Separation and Divorce for Men." *American Sociological Review* 66:246–268.

59. Shaw, Lois, and Catherine Hill. 2001. "The Gender Gap in Pension Coverage: What Does the Future Hold?" Institute for Women's Policy Research Publication E507. www.iwpr.org/pdf/e507.pdf (accessed September 18, 2008).

60. Bielby, William T., and Denise D. Bielby. 1992. "I Will Follow Him: Family Ties, Gender Role Beliefs, and Reluctance to Relocate for a Better Job." *American Journal of Sociology* 97:1241–1267; Moen, Phyllis (ed.). 2003. *It's About Time: Couples and Careers*. NY: Cornell University Press; Presser, Harriet B. 2005. *Working in a 24/7 Economy: Challenges for American Families*. NY: Russell Sage Foundation.

61. Burkhauser, Richard V., and Karen C. Holden. 1982. *A Challenge to Social Security: The Changing Roles of Women and Men in American Society*. NY: Academic Press, pp. 255–256.

62. Warren, Elizabeth, and Amelia Warren Tyagi. 2003. *The Two-Income Trap: Why Middle-Class Mothers and Fathers Are Going Broke*. NY: Basic Books.

63. Harrington Meyer, Madonna, and Eliza K. Pavalko. 1996. "Family, Work, and Access to Health Insurance Among Mature Women." *Journal of Health and Social Behavior* 37:311–325.

64. Men age 55 and over do face higher insurance premiums than women in some states, but the magnitude of the difference is much smaller. National Women's Law Center. 2008. "Nowhere to Turn: How the Individual Health Insurance Market Fails Women." Washington, D.C.: National Women's Law Center.

65. The nine states that do not prohibit insurers from denying coverage to victims of domestic violence are Arkansas, Idaho, Mississippi, North Carolina, North Dakota, Oklahoma, South Carolina, South Dakota, and Wyoming. National Women's Law Center. 2008. "Nowhere to Turn: How the Individual Health Insurance Market Fails Women." Washington, D.C.: National Women's Law Center.

66. National Center on Women and Aging. 2001. "If I Can Just Make it to 65…." MA: Institute on Assets and Social Policy, Brandeis University. iasp.brandeis.edu/womenandaging/If_I_Can_Just_Make_It.pdf (accessed May 26, 2009).

67. Patchias, Elizabeth M., and Judy Waxman. 2007. "Women and Health Coverage: The Affordability Gap." The Commonwealth Fund, April Issue Brief.

68. Lovell, Vicky. 2004. "No Time to Be Sick: Why Everyone Suffers When Workers Don't Have Paid Sick Leave." Washington, D.C.: Institute for Women's Policy Research.

69. Warren, Elizabeth, and Amelia Warren Tyagi. 2003. *The Two-Income Trap: Why Middle-Class Mothers and Fathers Are Going Broke*. NY: Basic Books.

70. McGarry, Kathleen, and Robert F. Schoeni. 2005. "Widow(er) Poverty and Out-of-Pocket Medical Expenditures near the End of Life." *The Journals of Gerontology Series B: Psychological Sciences and Social Sciences* 60:S160–S168.

71. www.ebri.org/pdf/briefspdf/EBRI_IB_12–20073.pdf (accessed June 8, 2009).

72. The sample is also limited to those households in which both parents are biological parents of the child. Kenney, Catherine T. 2008. "Father Doesn't Know Best? Parents' Control of Money and Children's Food Insecurity." *Journal of Marriage and Family* 70: 654–669.

73. Blumberg, Rae Lesser. 1991. "Income Under Female Versus Male Control: Hypotheses from a Theory of Gender Stratification and Data from the Third World." Chapter 4 in Rae Lesser Blumberg (ed.). *Gender, Family, and Economy: The Triple Overlap.* CA: Sage; Lundberg, Shelly J., Robert A. Pollak, and Terence J. Wales. 1997. "Do Husbands and Wives Pool Their Resources? Evidence from the United Kingdom Child Benefit." *The Journal of Human Resources* 32:463–480; Thomas, Duncan. 1990. "Intra-household Resource Allocation: An Inferential Approach." *Journal of Human Resources* 25:635–664.

74. Zhan, Min, and Michael Sherraden. 2003. "Assets, Expectations, and Children's Educational Achievement in Female-Headed Households." *Social Service Review* 77:191–211.

75. www.afpnet.org/ka/print_content.cfm?folder_id=2345&content_item_id=24400

76. Andreoni, James, Eleanor Brown, and Isaac Rischall. 2003. "Charitable Giving by Married Couples: Who Decides and Why Does It Matter?" *The Journal of Human Resources* 38:111–133; Ostrower, Francie. 1995. *Why the Wealthy Give: The Culture of Elite Philanthropy.* NJ: Princeton University Press.

77. Burgoyne, Carole B., and Alan Lewis. 1994. "Distributive Justice in Marriage: Equality or Equity?" *Journal of Community and Applied Social Psychology* 4:101–114; Kahn, Arnold, Virginia E. O'Leary, Judith E. Krulewitz, and Helmut Lamm. 1980. "Equity and Equality: Male and Female Means to a Just End." *Basic and Applied Social Psychology* 1:173–197.

78. Wilkinson, Richard G. 1996. *Unhealthy Societies: The Afflictions of Inequality.* NY: Routledge.

79. Yodanis, Carrie, and Sean Lauer. 2007. "Economic Inequality In and Outside of Marriage: Individual Resources and Institutional Context." *European Sociological Review* 23:573–583.

80. Baxter, Sarah. 2009. "Women Are Victors in 'Mancession.'" *The Sunday Times* June 7.

81. Coy, Peter. 2008. "The Slump: It's a Guy Thing." *BusinessWeek* May 12; Rampell, Catherine. 2009. "As Layoffs Surge, Women May Pass Men in Job Force." *New York Times* February 6.

82. Coy, Peter. 2008. "The Slump: It's a Guy Thing." *BusinessWeek* May 12.

83. National Women's Law Center. www.nwlc.org/details.cfm?id=3605&section=newsroom

84. Healy, Beth, and Julie Balise. 2009. "End of the 401(k) Match Leaves Workers in the Lurch." *The Boston Globe* May 31; Mincer, Jilian. 2009. "Many U.S. Employers

Cut 401(k) Matches." *The Wall Street Journal* March 25; Shin, Annys. 2008. "The Latest Bad News for Your 401(k)?" *The Washington Post* October 26.

85. Ehrenreich, Barbara. 2009. "Too Poor to Make the News." *New York Times* June 14.

Appendix

1. Although not all high-income households have a great deal of wealth, the oversample of high-income households includes a much higher percentage of high-wealth households than would be found in a strictly random sample.

2. Further information about the Survey of Consumer Finances can be found at www.federalreserve.gov/PUBS/oss/oss2/scfindex.html. For further information comparing the Survey of Consumer Finances with other household surveys of wealth, see Curtin, Richard F., Thomas Juster, and James Morgan. 1989. "Survey Estimates of Wealth: An Assessment of Quality." Pages 473–551 in Robert E. Lipsey and Helen Stone Tice (eds.). *The Measurement of Savings, Investment, and Wealth*. IL: University of Chicago Press; Oliver, Melvin L., and Thomas M. Shapiro. 2006. *Black Wealth/White Wealth: A New Perspective on Racial Inequality* (10th anniversary ed.). NY: Routledge; Wolff, Edward N. 2002. *Top Heavy: The Increasing Inequality of Wealth in America and What Can Be Done About It*. NY: The New Press, appendix.

3. The survey collects detailed financial information for the "primary economic unit" of the household: an economically dominant individual or couple (married or cohabitating as partners) and any persons in the household who are financially interdependent with the economically dominant person or couple. For purposes of simplicity, however, I use the term "household" throughout the book rather than the term "primary economic unit." For further information on the distinction between the primary economic unit and the household with respect to the collection of data, see Bucks, Brian K., Arthur B. Kennickell, and Kevin B. Moore. 2006. "Recent Changes in U.S. Family Finances: Evidence from the 2001 and 2004 Survey of Consumer Finances." *Federal Reserve Bulletin* Vol. 92, pp. A1-A38.

4. For further discussion of the changes in the survey and the consistent weight design employed by the Survey of Consumer Finances, see Kennickell, Arthur B., and R. Louise Woodburn. 1999. "Consistent Weight Design for the 1989, 1992, and 1995 SCFs, and the Distribution of Wealth." *Review of Income and Wealth* 45:193–214.

5. Two respondents stated that they preferred that the interview not be recorded.

6. Millman, Marcia. 1991. *Warm Hearts and Cold Cash: The Intimate Dynamics of Families and Money*. NY: The Free Press.

7. Winship, Christopher, and Larry Radbill. 1994. "Sampling Weights and Regression Analysis." *Sociological Methods and Research* 23:230–257.

References

AARP. 2006. "AARP European Leadership Study: European Experiences with Long-Term Care." http://assets.aarp.org/www.aarp.org_/cs/gap/ldrstudy_longterm.pdf

Abramovitz, Mimi, and Sandra Morgen. 2006. *Taxes Are a Woman's Issue*. NY: Feminist Press at the City University of New York.

Alexander, Linda Lewis, Judith H. Larosa, Helaine Bader, and Susan Garfield. 2007. *New Dimensions in Women's Health*. MA: Jones and Bartlett.

Alstott, Anne L. 2004. *No Exit: What Parents Owe Their Children and What Society Owes Parents*. NY: Oxford University Press.

American Bar Association. 1995. *ABA Guide to Wills and Estates: Everything You Need to Know About Wills, Trusts, Estates, and Taxes*. NY: Three Rivers Press.

Anderson, Deborah, Melissa Binder, and Kate Krause. 2003. "The Motherhood Wage Penalty Revisited: Experience, Heterogeneity, Work Effort, and Work-Schedule Flexibility." *Industrial and Labor Relations Review* 56:10–31.

Andreoni, James, Eleanor Brown, and Isaac Rischall. 2003. "Charitable Giving by Married Couples: Who Decides and Why Does It Matter?" *The Journal of Human Resources* 38:111–133.

Angel, Jacqueline L., Cynthia J. Buckley, Ronald J. Angel, and Maren A. Jimenez. 2003. "The Economic Consequences of Marital Disruption for Pre-Retirement Age African-American, Hispanic and Non-Hispanic White Women." Paper presented at the Population Association of America Annual Meeting in Minneapolis, Minnesota.

Angel, Jacqueline L., Maren A. Jimenez, and Ronald J. Angel. 2007. "The Economic Consequences of Widowhood for Older Minority Women." *The Gerontologist* 47:224–234.

Apicella, Coren L., Anna Dreber, Benjamin Campbell, Peter B. Gray, Moshe Hoffman, and Anthony C. Little. 2008. "Testosterone and Financial Risk Preferences." *Evolution and Human Behavior* 29:384–390.

Atlas, Riva D. 2001. "Why Juan Won't Save." *New York Times* June 20.

Ayres, Ian. 1991. "Fair Driving: Gender and Race Discrimination in Retail Car Negotiations." *Harvard Law Review* 104:817–872.

Bajtelsmit, Vickie L., and Nancy A. Jianakoplos. 2000. "Women and Pensions: A Decade of Progress?" Employee Benefit Research Institute Issue Brief Number 227, November..

Bajtelsmit, Vickie L., and Jack L. VanDerhei. 1997. "Risk Aversion and Pension Investment Choices." Chapter 4 in Michael S. Gordon, Olivia S. Mitchell, and Mac M. Twinney (eds.). *Positioning Pensions for the Twenty-First Century*. PA: Pension Research Council and the University of Pennsylvania Press.

Barber, Brad M., and Terrance Odean. 2001. "Boys Will Be Boys: Gender, Overconfidence, and Common Stock Investment." *The Quarterly Journal of Economics* 116:261–292.

Bardasi, Elena, and Janet C. Gornick. 2008. "Working for Less? Women's Part-Time Wage Penalties Across Countries." *Feminist Economics* 14:37–72.

Baxter, Janeen, and Mark Western. 2001. *Reconfigurations of Class and Gender*. CA: Stanford University Press.

Baxter, Sarah. 2009. "Women Are Victors in 'Mancession.'" *The Sunday Times* June 7.

Becker, Gary. 1991. *A Treatise on the Family*. MA: Harvard University Press.

Beeferman, Larry W. 2001. "Asset Development Policy: The New Opportunity." Asset Development Institute. The Heller School for Social Policy and Management, Brandeis University. October. www./iasp.brandeis.edu/pdfs/newopportunity.pdf

Beller, Andrea H., and John W. Graham. 1993. *Small Change: The Economics of Child Support*. CT: Yale University Press.

Bernasek, Alexandra, and Stephanie Shwiff. 2001. "Gender, Risk, and Retirement." *Journal of Economic Issues* 35:345–356.

Bielby, Denise, and William T. Bielby. 1984. "Work Commitment, Sex-Role Attitudes, and Women's Employment." *American Sociological Review* 49:234–247.

Bielby, William T., and James N. Baron. 1986. "Men and Women at Work: Sex Segregation and Statistical Discrimination." *American Journal of Sociology* 91:759–799.

Bielby, William T., and James N. Baron. 1984. "A Woman's Place Is with Other Women: Sex Segregation Within Organizations." Pages 25–55 in Barbara F. Reskin (ed.) *Sex Segregation in the Workplace*. Washington, D.C.: National Academy.

Bielby, William T., and Denise D. Bielby. 1992. "I Will Follow Him: Family Ties, Gender Role Beliefs, and Reluctance to Relocate for a Better Job." *American Journal of Sociology* 97:1241–1267.

Bittman, Michael, Paula England, Liana Sayer, Nancy Folbre, and George Matheson. 2003. "When Does Gender Trump Money? Bargaining and Time in Household Work." *American Journal of Sociology* 109:186–214.

Blair-Loy, Mary. 2003. *Competing Devotions: Career and Family Among Women Executives*. MA: Harvard University Press.

Blau, Francine D., Mary C. Brinton, and David B. Grusky (eds.). 2006. *The Declining Significance of Gender?* NY: Russell Sage Foundation.

Blau, Francine D., and Lawrence M. Kahn. 2006. "The Gender Pay Gap: Going, Going...but Not Gone." Chapter 2 in Francine D.Blau, Mary C. Brinton, and

David B. Grusky (eds.). *The Declining Significance of Gender?* NY: Russell Sage Foundation.

Blau, Francine D., and Lawrence M. Kahn. 2005. "Changes in the Labor Supply Behavior of Married Women: 1980–2000." NBER Working Paper 11230.

Blumberg, Rae Lesser. 1991. "Income Under Female Versus Male Control: Hypotheses from a Theory of Gender Stratification and Data from the Third World." Chapter 4 in Rae Lesser Blumberg (ed.). *Gender, Family, and Economy: The Triple Overlap.* CA: Sage.

Blumstein, Phillip, and Pepper Schwartz. 1985. *American Couples.* NY: Pocket Books.

Brandon, Peter D. 1999. "Income-Pooling Arrangements, Economic Constraints, and Married Mothers' Child Care Choices." *Journal of Family Issues* 20: 350–370.

Brimmer, Andrew. 1988. "Income, Wealth, and Investment Behavior in the Black Community." *American Economic Review* 78:151–155.

Brines, Julie. 1994. "Economic Dependency, Gender, and the Division of Labor at Home." *American Journal of Sociology* 100:652–688.

Brown, Philip H. 2009. "Dowry and Intrahousehold Bargaining: Evidence from China." *Journal of Human Resources* 44:25–46.

Brown, Ralph J. 1998. "Saving Rate Estimates for Single Persons by Income, Age, and Gender." *Journal of Legal Economics* 8:49–62.

Brush, Candida G., Nancy M. Carter, Patricia G. Greene, Myra M. Hart, and Elizabeth Gatewood. 2002. "The Role of Social Capital and Gender in Linking Financial Suppliers and Entrepreneurial Firms: A Framework for Future Research." *Venture Capital* 4:305–323.

Buckles, Kasey. 2008. "Women, Finances, and Children: Understanding the Returns to Delayed Childbearing for Working Women." *American Economic Review: Papers and Proceedings* 98:403–407.

Bucks, Brian K., Arthur B. Kennickell, and Kevin B. Moore. 2006. "Recent Changes in U.S. Family Finances: Evidence from the 2001 and 2004 Survey of Consumer Finances." *Federal Reserve Bulletin* Vol. 92, pp. A1-A38.

Budig, Michelle J., and Paula England. 2001. "The Wage Penalty for Motherhood." *American Sociological Review* 66:204–225.

Bumpass, Larry, James Sweet, and Teresa Castro Martin. 1990. "Changing Patterns of Remarriage." *Journal of Marriage and the Family* 52:747–756.

Burgoyne, Carole B. 1990. "Money in Marriage: How Patterns of Allocation Both Reflect and Conceal Power." *Sociological Review* 38:634–665.

Burgoyne, Carole B., and Alan Lewis. 1994. "Distributive Justice in Marriage: Equality or Equity?" *Journal of Community and Applied Social Psychology* 4:101–114.

Burke, Andrew E., Felix R. FitzRoy, and Michael A. Nolan. 2008. "What Makes a Die-Hard Entrepreneur? Beyond the 'Employee or Entrepreneur' Dichotomy." *Small Business Economics* 31:93–115.

Burkhauser, Richard V., and Karen C. Holden. 1982. *A Challenge to Social Security: The Changing Roles of Women and Men in American Society.* NY: Academic Press.

Burman, Leonard E., Elaine Maag, and Jeffrey Rohaly. 2005. "Tax Credits to Help Low-Income Families Pay for Child Care." Urban-Brookings Tax Policy Center, No. 14, July.

Buttner, E. Holly, and Dorothy P. Moore. 1997. "Women's Organizational Exodus to Entrepreneurship: Self-Reported Motivations and Correlates with Success." *Journal of Small Business Management* 35:34–46.

Carr, Deborah. 2004. "The Desire to Date and Remarry Among Older Widows and Widowers." *Journal of Marriage and Family* 66: 1051–1068.

Caskey, John P. 1994. *Fringe Banking: Check-Cashing Outlets, Pawnshops, and the Poor*. NY: Russell Sage Foundation.

Center for Disease Control. 2007. *National Vital Statistics Reports*. Vol. 56, No. 9. www. cdc.gov/nchs/data/nvsr/nvsr56/nvsr56_09.pdf

Chang, Mariko Lin. 2005. "With a Little Help from My Friends (and My Financial Planner)." *Social Forces* 83:1469–1498.

Charles, Kerwin K., and Erik Hurst. 2003. "The Correlation of Wealth Across Generations." *Journal of Political Economy* 111:1155–1182.

Cherlin, Andrew J. 1992. *Marriage, Divorce, Remarriage*. MA: Harvard University Press.

Chiteji, Ngina S., and Frank P. Stafford. 1999. "Portfolio Choices of Parents and Their Children as Young Adults: Asset Accumulation by African-American Families." *American Economic Review* 89:377–380.

Christopher, Karen, Paula England, Timothy M. Smeeding, and Katherin Ross Phillips. 2002. "The Gender Gap in Poverty in Modern Nations: Single Motherhood, the Market, and the State." *Sociological Perspectives* 45:219–242.

Chun, Hyuanbae, and Injae Lee. 2001. "Why Do Married Men Earn More: Productivity or Marriage Selection?" *Economic Inquiry* 39:307–319.

Clemence, Sara. 2005. "Real Estate vs. Stocks" *Forbes.com*. www.forbes.com/ lifestyle/2005/05/27/cx_sc_0527home.html?partner=sify

Cobb-Clark, Deborah A., and Vincent A. Hildebrand. 2006. "The Portfolio Choices of Hispanic Couples." *Social Science Quarterly* 87:1344–1363.

Cobb-Clark, Deborah A., and Vincent A. Hildebrand. 2006. "The Wealth of Mexican Americans." *The Journal of Human Resources* 41:841–868.

Cohn, Bob. 1998. "What a Wife's Worth." *Stanford Magazine* March/April.

Cole, R. A., and J. D. Wolken. 1995. "Financial Services Used by Small Businesses: Evidence from the 1993 National Survey of Small Business Finances." *Federal Reserve Bulletin* 629–667.

Coleman, Susan. 2002. "Constraints Faced by Women Small Business Owners: Evidence from the Data." *Journal of Developmental Entrepreneurship* 7:151–174.

Coltrane, Scott. 1996. *Family Man: Fatherhood, Housework, and Gender Equity*. NY: Oxford University Press.

Conley, Dalton. 1999. *Being Black, Living in the Red: Race, Wealth, and Social Policy in America*. CA: University of California Press.

Conley, Dalton, and Miriam Ryvicker. 2004. "The Price of Female Hardship: Gender, Inheritance, and Wealth Accumulation in the United States." *Journal of Income Distribution* 13:41–56.

Corporation for Enterprise Development. 2004. "Hidden in Plain Sight: A Look at the $335 Billion Federal Asset-Building Budget." Washington, D.C.: Corporation for Enterprise Development. www.cfed.org/knowledge_center/publications/savings_financial_security/hidden_in_plain_sight_a_look_at_the_335_billion_federal_asset-building_budget_long_version/index.html

Correll, Shelley J., Stephen Benard, and Im Paik. 2007. "Getting a Job: Is There a Motherhood Penalty?" *American Journal of Sociology* 112:1297–1338.

Coy, Peter. 2008. "The Slump: It's a Guy Thing." *BusinessWeek* May 12.

Crittenden, Ann. 2004. *If You've Raised Kids, You Can Manage Anything: Leadership Begins at Home*. NY: Penguin.

Cuddy, Amy J. C., Susan T. Fiske, and Peter Glick. 2004. "When Professionals Become Mothers, Warmth Doesn't Cut the Ice." *Journal of Social Issues* 60:701–718.

Curtin, Richard F., Thomas Juster, and James Morgan. 1989. "Survey Estimates of Wealth: An Assessment of Quality." Pages 473–551 in Robert E. Lipsey and Helen Stone Tice (eds.). *The Measurement of Savings, Investment, and Wealth*. IL: University of Chicago Press.

Deere, Carmen Diana, and Cheryl R. Doss. 2006. "The Gender Asset Gap: What Do We Know and Why Does It Matter?" *Feminist Economics* 12:1–50.

DePaulo, Bella. 2006. *Singled Out: How Singles Are Stereotyped, Stigmatized, and Ignored and Still Live Happily Ever After*. NY: St. Martin's Press.

Domhoff, G. William. 2002. *Who Rules America?* (4th ed.). NY: McGraw-Hill.

Doss, Cheryl. 2006. "The Effects of Intrahousehold Property Ownership on Expenditure Patterns in Ghana." *Journal of African Economies* 15:149–180.

Draut, Tamara. 2007. *Strapped: Why America's 20- and 30-Somethings Can't Get Ahead*. NY: Anchor Books.

Draut, Tamara, and Javier Silva. 2003. *Borrowing to Make Ends Meet: The Growth of Credit Card Debt in the 90s*. NY: Demos. http://www.demos-usa.org/pubs/borrowing_to_make_ends_meet.pdf#search='Borrowing%20to%20Make%20Ends%20Meet'

Duncan, Greg J., and Saul D. Hoffman. 1985. "A Reconsideration of the Economic Consequences of Marital Dissolution." *Demography* 22:485–497.

Edin, Kathryn, and Laura Lein. 1997. *Making Ends Meet: How Single Mothers Survive Welfare and Low-Wage Work*. NY: Russell Sage Foundation.

Edlund, Lena, and Wojciech Kopczuk. 2009. "Women, Wealth, and Mobility." *American Economic Review* 99:146–178.

Ehrenreich, Barbara. 2009. "Too Poor to Make the News." *New York Times* June 14.

Ehrenreich, Barbara. 2001. *Nickel and Dimed: On (Not) Getting By in America*. NY: Metropolitan Books.

Eller, Martha Britton. 1997. "Federal Taxation of Wealth Transfers, 1992–1995." *Statistics of Income Bulletin* 16:8–63. www.irs.gov/pub/irs-soi/92–95fedtaxwt.pdf

Elmelech, Yuval. 2008. *Transmitting Inequality: Wealth and the American Family*. Maryland: Rowman Littlefield.

Elmelech, Yuval. 2006. "Determinants of Intragroup Wealth Inequality Among Whites, Blacks, and Latinos." Chapter 3 in Gordon Nembhard, Jessica, and Ngina

Chiteji (eds.). *Wealth Accumulation and Communities of Color in the United States: Current Issues*. MI: University of Michigan Press.

England, Paula. 2001. "Gender and Access to Money: What Do Trends in Earnings and Household Poverty Tell Us?" Chapter 8 in Janeen Baxter and Mark Western (eds.). *Reconfigurations of Class and Gender*. CA: Stanford University Press.

England, Paula. 1992. *Comparable Worth: Theories and Evidence*. NY: Aldine de Gruyter.

England, Paula, and George Farkas. 1986. *Households, Employment, and Gender: A Social, Economic, and Demographic View*. NY: Aldine Publishing Company.

England, Paula, and Barbara Stanek Kilbourne. 1990. "Markets, Marriage and Other Mates: The Problem of Power." Chapter 6 in Roger Friedland and A. Robertson (eds.). *Beyond the Marketplace: Rethinking Economy and Society*. NY: Aldine de Gruyter.

Estes, Ralph, and Jinoos Hosseini. 1998. "The Gender Gap on Wall Street: An Empirical Analysis of Confidence in Investment Decision Making." *The Journal of Psychology* 122:577–590.

Even, William E., and David A. Macpherson. 1994. "Gender Differences in Pensions." *Journal of Human Resources* 29:555–587.

Fairlie, Robert W., Kanika Kapur, and Susan M. Gates. 2008. "Is Employer-Based Health Insurance a Barrier to Entrepreneurship?" RAND Institute for Civil Justice Working Paper.

Farkas, Janice I., and Angela M. O'Rand. 1998. "The Pension Mix for Women in Middle and Late Life: The Changing Employment Relationship." *Social Forces* 76:1007–1032.

Fernandez, Raquel, and Richard Rogerson. 2001. "Sorting and Long-Run Inequality." *Quarterly Journal of Economics* 116:1305–1341.

Fishbein, Allen J., and Patrick Woodall. 2006. "Women Are Prime Targets for Subprime Lending: Women Are Disproportionately Represented in High-Cost Mortgage Market." Washington, D.C.: Consumer Federation of America, December. www.consumerfed.org/pdfs/womenprimetargetsstudy120606.pdf (accessed September 11, 2008).

Folbre, Nancy. 2008. *Valuing Children: Rethinking the Economics of the Family*. MA: Harvard University Press.

Folbre, Nancy. 2001. *The Invisible Heart: Economics and Family Values*. NY: The New Press.

Forbes. 1989. "The Forbes Four Hundred." October 23.

Fuegen, Kathleen, Monica Biernat, Elizabeth Haines, and Kay Deaux. 2004. "Mothers and Fathers in the Workplace: How Gender and Parental Status Influence Judgments of Job-Related Competence." *Journal of Social Issues* 60:737–754.

Garcia, Jose, James Lardner, and Cindy Zeldin. 2008. *Up to Our Eyeballs: How Shady Lenders and Failed Economic Policies Are Drowning Americans in Debt*. NY: The New Press.

Garrett, Bowen, Len N. Nichols, and Emily K. Greenman. 2001. "Workers Without Health Insurance: Who Are They and How Can Policy Reach Them?" The Urban

Institute. www.communityvoices.org/Uploads/4c2xne45g5ezjq45414wni55_2002 0826102930.pdf (accessed January 31, 2008).

Gerson, Kathleen. 2010. *The Unfinished Revolution: How a New Generation Is Reshaping Family, Work, and Gender in America*. NY: Oxford University Press.

Glass, Jennifer. 2004. "Blessing or Curse: Work-Family Policies and Mother's Wage Growth over Time." *Work and Occupations* 31:367–394.

Glass, Jennifer. 2000. "Envisioning the Integration of Family and Work: Toward a Kinder, Gentler Workplace." *Contemporary Sociology* 29:129–143.

Goldin, Claudia. 1990. *Understanding the Gender Gap: An Economic History of American Women*. NY: Oxford University Press.

Goldstein, Joshua R., and Catherine T. Kenney. 2001. "Marriage Delayed or Marriage Forgone? New Cohort Forecasts of First Marriage for U.S. Women." *American Sociological Review* 66:506–519.

Gonzales, Felisa. 2008. "Hispanic Women in the United States, 2007." Washington, D.C.: Pew Hispanic Center.

Gordon, Michael S., Olivia S. Mitchell, and Marc M. Twinney. 1997. *Positioning Pensions for the Twenty-First Century*. PA: University of Pennsylvania Press.

Gordon Nembhard, Jessica, and Ngina Chiteji (eds.). 2006. *Wealth Accumulation and Communities of Color in the United States*. MI: The University of Michigan Press.

Gornick, Janet C., and Marcia K. Meyers. 2005. *Families That Work: Policies for Reconciling Parenthood and Employment*. NY: Russell Sage Foundation.

Gornick, Janet C., Teresa Munzi, Eva Sierminska, and Timothy Smeeding, 2006. "Older Women's Income and Wealth Packages: The Five-Legged Stool in Cross-National Perspective." Luxembourg Wealth Study Working Paper No. 3.

Gouskova, Elena, F., Thomas Juster, and Frank P. Stafford. 2006. "Trends and Turbulence: Allocations and Dynamics of American Family Portfolios, 1984–2001." Chapter 11 in Edward N. Wolff (ed.). *International Perspectives on Household Wealth*. MA: Edward Elgar.

Grall, Timothy S. 2006. "Custodial Mothers and Fathers and Their Child Support: 2003." Current Population Reports P60–230. Washington, D.C.: U.S. Census Bureau. http://www.census.gov/prod/2006pubs/p60–230.pdf (accessed September 10, 2008).

Gross, Daniel. 2000. *Bull Run: Wall Street, the Democrats, and the New Politics of Personal Finance*. NY: Public Affairs (member of the Perseus Books Group).

Grossbard-Shechtman, Shoshana. 1993. *On the Economics of Marriage: A Theory of Marriage, Labor, and Divorce*. CO: Westview Press.

Haas, Linda. 1992. *Equal Parenthood and Social Policy: A Study of Parental Leave in Sweden*. NY: SUNY Press.

Hao, Lingxin. 2007. *Color Lines, Country Lines: Race, Immigration, and Wealth Stratification in America*. NY: Russell Sage Foundation.

Hao, Lingxin. 1996. "Family Structure, Private Transfers, and the Economic Well-Being of Families with Children." *Social Forces* 75:269–292.

Harrington Meyer, Madonna, and Pamela Herd. 2007. *Market Friendly or Family Friendly? The State and Gender Inequality in Old Age*. NY: Russell Sage Foundation.

Harrington Meyer, Madonna, and Eliza K. Pavalko. 1996. "Family, Work, and Access to Health Insurance Among Mature Women." *Journal of Health and Social Behavior* 37:311–325.

Hartmann, Heidi. 2000. "Closing the Gap: Women's Economic Progress and Future Prospects." Chapter 9 in Ray F. Marshall (ed.). *Back to Shared Prosperity: The Growing Inequality of Wealth and Income in America*. NY: M. E. Sharpe.

He, Wan, Manisha Sengupta, Victoria A. Velkoff, and Kimberly A. DeBarros. 2005. *65+ in the United States: 2005*. Current Population Reports P23–209. Washington, D.C.: U.S. Census Bureau.

Healy, Beth, and Julie Balise. 2009. "End of the 401(k) Match Leaves Workers in the Lurch." *The Boston Globe* May 31.

Hegewisch, Ariane, and Janet C. Gornick. 2008. "Statutory Routes to Workplace Flexibility in Cross-National Perspective." Washington, D.C.: Institute for Women's Policy Research. www.iwpr.org/pdf/B258workplaceflex.pdf (accessed September 22, 2008).

Hersch, Joni. 1996. "Smoking, Seat Belts, and Other Risky Consumer Decisions: Differences by Gender and Race." *Managerial and Decision Economics* 17:471–481.

Hertz, Rosanna. 1986. *More Equal than Others: Men and Women in Dual Career Marriages*. CA: University of California Press.

Hewlett, Sylvia Ann. 2007. *Off-Ramps and On-Ramps: Keeping Talented Women on the Road to Success*. MA: Harvard Business School Press.

Hewlett, Sylvia Ann, and Cornel West. 1998. *The War Against Parents: What We Can Do for America's Beleaguered Moms and Dads*. NY: Houghton Mifflin Company.

Hinz, Richard P., David D. McCarthy, and John A. Turner. 1997. "Are Women Conservative Investors? Gender Differences in Participant-Directed Pension Investments." Chapter 6 in Michael S. Gordon, Olivia S. Mitchell, and Mac M. Twinney (eds.). *Positioning Pensions for the Twenty-First Century*. PA: Pension Research Council and the University of Pennsylvania Press.

Hirschl, Tomas A., Joyce Altobelli, and Mark R. Rank. 2003. "Does Marriage Increase the Odds of Affluence? Exploring the Life Course Probabilities." *Journal of Marriage and Family* 65:927–938.

Hochschild, Arlie. 1989. *The Second Shift*. NY: Avon.

Holden, Karen C., and Pamela J. Smock. 1991. "The Economic Costs of Marital Dissolution: Why Do Women Bear a Disproportionate Cost?" *Annual Review of Sociology* 17:51–78.

Horn, Laura. 2006. *Placing College Graduation Rates in Context: How 4-Year College Graduation Rates Vary with Selectivity and the Size of Low-Income Enrollment*. NCES 2007–161. U.S. Department of Education. Washington, D.C.: National Center for Educational Statistics. www.nces.ed.gov/pubs2007/2007161.pdf (accessed January 26, 2008).

Hudson, Michael. 1996. *Merchants of Misery: How Corporate America Profits from Poverty*. ME: Common Courage Press.

Institute for Women's Policy Research. 2009. "Fact Sheet: The Gender Wage Gap 2008." IWPR No. C350 April. www.iwpr.org/pdf/C350.pdf (accessed June 15, 2009).

Iqbal, Zahid, O. Sewon, and H. Young Baek. 2006. "Are Female Executives More Risk-Averse than Male Executives?" *Atlantic Economic Journal*. http://goliath. ecnext.com/coms2/summary_0199-689286_ITM

Insight Center for Community Economic Development. 2009. "Fact Sheet: Social Insurance and Communities of Color." Spring.

Jackson, Jesse L., Sr., and Jesse L. Jackson, Jr. 1999. *It's About the Money!* NY: Random House.

Jackson, Robert Max. 1998. *Destined for Equality: The Inevitable Rise of Women's Status*. MA: Harvard University Press.

Jacobs, Jerry A., and Kathleen Gerson. 2004. *The Time Divide: Work, Family, and Gender Inequality*. MA: Harvard University Press.

Jacobs, Lawrence R., and Theda Skocpol (eds). 2005. *Inequality and American Democracy: What We Know and What We Need to Learn*. NY: Russell Sage Foundation.

Jacobsen, Joyce P., and Rayack, Wendy L. 1996. "Do Men Whose Wives Work Really Earn Less?" *The American Economic Review* 86:268–273.

Joyce, Joyce Ann. 2007. *Women, Marriage and Wealth*. NY: Gordian Knot Books.

Kaba, Amadu Jacky. 2008. "Race, Gender and Progress: Are Black American Women the New Model Minority?" *Journal of African American Studies* 12:309–335.

Kaba, Amadu Jacky. 2005. "The Gradual Shift of Wealth and Power from African American Males to African American Females." *Journal of African American Studies* 9:33–44.

Kahn, Arnold, Virginia E. O'Leary, Judith E. Krulewitz, and Helmut Lamm. 1980. "Equity and Equality: Male and Female Means to a Just End." *Basic and Applied Social Psychology* 1:173–197.

Kalleberg, Arne L., and Kevin T. Leicht. 1991. "Gender and Organizational Performance: Determinants of Small Business Survival and Success." *Academy of Management Journal* 34:136–161.

Kamenetz, Anya. 2006. *Generation Debt: Why Now Is a Terrible Time to Be Young*. NY: Riverhead Books.

Keister, Lisa A. 2005. *Getting Rich: America's New Rich and How They Got That Way*. NY: Cambridge University Press.

Keister, Lisa A. 2000. *Wealth in America: Trends in Wealth Inequality*. NY: Cambridge University Press.

Kenney, Catherine T. 2008. "Father Doesn't Know Best? Parents' Control of Money and Children's Food Insecurity." *Journal of Marriage and Family* 70: 654–669.

Kennickell, Arthur B. 2006. "A Rolling Tide: Changes in the Distribution of Wealth in the US, 1989–2001." Chapter 2 in Edward N. Wolff (ed.). *International Perspectives on Household Wealth*. MA: Edward Elgar.

Kennickell, Arthur B., and R. Louise Woodburn. 1999. "Consistent Weight Design for the 1989, 1992, and 1995 SCFs, and the Distribution of Wealth." *Review of Income and Wealth* 45:193–214.

Kijakazi, Kilolo. 2003. "Impact of Unreported Social Security Earnings on Women and People of Color." Chapter 11 in Kathleen Buto, Martha Priddy Patterson,

William E. Spriggs, and Maya Rockeymoore (eds.). *Strengthening Community: Social Insurance in a Diverse America*. National Academy of Social Insurance.

Knoke, David. 1994. "Cui Bono? Employee Benefit Packages." *American Behavioral Scientist* 37:963–978.

Kochhar, Rakesh. 2004. "The Wealth of Hispanic Households: 1996 to 2002." Washington, D.C.: Pew Hispanic Center Report.

Kreider, Rose M., and Jason M. Fields. 2002. *Number, Timing, and Duration of Marriages and Divorces: 1996*. Current Population Report P70–80. Washington, D.C.: U.S. Census Bureau.

Krivo, Lauren J. 1995. "Immigrant Characteristics and Hispanic-Anglo Housing Inequality." *Demography* 32:599–615.

Land, Michael E. (ed.). 2003. *The Role of the Father in Child Development* (4th ed.). NY: Wiley.

Leigh, Wilhelmina A. 2006. "Issues for People of Color in the United States." Chapter 1 in Gordon Nembhard, Jessica, and Ngina Chiteji (eds.). *Wealth Accumulation and Communities of Color in the United States: Current Issues*. MI: University of Michigan Press.

Lewin, Tamar. 1994. "Men Whose Wives Work Earn Less, Studies Show." *New York Times* October 12.

Loscocco, Karyn A., Joyce Robinson, Richard H. Hall, and John K. Allen. 1991. "Gender and Small Business Success: An Inquiry into Women's Relative Disadvantage." *Social Forces* 70:65–85.

Lovell, Vicky. 2004. "No Time to Be Sick: Why Everyone Suffers When Workers Don't Have Paid Sick Leave." Washington, D.C.: Institute for Women's Policy Research.

Lui, Meizhu. 2009. "Laying the Foundation for National Prosperity: The Imperative of Closing the Racial Wealth Gap." Insight Center for Community Economic Development. March.

Lui, Meizhu, Barbara Robles, Betsy Leondar-Wright, Rose Brewer, and Rebecca Adamson, with United for a Fair Economy. 2006. *The Color of Wealth: The Story Behind the U.S. Racial Wealth Divide*. NY: The New Press.

Lundberg, Shelly J., Robert A. Pollak, and Terence J. Wales. 1997. "Do Husbands and Wives Pool Their Resources? Evidence from the United Kingdom Child Benefit." *The Journal of Human Resources* 32:463–480.

Lundberg, Shelly, and Elaina Rose. 2000. "Parenthood and the Earnings of Married Men and Women." *Labour Economics* 7:689–710.

Mabry, Tristan. 1999. "Black Investors Shy Away from Stocks." *Wall Street Journal* May 14.

Mahony, Rhona. 1995. *Kidding Ourselves: Breadwinning, Babies, and Bargaining Power*. NY: Basic Books.

Manning, Robert D. 2000. *Credit Card Nation: The Consequences of America's Addiction to Credit*. NY: Basic Books.

Mare, Robert D. 1991. "Five Decades of Educational Assortative Mating." *American Sociological Review* 56:15–32.

Marsden, Peter V., Arne L. Kalleberg, and Cynthia R. Cook. 1993. "Gender Differences in Organization Commitment." *Work and Occupations* 20:368–390.

Martin, Joyce A., Brady E. Hamilton, Paul D. Sutton, Stephanie J. Ventura, Fay Menacker, and Martha L. Munson. 2003. "Births: Final Data for 2002." National Vital Statistics Reports, Vol. 52, No. 10. U.S. Department of Health and Human Services.

Matthews, Linda. 1995. "Divorced Father's Case Raises Difficult Issues of Who Pays Tuition." *New York Times*, November 15.

Matthews, T. J., and Brady E. Hamilton. 2002. "Mean Age of Mother, 1970–2000." National Vital Statistics Reports, Vol. 51, No. 1. U.S. Department of Health and Human Services.

McCaffery, Edward J. 1997. *Taxing Women*. IL: University of Chicago Press.

McGarry, Kathleen, and Robert F. Schoeni. 2005. "Widow(er) Poverty and Out-of-Pocket Medical Expenditures near the End of Life." *The Journals of Gerontology Series B: Psychological Sciences and Social Sciences* 60:S160–S168.

McGhee, Heather, and Tamara Draut. 2004. *Retiring in the Red: The Growth of Debt Among Older Americans*. NY: Demos. http://www.demos-usa.org/pubs/Retiring_2ed.pdf#search='do%20women%20have%20higher%20credit%20card%20debt%20than%20men%3F'

McLanahan, Sara, and Erin Kelly. 2006. "The Feminization of Poverty: Past and Future." Chapter 7 in Janet Saltzman Chafetz (ed.). *Handbook of the Sociology of Gender*. NY: Plenum Publishing.

McLanahan, Sara, and Christine Percheski. 2008. "Family Structure and the Reproduction of Inequalities." *Annual Review of Sociology* 34:257–276.

McManus, Patricia A., and Thomas A. DiPrete. 2001. "Losers and Winners: The Financial Consequences of Separation and Divorce for Men." *American Sociological Review* 66:246–268.

Meers, Sharon, and Joanna Strober. 2009. *Getting to 50/50: How Working Couples Can Have It All by Sharing All*. NY: Bantam Books.

Menchik, Paul L. 1980. "Primogeniture, Equal Sharing, and the U.S. Distribution of Wealth." *The Quarterly Journal of Economics* 94:299–316.

Millman, Marcia. 1991. *Warm Hearts and Cold Cash: The Intimate Dynamics of Families and Money*. NY: The Free Press.

Mincer, Jilian. 2009. "Many U.S. Employers Cut 401(k) Matches." *The Wall Street Journal* March 25.

Mincy, Ronald B. 2006. *Black Males Left Behind*. Washington, D.C.: Urban Institute Press.

Mishel, Lawrence, Jared Bernstein, and Sylvia Allegretto. 2007. *The State of Working America, 2006/2007*. NY: ILR Press.

Misra, Joya, Michelle Budig, and Stephanie Moller. 2006. "Reconciliation Policies and the Effects of Motherhood on Employment, Earnings, and Poverty." Luxembourg Income Study Working Paper No. 429.

Mitchell, Olivia S., Phillip B. Levine, and John W. Phillips. 1999. "The Impact of Pay Inequality, Occupational Segregation, and Lifetime Work Experience on the

Retirement Income of Women and Minorities." Washington, D.C.: AARP Public Policy Institute.

Moen, Phyllis (ed.). 2003. *It's About Time: Couples and Careers*. NY: Cornell University Press.

Moran, Beverly (ed.). 2008. *Race and Wealth Disparities: A Multidisciplinary Discourse*. MD: Rowman and Littlefield.

Morris, Betsy. 1998. "It's Her Job Too: Lorna Wendt's $20 Million Divorce Case Is the Shot Heard 'Round the Water Cooler." *Fortune* February 2.

Nam, Yunju. 2008. "Welfare Reform and Asset Accumulation: Asset Limit Changes, Financial Assets, and Vehicle Ownership." *Social Science Quarterly* 89:133–154.

National Center on Women and Aging. 2001. "If I Can Just Make It to 65..." MA: Institute on Assets and Social Policy, Brandeis University. iasp.brandeis.edu/womenandaging/If_I_Can_Just_ Make_It.pdf (accessed May 26, 2009).

National Hispanic Council on Aging. N. d. "The Economic Security of Hispanic Older Adults in the United States." www.nhcoa.org/economic_security.php (accessed March 20, 2009).

National Women's Law Center. 2008. "Nowhere to Turn: How the Individual Health Insurance Market Fails Women." Washington, D.C.: National Women's Law Center.

Nelson, Robert L., and William P. Bridges. 1999. *Legalizing Gender Inequality: Courts, Markets, and Unequal Pay for Women in America*. NY: Cambridge University Press.

Newcomb, Michael D., and Jerome Rabow. 1999. "Gender, Socialization, and Money." *Journal of Applied Social Psychology* 29:582–869.

Newman, Katherine S., and Victor Tan Chen. 2007. *The Missing Class: Portraits of the Near Poor in America*. MA: Beacon Press.

Nock, Steven L. 1998. *Marriage in Men's Lives*. NY: Oxford University Press.

Oliver, Melvin L., and Thomas M. Shapiro. 2006. *Black Wealth/White Wealth: A New Perspective on Racial Inequality* (10th anniversary ed.). NY: Routledge.

Ong, Paul. 2002. "Car Ownership and Welfare-to-Work." *Journal of Policy Analysis and Management* 21:239–252.

Ong, Paul, and R. Varisa Patraporn. 2006. "Asian Americans and Wealth." Chapter 7 in Gordon Nembhard, Jessica, and Ngina Chiteji (eds.). *Wealth Accumulation and Communities of Color in the United States: Current Issues*. MI: University of Michigan Press.

O'Rand, Angela M. 1986. "The Hidden Payroll: Employee Benefits and the Structure of Workplace Inequality." *Sociological Forum* 1:657–683.

O'Rand, Angela M., and Kim M. Shuey. 2007. "Gender and the Devolution of Pension Risks in the US." *Current Sociology* 55:287–304.

Orloff, Ann Shola. 1993. "Gender and the Social Rights of Citizenship: The Comparative Analysis of Gender Relations and Welfare States." *American Sociological Review* 58:303–328.

Orszag, Peter, and Robert Greenstein. 2005. "Toward Progressive Pensions: A Summary of the U.S. Pension System and Proposals for Reform." Chapter 13 in Michael Sherraden (ed.). *Inclusion in the American Dream: Assets, Poverty, and Public Policy*. NY: Oxford University Press.

Osilli, Una Okonkwo, and Anna Paulson. 2004. "Prospects for Immigrant-Native Wealth Assimilation: Evidence from Financial Market Participation." Working Paper 04–18. Federal Reserve Bank of Chicago.

Ostrower, Francie. 1995. *Why the Wealthy Give: The Culture of Elite Philanthropy*. NJ: Princeton University Press.

Pahl, Jan. 1983. "The Allocation of Money and the Structuring of Inequality Within Marriage." *The Sociological Review* 31:237–262.

Pahl, Jan. 1980. "Patterns of Money Management Within Marriage." *Journal of Social Policy* 9:313–335.

Papke, Leslie E. 1998. "How Are Participants Investing Their Accounts in Participant-Directed Individual Account Pension Plans?" *The American Economic Review* 88:212–216.

Patchias, Elizabeth M., and Judy Waxman. 2007. "Women and Health Coverage: The Affordability Gap." The Commonwealth Fund, April Issue Brief.

Paulin, Geoffrey D., and Yoon G. Lee. 2002. "Expenditures of Single Parents: How Does Gender Figure In?" *Monthly Labor Review* 125:16–37.

Pearce, Diana. 1978. "The Feminization of Poverty: Women, Work and Welfare." *Urban and Social Change Review* 11:28–36.

Penn, Mark. 2009. "Guys Left Behind (GLBs)." *The Wall Street Journal* June 2.

Peterson, Richard R. 1996. "A Re-Evaluation of the Economic Consequences of Divorce." *American Sociological Review* 61:528–536.

Peterson, Trond, and Laurie A. Morgan. 1995. "Separate and Unequal. Occupation-Establishment Sex Segregation and the Gender Wage Gap." *American Journal of Sociology* 101:329–361.

Phipps, Shelley, and Peter Burton. 1998. "What's Mine Is Yours? The Influence of Male and Female Incomes on Patterns of Household Expenditure." *Economica* 65:599–613.

Presser, Harriet B. 2005. *Working in a 24/7 Economy: Challenges for American Families*. NY: Russell Sage Foundation.

Projector, Dorothy S. 1964. "Survey of Financial Characteristics of Consumers." *Federal Reserve Bulletin* 51:285–293.

Pruett, Kyle D. 2000. *Fatherneed: Why Father Care Is as Essential as Mother Care for Your Child*. NY: Free Press.

Purcell, Patrick J. 2003. "Pension Issues: Lump Sum Distributions and Income Security." Washington, D.C.: Congressional Research Service, The Library of Congress.

Pyne, Solana. 2001. "The Push for Insurance to Cover Birth Control." *Newsday* September 4.

Quadagno, Jill. 1988. "Women's Access to Pensions and the Structure of Eligibility Rules: Systems of Production and Reproduction." *The Sociological Quarterly* 29:541–558.

Quisumbing, Agnes R., and John A. Maluccio. 2003. "Resources at Marriage and Intrahousehold Allocation: Evidence from Bangladesh, Ethiopia, Indonesia, and South Africa." *Oxford Bulletin of Economics and Statistics* 65:283–327.

Rampell, Catherine. 2009. "As Layoffs Surge, Women May Pass Men in Job Force." *New York Times* February 6.

Raphael, Steven, and Lorien Rice. 2002. "Car Ownership, Employment, and Earnings," *Journal of Urban Economics* 52:109–130.

Raymond, Joan. 2001. "The Ex-Files—Corporate Marketing Campaigns Focusing on Divorced Women." *American Demographics* February.

Reuters. 2000. "Overly Cautious Savers Risk Losing a Fortune." *New York Times*. November 19.

Rhodes, Elizabeth. 2001 "While He Plays, She Buys." *Seattle Times* December 8.

Ridgeway, Cecilia L., and Shelley J. Correll. 2004. "Motherhood as a Status Characteristic." *Journal of Social Issues* 60:683–700.

Roberts, Sam. 2007. "For Young Earners in Big City, a Gap in Women's Favor." *New York Times* August 3.

Robles, Barbara J. 2006. "Wealth Creation in Latino Communities." Chapter 10 in Gordon Nembhard, Jessica, and Ngina Chiteji (eds.). *Wealth Accumulation and Communities of Color in the United States: Current Issues*. MI: University of Michigan Press.

Rose, Stephen J., and Heidi I. Hartmann. 2004. "Still a Man's Labor Market: The Long-Term Earnings Gap." Washington, D.C.: Institute for Women's Policy Research.

Rubenstein, Carin. 1981. "Money and Self Esteem, Relationships, Secrecy, Envy, and Satisfaction." *Psychology Today* (May):29–44.

Rubin, Lillian B. 1992. *Worlds of Pain: Life in the Working-Class Family*. NY: Basic Books.

Schmidt, Lucie, and Purvi Sevak. 2006. "Gender, Marriage, and Asset Accumulation in the United States." *Feminist Economics* 12:139–166.

Schoen, Robert, and Robin M.Weinick. 1993. "The Slowing Metabolism of Marriage: Figures from 1988 U.S. Marital Status Life Tables." *Demography* 30:737–746.

Schreiner, Marik, Michael Sherraden, Margaret Clancy, Lissa Johnson, Jami Curley, Min Zhan, Sondra G. Beverly, and Michal Grinstein-Weiss. 2005. "Assets and the Poor: Evidence from Individual Development Accounts." Chapter 10 in Michael Sherraden (ed.). *Inclusion in the American Dream: Assets, Poverty, and Public Policy*. NY: Oxford University Press.

Seccombe, Karen. 1993. "Employer Sponsored Medical Benefits: The Influence of Occupational Characteristics and Gender." *The Sociological Quarterly* 34:557–580.

Shapiro, Thomas M. 2004. *The Hidden Cost of Being African American: How Wealth Perpetuates Inequality*. NY: Oxford University Press.

Shapiro, Thomas M., and Edward N. Wolff (eds.). 2001. *Assets for the Poor: The Benefits of Spreading Asset Ownership*. NY: Russell Sage Foundation.

Shaw, Lois, and Catherine Hill. 2001. "The Gender Gap in Pension Coverage: What Does the Future Hold?" Institute for Women's Policy Research Publication E507. www.iwpr.org/pdf/e507.pdf (accessed September 18, 2008).

Sherraden, Michael (ed.). 2005. *Inclusion in the American Dream: Assets, Poverty, and Public Policy*. NY: Oxford University Press.

Sherraden, Michael. 2001. "Asset-Building Policy and Programs for the Poor." Chapter 9 in Thomas M. Shapiro and Edward N. Wolff (eds.). *Assets for the Poor: The Benefits of Spreading Asset Ownership*. NY: Russell Sage Foundation.

Sherraden, Michael. 1991. *Assets and the Poor: A New American Welfare Policy*. NY: Sharpe.

Shin, Annys. 2008. "The Latest Bad News for Your 401(k)?" *The Washington Post* October 26.

Shuey, Kim M., and Angela M. O'Rand. 2004. "New Risks for Workers: Pensions, Labor Markets, and Gender." *Annual Review of Sociology* 30:453–477.

Sierminska, Eva, Andera Brandolini, and Timothy M. Smeeding. 2006. "Comparing Wealth Distribution Across Rich Countries: First Results from the Luxembourg Wealth Study." Luxembourg Wealth Study Working Paper No. 1. www.lisproject. org/publications/lwswps/lws1.pdf (accessed September 18, 2008).

Simms, Margaret C. 2008. "Weathering Job Loss: Unemployment Insurance." New Safety Net Paper 6. The Urban Institute. July.

Smeeding, Timothy M. 1999. *Social Security Reform: Improving Benefit Adequacy and Economic Security for Women*. Center for Retirement Research Working Paper No. 16/1999. http://escholarship.bc.edu/retirement_papers/25 (accessed January 7, 2008).

Sorensen, Annemette. 2003. "Economic Relations Between Women and Men: New Realities and the Re-Interpretation of Dependence." *Advances in Life Course Research* 8:281–297.

Sorensen, Annemette. 1994. "Women, Family and Class." *Annual Review of Sociology* 20:27–47.

Sorensen, Annemette, and Sara McLanahan. 1987. "Married Women's Economic Dependency, 1940–1980." *American Journal of Sociology* 93:659–687.

Stern, Mark J. 2001. "The Un(credit)worthy Poor: Historical Perspectives on Policies to Expand Assets and Credit." Chapter 8 in Thomas M. Shapiro and Edward N. Wolff (eds.). *Assets for the Poor: The Benefits of Spreading Asset Ownership*. NY: Russell Sage Foundation.

Stern, Sharon M. 2008. "Poverty Dynamics: 2001–2003." May 15. http://www.census. gov/hhes/www/poverty/dynamics01/pdf/PovertyDynamics.pdf (accessed June 3, 2008).

Stolberg, Sheryl Gay. 2009. "Obama Signs Equal-Pay Legislation." *New York Times* January 30.

Stone, Pamela. 2007. *Opting Out? Why Women Really Quit Careers and Head Home*. CA: University of California Press.

Sullivan, Teresa A., Elizabeth Warren, and Jay Lawrence Westbrook. 2002. *The Fragile Middle Class: Americans in Debt*. CT: Yale University Press.

Swartz, Katherine. 2006. *Reinsuring Health: Why More Middle-Class People Are Uninsured and What Government Can Do*. NY: Russell Sage Foundation.

Sweeney, Megan M. 1997. "Remarriage of Women and Men After Divorce: The Role of Socioeconomic Prospects." *Journal of Family Issues* 18:479–502.

Tan, Amy. 1989. *The Joy Luck Club*. NY: Ivy Books.

Thomas, Adam, and Isabel Sawhill. 2005. "For Love and Money? The Impact of Family Structure on Family Income." *The Future of Children* 15:57–74.

Thomas, Duncan. 1990. "Intra-household Resource Allocation: An Inferential Approach." *Journal of Human Resources* 25:635–664.

Thomas, Paulette. 2000. "At 'Camp,' Women Learn to Pitch Deals to Investors." *The Wall Street Journal* July 18.

Tichenor, Veronica Jaris. 2005. *Earning More and Getting Less: Why Successful Wives Can't Buy Equality*. NJ: Rutgers University Press.

Townsend, Nicholas W. 2002. *The Package Deal: Marriage, Work, and Fatherhood in Men's Lives*. PA: Temple University Press.

Treas, Judith. 1993. "Money in the Bank: Transaction Costs and the Economic Organization of Marriage." *American Sociological Review* 58:723–734.

Treas, Judith, and Esther De Ruuter. 2008. "Earnings and Expenditures on Household Services in Married and Cohabiting Unions." *Journal of Marriage and the Family* 70:796–805.

Updegrave, Walter. 2005. "Is Real Estate Right for Your IRA?" August 11. www.money.cnn.com/2005/08/11/pf/updegrave_0509/index.htm

U.S. Bureau of Labor Statistics. 2005. "Highlights of Women's Earnings in 2004." Report 987. Washington, D.C. www.bls.gov/cps/cpswom2004.pdf

U.S. Census Bureau. 2008. *Statistical Abstract*. Table 58. http://www.census.gov/compendia/statab/tables/08s0058.pdf

U.S. Census Bureau. 2007. Detailed Tables: Number, Timing, and Duration of Marriages and Divorces 2004, Table 5. www.census.gov/population/www/socdemo/marr-div/2004detailed_tables.html.U.S. Census Bureau. 2006. *2002 Survey of Business Owners, Company Summary*. Washington, D.C.: U.S. Department of Commerce.

U.S. Census Bureau. 1995. "Two Different Worlds: Men and Women from 9 to 5." Statistical Brief SB94–24, February.

U.S. Department of Education, National Center for Educational Statistics. 2004. "The Condition of Education 2004." NCES 2004–077. Washington, D.C.: U.S. Government Printing Office. www.nces.ed.gov/pubs2004/2004077.pdf (accessed July 24, 2008).

U.S. Department of Labor. 2009. "Employer Costs for Employee Compensation—March 2009." www.bls.gov/news.release/pdf/ecec.pdf (accessed June 10, 2009).

U.S. Department of Labor. 2008. "Women in the Labor Force: A Databook" (2008 ed.). www.bls.gov/cps/wlf-databook2008.htm (accessed June 15, 2009).

U.S. Department of Labor. 2007. "Labor Force Characteristics by Race and Ethnicity, 2007." http://www.bls.gov/cps/cpsrace2007.pdf (accessed June 15, 2009).

U.S. General Accounting Office. 2000. "Contingent Workers: Incomes and Benefits Lag Behind Those of the Rest of the Workforce." www.gao.gov/archive/2000/he00076.pdf (accessed March 14, 2008).

Velamuri, Malathi R. 2008. "Taxes, Health Insurance and Women's Self-Employment." Social Science Research Network. http://ssrn.com/abstract=1141507

Waite, Linda J., and Maggie Gallagher. 2000. *The Case for Marriage: Why Married People Are Happier, Healthier, and Better Off Financially*. NY: Broadway Books.

Waldfogel, Jane. 1997. "The Effects of Children on Women's Wages." *American Sociological Review* 62:209–217.

Warren, Elizabeth, and Amelia Warren Tyagi. 2003. *The Two-Income Trap: Why Middle-Class Mothers and Fathers Are Going Broke*. NY: Basic Books.

Warren, Tracy, Karen Rowlingson, and Claire Whyley. 2001. "Female Finances: Gender Wage Gaps, Gender Asset Gaps." *Work, Employment and Society* 15:465–488.

Weir, David R., Robert J. Willis, and Purvi Sevak. 2002. *The Economic Consequences of Widowhood*. University of Michigan Retirement Research Center Working Paper 2002–023.

Weitzman, Lenore. 1996. "The Economic Consequences of Divorce Are Still Unequal: Comment on Peterson." *American Sociological Review* 61:537–538.

Weller, Christian. 2006. "Drowning in Debt: America's Middle Class Falls Deeper in Debt as Income Growth Slows and Costs Climb." Center for American Progress. www.americanprogress.org/issues/2006/05/b1655517.html (accessed May 6, 2009).

Weller, Christian, and Jessica Lynch. 2009. "Household Wealth in Freefall: America's Private Safety Net in Tatters." Center for American Progress. www.americanprogress.org/issues/2009/04/pdf/wealth_declines.pdf (accessed May 7, 2009).

Weller, Christian, and Edward N. Wolff. 2005. *Retirement Income: The Crucial Role of Social Security*. Washington, D.C.: Economic Policy Institute.

West, Candace, and Donald Zimmerman. 1987. "Doing Gender." *Gender and Society* 1:125–151.

Wheary, Jennifer, and Tamara Draut. 2007. "Who Pays? The Winners and Losers of Credit Card Deregulation." Washington, D.C.: Demos, August 1. www.demos.org/pub1463.cfm (accessed July 22, 2008).

Wheary, Jennifer, Thomas M. Shapiro, and Tamara Draut. 2007. "By a Thread: The New Experience of America's Middle Class." Briefing Paper. Washington, D.C.: Demos.

Whittelsey, Frances Cerra, and Marcia Carroll. 1995. *Women Pay More*. NY: The New Press.

Wilkinson, Richard G. 1996. *Unhealthy Societies: The Afflictions of Inequality*. NY: Routledge.

Williams, Joan. 2000. *Unbending Gender: Why Family and Work Conflict and What to Do About It*. NY: Oxford University Press.

Williams, Joan C., and Holly Cohen Cooper. 2004. "The Public Policy of Motherhood." *Journal of Social Issues* 60:849–865.

Williams, Robert J. 2003. "Women on Corporate Boards of Directors and Their Influence on Corporate Philanthropy." *Journal of Business Ethics* 42:1–10.

Wilmoth, Janet, and Gregor Koso. 2002. "Does Marital History Matter? Marital Status and Wealth Outcomes Among Preretirement Adults." *Journal of Marriage and Family* 64:254–268.

Wilson, William Julius. 2009. *More than Just Race: Being Black and Poor in the Inner City*. NY: W.W. Norton and Company.

Winship, Christopher, and Larry Radbill. 1994. "Sampling Weights and Regression Analysis." *Sociological Methods and Research* 23:230–257.

Wolff, Edward N. 2007. "Recent Trends in Household Wealth in the United States: Rising Debt and the Middle-Class Squeeze." Levy Economics Institute Working Paper No. 502. www.levy.org/pubs/wp_502.pdf

Wolff, Edward N. (ed.). 2006. *International Perspectives on Household Wealth*. MA: Edward Elgar.

Wolff, Edward N. 2002. *Top Heavy: The Increasing Inequality of Wealth in America and What Can Be Done About It*. NY: The New Press.

Wolff, Edward N. 2001. "Recent Trends in Wealth Ownership, from 1983 to 1998." Chapter 2 in Thomas M. Shapiro and Edward N. Wolff (eds.). *Assets for the Poor: The Benefits of Spreading Asset Ownership*. NY: Russell Sage Foundation.

Wolff, Edward N. 1998. "Recent Trends in the Size Distribution of Household Wealth." *Journal of Economic Perspectives* 12:131–150.

Woolf, Virginia. 1929. *A Room of One's Own*. NY: Harcourt Brace Jovanovich.

Yamashita, Takashi. January 2009. "Keeping up with the Joneses in McMansions: Changes in Wealth Inequality between College and High-School Graduates." (unpublished manuscript) Department of Economics, Reed College. academic.reed.edu/economics/yamashita/McMansions.pdf

Yamokoski, Alexis, and Lisa A. Keister. 2006. "The Wealth of Single Women: Marital Status and Parenthood in the Asset Accumulation of Young Baby Boomers in the United States." *Feminist Economics* 12:167–194.

Yodanis, Carrie, and Sean Lauer. 2007. "Economic Inequality In and Outside of Marriage: Individual Resources and Institutional Context." *European Sociological Review* 23:573–583.

Zelizer, Viviana. 1997. *The Social Meaning of Money*. NJ: Princeton University Press.

Zhan, Min, and Michael Sherraden. 2003. "Assets, Expectations, and Children's Educational Achievement in Female-Headed Households." *Social Service Review* 77:191–211.

Zissimopoulos, Julie M., and Lynn A. Karoly. 2003. "Transitions to Self-Employment at Older Ages: The Role of Wealth, Health, Health Insurance, and Other Factors." Rand Working Paper 135. www.rand.org/pubs/working_papers/WR135/WR135.pdf (accessed September 22, 2008).

Index